BLACK&DECKER®

W9-CBK-912

The Complete Guide to
Dream
Kitchens

Creative Publishing
international

CHANHASSEN, MINNESOTA
www.creativepub.com

Creative Publishing international

Copyright © 2007
Creative Publishing international, Inc.
18705 Lake Drive East
Chanhassen, Minnesota 55317
1-800-328-3895
www.creativepub.com

Printed at R. R. Donnelley

10 9 8 7 6 5 4 3 2 1

Library of Congress Cataloging-in-Publication Data

The complete guide to dream kitchens.
        p. cm.
    "Black & Decker."
    Summary: "Shows homeowners what's hot and what's not, and
gives practical information on how they can achieve the kitchens of
their fantasies. Recent innovations in planning and room layout are
covered in detail, and the merits of premium building materials and
appliances are discussed and compared. Also gives many actual how-
to projects for creating luxury kitchens with professional results"--
Provided by publisher.
    Includes index.
    ISBN-13: 978-1-58923-304-1 (soft cover)
    ISBN-10: 1-58923-304-2 (soft cover)
    1. Kitchens--Remodeling. I. Title.

    TH4816.3.K58 C6543
    643'.3--dc22

2006101333

President/CEO: Ken Fund
VP for Sales & Marketing: Peter Ackroyd

Home Improvement Group

Publisher: Bryan Trandem
Managing Editor: Tracy Stanley
Senior Editor: Mark Johanson
Editor: Jennifer Gehlhar

Creative Director: Michele Lanci-Altomare
Senior Design Manager: Brad Springer
Design Managers: Jon Simpson, Mary Rohl

Director of Photography: Tim Himsel
Lead Photographer: Steve Galvin
Photo Coordinators: Julie Caruso, Joanne Wawra
Shop Manager: Randy Austin

Production Managers: Linda Halls, Laura Hokkanen

Editor: Sarah Lynch
Page Layout Artist: Kari Johnston
Photographers: Andrea Rugg, Joel Schnell
Shop Help: Glenn Austin, Sean Brennan and John Webb
Cover Photograph: © Karen Melvin for Rebekah Fellers
  Interiors, Cincinnati, OH

THE COMPLETE GUIDE TO DREAM KITCHENS
Created by: The Editors of Creative Publishing international, Inc., in cooperation with Black & Decker.
Black & Decker® is a trademark of The Black & Decker Corporation and is used under license.

NOTICE TO READERS

For safety, use caution, care and good judgment when following the procedures described in this book. The
Publisher and Black& Decker cannot assume responsibility for any damage to property or injury to persons
as a result of misuse of the information provided.

The techniques shown in this book are general techniques for various applications. In some instances,
additional techniques not shown in this book may be required. Always follow manufacturers„ instructions included
with products, since deviating from the directions may void warranties. The projects in this book vary widely as to
skill levels required: some may not be appropriate for all do-it-yourselfers, and some may require professional help.

Consult your local Building Department for information on building permits, codes and other laws as they
apply to your project.

Contents

Complete Guide to Dream Kitchens

Introduction

Today's kitchen feels more like the heart of the home than ever. As we spend more and more time in the kitchen—not just cooking and eating, but also entertaining, socializing and running our households, we realize the benefit of having a pleasant, efficient central space. The ideal kitchen serves all these needs. It is spacious, well organized and well lit. Unfortunately, many real kitchens are cramped, poorly designed and badly lit. Here's where *The Comple Guide to Dream Kitchens* can help.

Kitchens in older pre-war homes often still reflect a time when built-in cabinets were not standard, pantries and ice chests stored foods, and tables doubled as work surfaces and gathering places. Mid-century kitchens may feature built-in cabinets and niches for modern appliances, but often lack proper task lighting and a place for casual dining. Contemporary kitchens, designed in the 1980s and '90s, often focused too much attention to details such as lighting and materials, leaving little in the realm of warmth and functionality. The point is, most kitchens today need to be remodeled to fit the current owners' needs, or upgraded to improve the value of a home.

You may like almost everything about your current kitchen, but wish it weren't so dark, or you find that with the kids it's starting to feel cramped. You may like the charm of your old house, but hate the tiny galley kitchen. All these and a hundred other factors give you a good reason for sprucing up, fixing up, reconfiguring, or tearing out and starting over.

The Complete Guide to Dream Kitchens is the place to start regardless of where you are on the kitchen improvement continuum. In this book, we cover dozens of ways to make your kitchen brighter and easier to use—from painting the walls to refacing the cabinets, updating the lighting or raising the dishwasher or installing pull-out shelves.

We also cover some of the more advanced kitchen makeovers, such as installing all-new cabinets and countertops, replacing the flooring and adding a range hood. These are all projects that can be done by most do-it-yourselfers with moderate skills.

To offer inspiration, we have included an overview section in the beginning of the book that includes a portfolio of kitchens to help you determine your style, as well as a chapter on designing and planning your dream kitchen. Complete with do's and don'ts that will help you determine the details needed to transform your kitchen into a perfectly customized working space on budget. The chapter on remodeling will also offer advice on when to hire out some of the tasks and how to work with a contractor.

Throughout this book, you'll find pointers about eco-friendly options, shopping tips to clue you in on features to look for, and notes on Universal Design, which creates accessibility to a wide range of people. But above all, you'll see exactly how to complete the remodeling projects that can make your dream kitchen real.

Planning & Designing
Your Dream Kitchen

Kitchens Portfolio

The initial step for any home improvement project is to assess the space you already have, and to develop the look of your dream remodel. Most people know right away whether they consider themselves a modernist or a traditionalist, but the growing selection of materials, appliances and upgrades means that selecting your style is not that simple anymore, especially when it comes to kitchens. With so many customizable options—from cabinet hardware to floor tiles—the possibilities can seem endless. Whether you're looking for a dramatic transformation or simply an easy update, consider the vast selection as an opportunity to make your dream kitchen come true.

In an effort to make things easier, we've compiled a portfolio of kitchens in every size and style. As you browse the following pages—and subsequent chapters— look for kitchens that you find aesthetically appealing, while keeping an eye out for elements or ideas to add to your kitchen wish list.

In This Chapter

- Efficient Kitchens
- Country/Rustic Kitchens
- Traditional Kitchens
- Contemporary Kitchens
- Professional Kitchens
- Multipurpose Kitchens
- Green Kitchens
- Kitchens that Work
- Kitchens that Flow
- Kitchens with Style
- The Accessible Kitchen

Efficient Kitchens

For a well-planned kitchen, size should not necessarily matter. But, as anyone who has tried preparing an elaborate meal in a cramped galley kitchen can attest, a roomy kitchen with plenty of counter space and storage solutions can truly be a delight. If space constraints are insurmountable, adding tidy storage solutions and reconfiguring the floor plan can go a long way toward making your kitchen more enjoyable. If you have an abundance of square footage, make good use of the space so that corners and niches are used to best advantage and the room doesn't feel cavernous.

The vaulted ceiling and repeated use of squares—from the slate floors to the panes in the glass-fronted cabinets—makes this spacious kitchen seems almost institutional in its size, but a warm palette of gray and green along with plenty of natural light keeps the room feeling friendly.

This compact kitchen (above) makes the most of the space, with cabinets that extend all the way up to the ceiling. Built-ins such as the microwave and wall oven, combined with a slender pot rack, keep everything looking well organized.

This galley kitchen (left), though small, features stainless steel countertops, stove and vent. The beautiful wood cabinets and slate floor lend a feeling of warmth to this cozy space.

Country/Rustic Kitchens

The classic country kitchen will never fall out of fashion. The atmosphere created by a palette of natural wood finishes and rustic elements like rough-hewn stone and brick feels warm and welcoming. Farmhouse throwbacks like a table made of well-worn solid wood, a porcelain apron-front sink and glass-paned cabinets reinforced with open wire fabric add a touch of nostalgia. Open storage offers the chance to show off a collection of country pottery.

A combination of slate and wood come together for a classic rustic look in this double-height kitchen. Because it's part of the great room, this kitchen must stylistically match the rest of the space.

The Shaker style cabinetry (above) and colonial colors in this kitchen combine with knotty wood flooring for an old-fashioned yet completely fresh look.

Simple, geometric lines, (left) warm wood tones and natural stone countertops can be found in kitchens of just about any style. But this kitchen makes clever use of a couple of additional details to pull a feeling of rustic appeal from these raw elements. Specifically, the blue-and-white patterned tile backsplash behind the stovetop and the horizontal shiplap-style paneling signal the fact that this is a country kitchen.

Traditional Kitchens

The definition of "traditional style" shifts continually over time, to the extent that it can be virtually meaningless. Derivative terms, such as the current "transitional," suggest that traditional elements are mixed with more modern pieces to create a kitchen that incorporates classic styles in an updated manner. For example, a kitchen that must double as a space for entertaining can include traditional elements like framed cabinets painted white or café curtains that, when combined with nontraditional elements, can lean in almost any direction, from contemporary to rustic. Traditionally styled furnishings can also help tone down the industrial feel of professional-grade appliances.

Classic crown moldings and shelves left open for display are two elements of the traditional kitchen. Here, retro-styled hardware in brushed nickel helps further soften the look.

This classic look carries on the long-standing tradition of painted cabinetry in the kitchen. Darker countertops and shades soften the room. Subway tile and a fireclay sink add extra reflection.

Your grandparents might not call this kitchen traditional, but if you look closely you'll see that only the stainless steel side-by-side refrigerator would be a complete anachronism in a turn-of-the-century kitchen. From the pot rack to the diagonal pattern of the backsplash to the sturdy, turned island legs, most of the elements of this design are updated versions of very traditional kitchen components.

Contemporary Kitchens

Modern design strives to retain function while putting a premium on form. Contemporary features such as minimalist touch-latch cabinets or high-tech countertops help create an orderly atmosphere for hardworking chefs and an uncluttered space for those who stop only at the coffeemaker on their way through the kitchen. In a home dedicated to a contemporary look, the kitchen can easily be designed to maintain a stylistic flow with the rest of the house.

The contrast of black marble and white laminate presents a clear definition for the contemporary kitchen. Frosted glass cabinet doors and hardware pulls that look like minimalist rods work with chrome accents to create a streamlined effect.

Sleek, smooth and polished surfaces (left) were chosen for this moderate-sized contemporary kitchen.

Modern curves (below) often work just as well as right angles to create a contemporary atmosphere. This island bar area has a swooping cutaway that serves as the focal point for the entire room.

Stainless steel makes any kitchen look more contemporary, but it must be handled with some care from a design standpoint (and from a fingerprint-smudging standpoint). Here, the juxtaposition of the warm wood floor and the light, airy color schemes prevent the masses of stainless steel from causing the kitchen to look industrial and cold.

Contemporary kitchens borrow design components from public spaces, where most of the cutting-edge interior design occurs. From the retro-lounge swoop of the countertop to the gleaming black and steel surfaces, this kitchen recalls the look and feel of an uptown bistro, but with just enough homey design touches to maintain a residential feeling.

Color trends go a long way toward placing your kitchen in the high-end design continuum. While bright, fun colors are currently on-trend (and happily so, a lot of kitchen owners feel), the predominant tones of high-end design are sure to change soon. Luckily, the changes typically can be accommodated with a gallon or two of paint.

Black and white is a truly unique color combination because it manages to look contemporary no matter when you deploy it, and even in otherwise traditional settings. The sleek lines and minimalist feeling of this kitchen would look contemporary even with very high tone colors.

Professional Kitchens

If there is one trend that has changed the face of kitchens in the 21st century, it's the blurring of the line between consumer and professional-grade kitchen appliances. State-of-the-art ranges and refrigerators, and materials such as stainless-steel countertops that previously were reserved for restaurant kitchens have made their way to every level of the consumer marketplace. Evidence of this trend can be found in six-burner gas ranges, stainless steel backsplashes and glass-fronted refrigerators. The trick here, however, is to find a happy medium between a kitchen outfitted to feed an army and one that can serve as your everyday home base (and also be created on a family budget).

Although its visual effect is minimized by the wood panel door coverings and trimwork (above), a large side-by-side refrigerator is a hallmark of a restaurant-inspired kitchen. Other giveaways include massive amounts of countertop and island worksurface.

A highly efficient work triangle is a must for the serious home chef, especially when his or her kitchen is somewhat limited in available floorspace. And as always, the big-buck range is a centerpiece that sends an unmistakable message.

A six-burner gas range with double oven and warming bins, combined with a host of high-tech smaller appliances and thoroughly modern cabinetry give this kitchen its professional appearance and functionality.

Multipurpose Kitchens

Whether the extra function is a place where the kids do their homework, a home office or a showplace room for entertaining, today's kitchens have grown from spaces reserved for preparing meals into the central hubs of our homes. Adding a computer workstation, a casual dining counter or just opening up the kitchen to the living room will increase the time spent in a kitchen. For these rooms, space planning is the key, so that homework doesn't bump into the griddle and guests aren't blocking the path to the sink. It's always wise to choose extra durable materials and sturdy furnishings for a kitchen that you'd like to play so many roles.

Homework has become yet another function of the kitchen. A spacious breakfast bar offers a comfortable, supervised space where kids can finish up school work while dinner is being prepared.

A small wine station (left) in one corner of a kitchen can help keep hostess duties out of the way of other entertaining and food preparation. It can also serve as an extra prep area or beverage station for kids' drinks.

You won't need to travel far to take your lunchbreak when you're working in this home office. By repeating design elements (particularly the cabinetry) the designer of this multipurpose kitchen has knit the office area, dining area and food prep area together almost seamlessly.

Green Kitchens

The growing popularity of eco-friendly designs is changing the look of kitchens. From sustainable bamboo flooring to an ultra-efficient dishwasher, choosing materials and appliances that lower our impact on the environment is always a smart choice. Accordingly, the selection of renewable and recycled surface materials—for floors and countertops—is increasing to meet the demand with more durable and elegant options coming into the market every year.

Not only does a green kitchen support the environment, it should also accommodate the popularity of increasingly healthy eating and cooking habits. This kitchen has plenty of warm woods, metals and natural light as well as central and convenient storage for fresh organic produce under the island.

Maybe you've heard the eco-friendly terms—recycled, renewable, salvaged, sustainable, low-emissions, low-VOC—so many times that you've come to assume that practically all the options are "green." The fact is that eco-friendly materials and resources are often a little harder to find, a little more expensive and a little less familiar than our standard kitchen materials, but a growing selection is out there and the choice is yours. Here are a few terms to become familiar with:

- **Salvaged wood** refers either to materials that have been reclaimed for an existing structure or job site, or old hardwoods that have been saved from demolished buildings and can be remilled for new use.

- **FSC-certified wood** has been certified by the Forest Stewardship Council (FSC), which is an accredited international organization promoting the use of environmentally and socially responsible foresting techniques.

- **Renewable materials,** such as bamboo, cork or grass, are generally plants that grow quickly enough to replenish the resources at the relative rate of demand.

- **VOC emissions**—short for volatile organic compounds— refer to the toxic vapors that are a result of manufacturing processes. Many materials, paints and finishes are now available in variations that offgas less VOC.

- **Long-lasting materials** from local suppliers are another way to avoid wasted energy and resources, because they don't have to be imported and do not have to be replaced as frequently.

Renewable building materials like the bamboo flooring and cabinet cases shown here represent cutting edge design while preserving natural resources. Bamboo (which is actually a grass) is durable, fast growing and requires little water or fertilizer when it grows in the wild.

Conserving resources can make a design statement as well as an environmental one. Although it is hardly a prerequisite, most "green" kitchens have a distinctly Oriental or Zen ambiance.

The addition of dishwasher drawers can be an effective energy- and water-saving trick, since you only have to run one if its full. Efficient appliances consume less energy, and typically, natural materials such as this stone backsplash require less energy to produce than manmade materials.

Natural light is free and readily available, making it a central player in any green kitchen. Light surfaces and colors and good design planning enhance the effect of the natural light, reducing the need to supplement it with task light.

Kitchens That Work

Performance is the ultimate goal of a kitchen. While it's fun to dream about marble countertops and shiny new faucets, if your new kitchen is an inefficient place to prepare food then your design most likely has failed.

How much time could be saved if all the ingredients and tools you needed to make dinner were there within arm's reach? Consider the peace of mind achieved by having a child's play area within earshot—and sightlines—of the kitchen. How much easier would it be to unload the groceries to a large island countertop en route to the fridge? Think of the luxuries a new range hood could afford with better stove-top lighting and ventilation.

It's easy to get used to doing things the hard way, and sometimes it's difficult to even imagine an alternate solution. But when it comes to kitchen design, there's always a simpler way to do things. Consider the fact that an entire industry is continuously inventing new ways to speed up food preparation or streamline tasks like dish washing. Now step back and think about all the ways that your kitchen could help make life easier:

Are your appliances slowing you down? The technology of ovens, refrigerators, microwaves—even toasters—seems to advance at a rapid pace, so investing in new up-to-minute appliances can often be a quick and easy way to upgrade a kitchen.

Is lack of storage creating clutter? Extending cabinets all the way up to the ceiling or adding more shelves inside existing cabinets can go a long way toward eliminating the mess of disorganized storage and crowded countertops.

Do you often have to transport ingredients and hot serving plates clear across the room? A look at the layout and reshuffling of the floor plan can instantly afford a more logical work flow.

Kitchens invite conviviality, so why not plan for it? By creating dedicated seating and eating areas adjacent to the kitchen, a chef who enjoys entertaining can insert himself or herself into the fun without creating obstacles that can threaten the delicate timing of a gourmet meal.

A compact food prep area (above) is balanced perfectly by a defined eating area. Careful attention to storage solutions greatly increases efficiency, making for a hardworking kitchen of the highest order.

Living in an apartment or small townhome with a modest kitchen (left) can mean you need to incorporate other elements into the room's function (see Multipurpose Kitchens, page 22). Choose appliances that blend with your decor and use cabinetry to tie it all together visually.

Kitchens That Flow

Kitchens that flow make good use of space and direct both diners and cooks so they can stay out of each other's way when they are engaged in the conflicting functions of eating and preparing food. And if you wish to extract even more use out of the space by setting it up for entertaining or other purposes, you'll need to pay even more attention to layout to ensure efficient work flow. Even if you plan to do all of the work yourself, establishing the layout to create a good flow may be the one task where it makes sense for you to enlist the advice of a professional designer. But in any case, start the process with some basic questions.

A few questions to consider:

- Will a readjustment of appliances do the trick?
- What about the addition of an island or an added peninsula?
- Can you work within your existing square footage of your kitchen?
- Do you need to expand into another room/open up to the living area?
- Do you need to "bump out" a wall for even more space?

This kitchen cuts corners to create a smoother working experience through the space. Note the way the sinks are set into the corners to maximize the counter space.

Even a galley kitchen (left) can be laid out to create efficient workflow. In a two-sided galley, the main issues are to leave enough space between opposing sides and to locate the sink and stove close together.

Flow is as important for the eye as it is for the feet (below). If you direct the feet to move toward an eye-catching feature, like this picture window with stunning skyline view, the eye tends to keep going after the feet stop.

Kitchens With Style

Once you've thought a little bit about layout and function, go ahead and turn your attention to the design details that make the kitchen the heart of the home: in other words, style.

Style is a bit tricky as far as design concepts go. Just as our own styles differ, so do our ideas about what style means. For some, it may be a subscription to an established design motif, such as Arts and Crafts or Art Deco or French Provincial. But for others, style is more of a personal reflection. It is something we each develop, deliberately or simply by virtue of living. Whether you aspire to a style that is instantly recognizable in design magazines or you simply want to make your kitchen look like you, the task can usually be achieved with just a few simple accessories and focal points. In other words, you don't need to go out and buy a Neoclassical style refrigerator to create a kitchen that evokes a Neoclassical image. A couple of columnar plant stands and an arched wall niche will get you a lot closer to the goal.

This kitchen is all about style, from the different materials and styles used in the cabinets—note how the sink section is raised up on legs—to the colors and materials. Here a mix of painted wood, dark stained wood floors and mottled stone tile adds interest from every angle.

Style can come from relentlessly repeating the use of a material (above) until there is no mistaking its dominant presence. If your goal is to create a bold, contemporary style that is designed to impress, for example, surround yourself in stainless steel.

Lighting provides an obvious avenue (left) to exhibit style, partly because lighting fixtures are often designed with very specific style objectives in mind. Reflecting light adds to the effect.

Style can be backward looking or forward looking. It can seek to recall a specific worldview or it can try and establish or predict a new one. This kitchen falls more in the latter category.

Colors can say a lot about your personal sense of style. Practically everyone has a favorite color or color scheme. When you are choosing the colors for your new kitchen, put your favorite colors at the top of the list and see what you can do to make them work. You'll probably be surprised how easy it is to incorporate them.

Choose a favorite item and make it a centerpiece. It can be a work of art, a furnishing or even something that you'd never expect to find in a kitchen.

The Accessible Kitchen

Universal Design and Accessible Design are the terms used by architects, engineers and product designers to describe making accommodations for the needs of every type of person, regardless of age and physical ability. For example, large handled tools, contrasting typeface, wide doorways and smooth flooring are all results of Universal Design research. In the kitchen, the consideration of accessibility must be more extensive than almost anywhere else in the home. From safety lighting, to pull out shelves, to the height of counters, planning a kitchen that everyone can easily use requires careful forethought. There are tips on Universal Design throughout this book, offering advice on accessibility for many of the standard kitchen elements.

Universal design for kitchen cabinets puts the majority of items in the comfortable reach zone between 2 and 5 feet above the floor. Using pop-up and pull-down shelves can extend this area. Full-extension hardware on drawers and pull-out shelves eliminates reaching and fumbling for unseen items at the back of drawers and cabinets. Base cabinets installed at various heights serve users of different heights. Hanging some sections of upper cabinets at 12" to 15" above the countertop—rather than 18"—makes it easier to see and access items.

A full-length pantry also increases the amount of storage space in the comfortable reach zone. A pull-out pantry allows for easier viewing of the contents, but make sure the hardware is top quality and operates easily and smoothly. An appliance garage, a cabinet with a tambour door that sits on the countertop, is an excellent way to efficiently use corner space and store heavy or frequently used appliances out of sight. Make sure an electrical outlet or two are inside the garage.

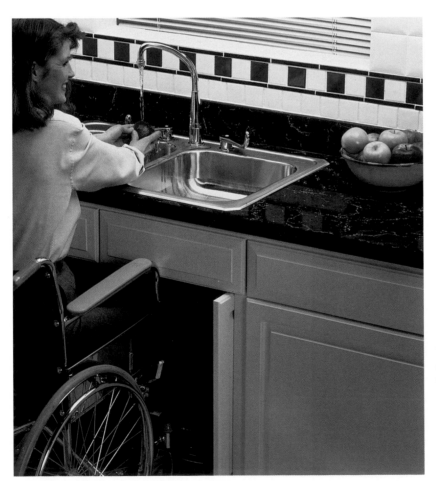

Universal Tips ▸

- Magnetic touch latches or c-shaped handles are the easiest to open.

- Avoid gloss cabinet finishes to reduce glare for the vision impaired.

- Countertops at a variety of heights should be ergonomically correct for a range of different users.

Countertop height and ease of fixture operation are two of the most important aspects of universal design. If your kitchen remodeling project needs to accommodate a person with special needs, most states have agencies that can offer you specific advice for your situation.

Store commonly used plates and dinnerware in deep drawers in your base cabinets for easy access.

Revolving corner systems are efficient and affordable.

Pull-out, expanding shelves bring the contents of the corner out to you.

Kitchen Elements

Like anything made in a kitchen, the success of a kitchen remodel depends on selecting the freshest and best ingredients. This means the cabinets, countertops, fixtures, appliances, flooring, and lighting. The materials for the cabinets and countertops should be suitable to your lifestyle, and offer the highest quality in your price range. Appliances should be energy-efficient while accommodating all the needs of your dream kitchen. Floors need to be durable and easy-to-clean, considering the high amount of foot traffic and inevitable spills. The style of fixtures and hardware should complement the overall look of the space—don't run out of steam when it comes to selecting these details, as they are the pieces that will be touched each day.

Be sure to set priorities. Knowing your budget before you even get started will help narrow down the elements to those in your price range. Splurge on the one ingredient that means the most to you, whether it's a six-burner range, wide-plank wood floors or nickel-plated hardware. Decide where you need or want high-quality elements and how you can incorporate green materials.

Finally, keep in mind that not all of these examples are achieved through do-it-yourself projects. Some projects are best left for professional installation, so if you want to keep this a DIY remodel, choose features that are within your skill level.

In This Chapter
- Cabinets
- Countertops
- Fixtures & Appliances
- Flooring
- Lighting
- Color & Materials

Cabinets

When purchasing cabinets, you have a number of decisions to make. First you need to decide if you want to go with stock, semi-custom or custom cabinets. Then you need to choose between face-frame or frameless styles. Materials, door and drawer styles, and finishes must also be decided upon. And finally, you'll need to consider the wide range of specialty features, add-ons and hardware available.

Cabinets are generally divided into three categories: stock, semi-custom and custom. Stock cabinets and some semi-custom cabinets are available for homeowners to install themselves; custom cabinets are invariably installed by the fabricator or designated installer.

There's a growing trend in "unfitted" kitchen systems, too. Seen most frequently in European kitchens, the cabinets and shelves are modular—like pieces of storage furniture—rather than built-in, or fitted. There are several manufacturers that sell unfitted storage units but another option is to incorporate some less-expected items—a storage locker as a pantry or a china cabinet for displaying dishes—in lieu of standard cabinets.

Stock

Stock cabinets are available as either ready-to-assemble (RTA) or ready-to-install. Ready-to-assemble cabinets, also referred to as knock-down or flat-pack, are shipped as flat components that the consumer puts together using connecting hardware.

In other words, in addition to installing the cabinets, you have to assemble them. Your options will be limited if you chose RTA cabinets, but because many of them are created by European designers, you will be able to achieve a slightly different look than the standard American stock cabinet. Be aware that some RTA cabinets are made with low-quality materials—½" particleboard and plastic veneer for example. But, just because a cabinet is shipped flat does not necessarily mean it is poorly constructed. Carefully inspect samples of assembled cabinets to check material quality and engineering quality. If possible, also look at assembly directions to check for clarity.

Ready-to-install cabinets are available in a number of quality levels, from utility units suitable for a workshop or a weekend home, to good-quality, long-lasting kitchen classics. Standard stock cabinets range from 6" to 42" wide, in 3" increments. Most sizes are readily available, though they may need to be shipped from a warehouse. Also available with stock cabinets are filler strips and trim moldings.

Semi-Custom

Semi-custom cabinets are also factory-made to standard sizes, but they offer far more options in finish, size, features and materials than stock cabinets. These are typically sold in showrooms and are priced between stock and custom cabinets. Semi-custom is the best choice for homeowners who want better-quality cabinets with some special features but don't want to pay the high prices for a custom product. You should allow three to eight weeks lead time when ordering semi-custom cabinets.

Custom

Custom cabinets offer the most in terms of options. These cabinets are designed, built and installed to fit a unique space. It is wise to shop around before settling on a custom cabinetmaker, as price, quality and availability will vary widely. The minimum lead time for custom cabinet construction is six weeks in most markets. When you get bids, find out if the lead time is from acceptance of the bid, or from when the condition of the kitchen allows the cabinetmaker to take accurate measurements. Remember that exotic or difficult-to-machine materials and intricate custom designs will end up costing you more.

Perhaps more than any other kitchen feature, cabinets define the tone and overall appearance of a kitchen. They can be light and casual, dark and formal, or just about anywhere in between.

Standard Stock Cabinets ▶

Base cabinets (without countertop)
Height	34½"
Depth	24"
Width	6" to 42", in 3" increments

Wall cabinets
Height	12", 15", 18", 24", 30", 36"
Depth	12"
Width	6" to 36", in 3" increments

Oven cabinets
Height	83", 95"
Depth	24"
Width	30", 33"

Pantry cabinets
Height	83", 95"
Depth	24"
Width	18", 24"

Face-frame vs. Frameless

Once you have decided whether you will be purchasing factory-made or custom cabinets, you need to decide which type of cabinet: face-frame or frameless.

Face-frame cabinets have frames made of solid wood around the front of the cabinet box. Because the frame extends into cabinet space, the door openings will be reduced and a certain amount of "dead" space exists within the cabinet behind the frames. The hinges for doors on face-frame cabinets mount on the frame. The door itself may be flush within the frame or raised above it. Flush-fitting doors were common on older cabinets, but because they require a precise fit, which means more time and craftsmanship, they will be more expensive and more difficult to find.

Frameless cabinets are often referred to as "Eurostyle." These cabinets do not have a face frame and the doors and drawers span the entire width of the carcass, which allows for easier access and a bit more storage space. The doors are mounted using cup hinges, which are invisible when the doors are closed. Frameless cabinets have a streamlined look, which makes them feel more contemporary in style. One drawback of frameless cabinets is that they do not have the added strength of the face frame, so it is critical that they are solidly constructed and properly installed.

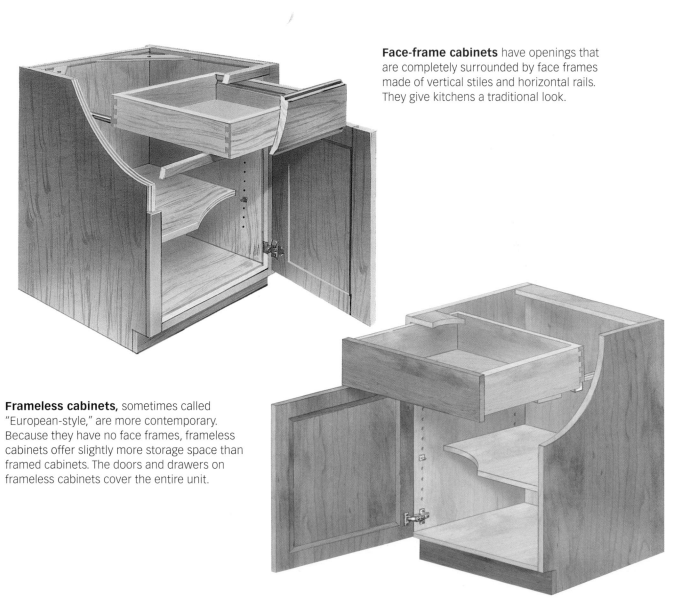

Face-frame cabinets have openings that are completely surrounded by face frames made of vertical stiles and horizontal rails. They give kitchens a traditional look.

Frameless cabinets, sometimes called "European-style," are more contemporary. Because they have no face frames, frameless cabinets offer slightly more storage space than framed cabinets. The doors and drawers on frameless cabinets cover the entire unit.

Custom cabinets (above) are expensive, but many designers prefer them because they offer endless design opportunities and they tend to be better constructed than stock cabinets or ready-to-assemble cabinets. Most custom cabinets have all-wood drawer fronts and doors, usually made with quality hardwood that's suitable for a fine wood finish.

Metallic (left) and other nonwood finishes bring interesting new textures and colors into your kitchen. They also allow you to incorporate lighter tones to brighten the kitchen and reflect light.

Doors & Drawers

Doors and drawer fronts are available in many styles made from a variety of woods and wood-finish options. If you are not a fan of woodgrain, another option is the "foil" clad door. These have the look of a raised-panel door, but are made of medium-density fiberboard (MDF) coated with a durable vinyl material. Doors can also have glass or a variety of other materials including laminate, fabric, wire mesh, and decorative metal fronts, instead of wood panels.

The door style, material and finish will be a major factor in determining the cost of your cabinets. The least expensive cabinets are the frameless style with a flat-slab door or a flat-panel door. Picture frame, cathedral, raised-panel, slatted and glass with individual panes are all more expensive door options.

Glass lites add interest and gleam to a kitchen, but if you are not a stickler for cabinet organization look for multi-lite doors with frosted or textured glass.

Overlay frame-and-panel doors (left) provide some depth and relief to a flat bank of cabinets, and they are easier to hang than some other types. Structurally, they are the same as raised panel doors, except with simpler profiles.

Stainless steel cabinets with glass doors (below) give a sleek, industrial look to a kitchen. At one time, metal kitchen cabinets were inexpensive and very common, but these days they are a high-end option.

Hardware

Your cabinet hardware—the door and drawer pulls and hinges—is another way to customize the look of your kitchen. Whether stylized organic shapes or classic ceramic knobs, the hardware on cabinets can really help define the style of your kitchen. Many cast-metal or handmade ceramic pulls are available in a wide variety of shapes and sizes. Since these pieces are often priced individually, they can often add up when all is said and done. Eclectic styles are increasingly trendy, however, so it's fine to have a few decorative pulls mixed in with the basic less-expensive versions. Consider adding ornamental pulls just to the top drawers or on upper cabinets only.

Touch-latch cabinet closures are another trendy option that offers a modern look. Keep in mind that not having drawer and door pulls can mean that the fronts of cabinets and drawers have to be cleaned more frequently.

Hinges may be fully concealed or semi-concealed on face-frame cabinets, but frameless cabinets always have concealed hinges. One area not to skimp on with concealed hinges is their adjustability. Ideally they should have side, height and depth adjustments. No-mortise hinges for semi-concealed hinges reduce labor because they mount on top of the cabinet and door surface with no need for cutting mortises.

Unique cabinet hardware can transform ordinary millwork into a design highlight that helps set the overall tone and feeling of the kitchen.

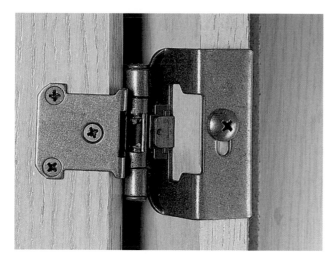

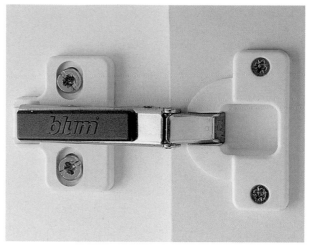

Hinges on framed cabinets are screwed directly to the face frames. Better cabinets have adjustable hinges that allow door realignment.

Hinges on frameless cabinets are screwed directly to the inside of the cabinet, eliminating the need for face frames. Hinges are hidden, providing a cleaner look.

Drawer hardware usually mounts to a drawer front or false front with mounting bolts that are driven through the back face of the drawer front and into threaded rods on the hardware. The spacing of the guide holes is not uniform, so the drawer fronts do not come predrilled.

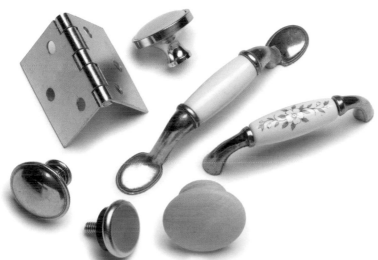

Pulls come in an array of styles, from simple wooden knobs to elaborate or whimsical art pieces. Think about your hardware selections while you are budgeting for the project. Cabinet hardware is one of those hidden costs that is easy to overlook (especially if you want to invest in some handcrafted hardware for a unique look).

Cabinets & Universal Design

When considering a design for kitchen cabinets, the issue of accessibility should be a priority. Cabinets that require constant bending down would be inappropriate for someone with a bad back.

Shelves so high you need a step stool are not the safest bet for someone who is elderly. Considering the needs of users—and future users—is a smart way to start planning for a new kitchen.

Pull-out shelves offer the ultimate in easy access, not just for operators with restricted movement. If someone in your household requires a wheelchair, design your new cabinets so they have a full 8"-tall toe-kick area, not just the standard 2½" to 3" seen here.

Accessible Cabinets ▶

Making a kitchen accessible to wheelchair users involves incorporating open, roll-in space in the base cabinets so that sink, cooktop and countertops are within reach. Roll-in cabinets have no bottom or toe kick. The roll-in space can be concealed with a fold-away door. All other base cabinets should be modified to have an 8" toe kick. If upper cabinets are used, they need to have pull-down shelving. Base cabinets with pull-out shelves and pantries with lazy Susans are the best storage options.

Universal Design ▸

Design your kitchen around a clear, circular space of at least 5 ft. in diameter to provide room for a wheelchair. If your kitchen doesn't have 60" of clear space, allow 48" for pathways. Plan for 30 to 48" of clear approach space in front of all appliances and workstations.

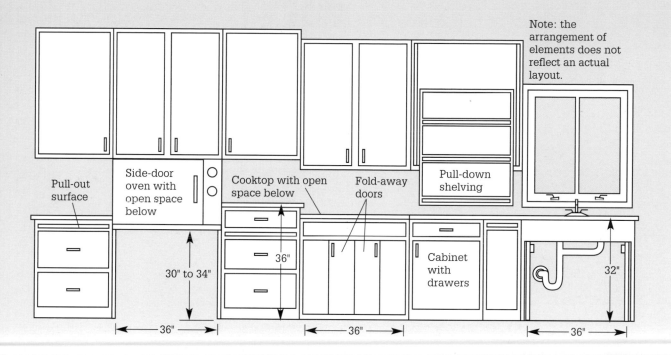

Note: the arrangement of elements does not reflect an actual layout.

Pull-out surface

Side-door oven with open space below

Cooktop with open space below

Fold-away doors

Pull-down shelving

Cabinet with drawers

30" to 34"

36"

36"

36"

32"

36"

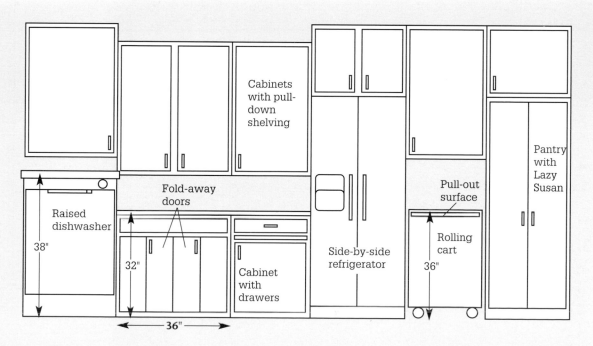

Cabinets with pull-down shelving

Raised dishwasher

Fold-away doors

Cabinet with drawers

Side-by-side refrigerator

Pull-out surface

Rolling cart

Pantry with Lazy Susan

38"

32"

36"

36"

Countertops

More than simply a worksurface, a kitchen countertop can dazzle with the look-at-me drama of mottled granite, or bring together a country theme with honed soapstone and butcher block. But durability and maintenance are generally the primary concerns when it comes to countertops. Some materials, like granite, can withstand the heat of pots and pans, so are better suited for heavy-duty cooks. Others, including laminate, are affordable options that come in a wide variety of modern colors. There are many choices in countertops, from the less-expensive laminate, through ceramic and stone tile, to concrete and wood, to high-end granite and marble.

Countertop options for your kitchen depend on how much you are willing to spend, whether you will be doing it yourself or contracting it out, and what look you want to achieve. When choosing countertops, remember that you do not need to have a uniform countertop. Many people choose to use more expensive countertop materials as accents or for islands rather than for the entire kitchen.

Fabricated countertop material like quartz and solid-surface is virtually impenetrable to water and if it becomes scratched, minor damage can easily be buffed out.

A custom laminate countertop allows for numerous edging and backsplash options. While it can be trickier than you might think, making your own plastic laminate countertops is a doable DIY job (see pages 164 to 171).

Laminate

Laminate countertops are formed from layers of resin-saturated paper and plastic that are bonded under pressure, then given a protective coating. The laminate is bonded to a substrate to create the countertop. Also available is through-color laminate in which the surface color runs all the way through. This product doesn't have the dark edge of standard laminate and does not show surface damage as easily, but it is two to three times more expensive.

The cheapest laminate countertop is ready-made post-form. A post-form countertop comprises a backsplash, counter and bullnose front apron formed into one seamless piece. Home centers carry post-form countertop options available at various lengths in a few stock colors. You can also have a custom post-form countertop made, which will be slightly more expensive. You can install this yourself, or often have it delivered and installed by the fabricator.

A custom laminate countertop is distinguished from a post-form countertop by the square backsplash and seam between the backsplash and the countertop. Because the laminate used for custom surfaces is slightly thicker than that used for post-form, it is a little bit sturdier. You can order custom laminate countertops to be fabricated for you, or you can make your own.

A limitation of the laminate countertops is that sinks must be drop-in, not undermounted. Though the laminate itself is waterproof, the particleboard or plywood it is attached to will swell if it gets wet. Laminate is also not as heat-proof or scratch-proof as other countertop materials. To get the most out of your laminate countertop, do not use scouring pads or abrasive cleansers, always use a cutting board, and never place hot pots and pans directly on the surface.

Ceramic & Stone Tile

Ceramic tile and stone tile countertops are popular, mid-priced options. If you like the look of granite, but don't want to pay the price, granite tiles can create a similar look for substantially less, especially if you do the installation yourself. When selecting tiles for countertops, make sure they are floor tiles—wall tiles will not stand up to the wear and tear of countertop use.

Two major drawbacks of ceramic or stone tile are its hardness and the grout lines. Glassware and pottery will break and chip readily when knocked or dropped against this surface. Grout lines make the surface uneven and difficult to keep clean. Standard grout needs to be sealed on an annual basis to prevent it from staining. Newer, epoxy-based grout should be considered for countertops as it does not require sealing or upkeep. Using tiles for a backsplash is an excellent way to get the look of tile near the countertop.

A tiled countertop is a heat-resistant surface that is good for surrounding a cooktop because you can set hot pans on it. On the down side, the grout lines stain easily and can crack over time.

Concrete

Concrete is quickly becoming a popular countertop choice. It is a custom option, but is not as expensive as granite. It can be cast in place as a moderate to difficult DIY project, or off site with the help of professionals. Concrete can be dyed or stained in many different colors, and treated to have a number of finishes. Dish-drying rails or ornamental objects can be embedded in the concrete for added functionality or just to make it more unique.

Concrete needs to be sealed regularly, and it will permanently stain if not. Acidic foods will etch the surface. Like ceramic tile and stone surfaces, it has no give, so expect a greater number of broken glasses and plates. Custom concrete sinks integrated as part of the counter are also available.

Concrete countertops can be fabricated right on site, eliminating any surprises. Multiple layers of dye can be applied until the color suits your design.

Wood countertops may be highly polished, or oiled for a matte look. Either way, wood is a versatile and beautiful countertop.

Butcher Block & Wood

New finishes and sealants have made wood more amenable for kitchen applications, where historically the amount of water splashed around a sink would ruin a wood surface.

The best option in wood countertops is butcher block, which can be ordered and installed as a moderate DIY project. Butcher block is made up of small pieces of wood glued together into a slab. It's generally categorized as either end grain, which is composed of vertical pieces of wood, or edge grain, made up long strips of wood. The thickness of stock slabs can vary, from 1½" for the standard countertop to 4" for an island or small-section installation.

Many people think that butcher block is convenient because you no longer need cutting boards, but it's a poor idea to use them as direct cutting surfaces. Every nick and cut will collect dirt and will darken differently when reoiled. For basic hygiene, surfaces used to cut meat and fish need to be removable so they can be thoroughly washed in hot soapy water. Another important thing to note is that wood, no matter how well it is sealed, will continue to expand and contract in relation to humidity levels, so installation of a wood countertop requires flexible attachments.

Solid-surface countertops are easy to restore. Light sanding will remove surface scratches, burns, and stains; more significant damage requires professional restoration. Since its introduction in the early 1970s, solid surface material has quickly become one of the most popular counter materials on the market. It resists low heat, marks, and scratches. And because the color goes all the way through the material, minor damage simply can be sanded or polished away.

Stainless steel counters and backsplashes work with stainless steel appliances to make this galley kitchen as easy to look at as it is to clean. The stainless surfaces softly reflect light, making the space seem more spacious than it actually is.

Quartz countertops are similar to solid surface in appearance, but because they do not contain plastic resins or binders they are much more heat resistant. Manufacturers also claim the material is completely impervious to water or moisture.

Solid Surface

Solid-surface countertops, commonly described by the common brand name Corian™, are popular but more expensive options. As the name implies, these countertops are solid color from top to bottom. Pieces are joined with a bonding compound that leaves no visible seam line.

An advantage of solid surface materials is that it can be used with the same seamless bonding. Sinks are available in three or four basic color options. Solid-surface countertops can be shaped and inlaid, it comes in many colors and patterns, it is durable and it can be repaired.

Solid surface should not be used as a cutting board and hot pans cannot be placed directly on the surface. Most spills are easily cleaned with soap and water. If staining, etching or scorching occurs, it can be rubbed out with fine abrasives, though gloss surfaces will need to be buffed to regain their shine.

Though solid surface materials are easily worked with standard hand tools, do-it-yourselfers may have difficulty purchasing the materials and bonding agents. If a non-licensed installer installs one of those countertops, the manufacturer will not honor any product warranties.

Edging options with solid surface are many. Because the material is easily cut with a router, the edges can be formed in a number of profiles, though there are two or three standard edges. Also possible are edgings with contrasting colors or patterns.

Quartz Surfaces

Quartz surfaces are manufactured from 93% quartz and 7% pigments, resins and binders. Regardless of the manufacturer, all quartz surfaces are manufactured using equipment and formulas developed by Breton Stone. The difference in appearance among products is due to the type of quartz used.

This surface is unscratchable, non-porous, non-staining, does not need to be sealed, and will not scorch or mar from high heat. Though as hard as granite, it has more inherent flexibility, so surface cracking does not occur. The surface is cool to the touch, like granite and marble. Installation is the same as granite. Because it is a pigmented product, color choices are numerous.

Stainless Steel

Though slightly more expensive than sold surface or quartz, stainless steel is an impervious material that doesn't stain, can handle hot pots, and can be fabricated into seamless countertops and sinks. Stainless steel countertops for residential use are usually bonded to plywood or particleboard to quiet the noise and prevent denting. Sinks can either be fabricated as part of the countertop, or, more likely, welded in. Either way, it is a seamless application. The biggest downside is that stainless steel shows fingerprints and watermarks, especially on a polished surface, so it's best to get a matte or satin surface.

Natural stone countertops (above) like this marble counter are beautiful and have a certain warmth that can elude manmade materials. They're also heat resistant and highly durable. But they can be quite expensive and are susceptible to staining.

The beauty and elegance of granite (right) is also available as stone tiles. These tiles are installed in the same manner as ceramic tiles.

Stone

Soapstone, slate, marble and granite are all used for countertops. These countertops are also very heavy, and except for sandstone, require specialized cutting and shaping tools. Though they are all quarried stone, and are all fairly expensive, they have numerous differences.

Soapstone has been used for kitchen countertops and sinks for hundreds of years. Though the stone itself is easily workable with non-specialized tools, its surface is non-absorbent and unaffected by either acids or alkalis. The surface will age to a glossy patina, or it can be oiled to achieve this finish. Surface stains are also limited to the surface and easily rubbed or sanded out.

Slate for countertops is durable, hard and dense. Scratches can be rubbed out if necessary. Like soapstone, its surface is non-absorbing and does not require sealing. Slate comes in shades of green, purple, gray and black, with a rare red available at higher cost.

Marble has long been popular for rolling pins and surfaces for pastry and candy making because it is cool to the touch. The advantage of a small movable marble surface is that it can be placed in the refrigerator to provide an even cooler surface. The beauty of marble comes from its veining patterns—unfortunately these are mini faultlines along which the stone will easily break, especially if improperly installed. Some marbles are as hard as granite, but most are fairly soft and scratch or chip easily, and all are susceptible to staining and will be etched by acid.

Granite is the hardest of the stone countertops. It comes in an ever-increasing array of colors—ranging from whites and blacks to pinks, reds, yellows and greens—as more countries begin exporting their local granites. No two pieces of stone will be identical, so if your countertop is large, it should be cut from the same piece or adjoining pieces to get the best possible match. The main drawback of granite is that it must be sealed to prevent staining. Sealing is usually needed once or twice a year.

For all stone countertops, a honed or matte surface is recommended—a polished surface is a mirror gloss finish, which creates unnecessary glare and reveals surface scratches and spotting more easily.

Green Design

Stone countertops are good green options since they will not outgas hazardous chemicals. Where the stone is quarried is of concern. European and North American sources have to meet strict environmental and safety standards and generally have well-paid work forces. Some concerns have been raised about granite emitting radon, but no conclusive risks have been documented.

A soapstone countertop with a soapstone sink creates a one-of-a-kind rustic look.

Fixtures & Appliances

Selecting the right appliances and fixtures for your kitchen update or remodeling project requires a balancing act, with cost, energy efficiency, performance, and style thrown into the mix. It's fun to look through magazines and at the cutting edge kitchens featured, but be prepared for sticker shock when you are ready to make your selections.

Focus on the features you really need and want, and look for appliances and fixtures that offer those options. For instance, a stainless steel kitchen may be appealing—but if your main goal is easy cleanup, you will be disappointed to discover that stainless steel prominently displays fingerprints and water marks.

As you read this section, consider what options you cannot live without, as well as those you just don't need. This will help you narrow your choices when you begin looking at the costs of various options.

Ranges, Cooktops & Ovens

A range, or stove, combines an oven and a cooktop in one unit. Ranges often cost less than two separate units, and take up less space. Choosing separate units, however, gives you flexibility in placement and may allow you access to features not available in a range. Cooktops can be placed in practically any enclosed cabinet with countertop. Ovens can be placed in islands, under counters and at varying heights on the wall.

The first decision to make for any of these items is what type of power to use. Gas is the favorite cooktop fuel of chefs and serious home cooks because it has immediate heat control. Electric cooktops are slower to heat and cool and are not as obviously "on" because there is no visible flame. Many bakers prefer an electric oven because the heat is more even. A solution is to either use separate components or to purchase a dual-fuel range that has an electric oven and a gas cooktop.

The gas cooktop has the reputation of being difficult to clean, though sealed burners make this less of an issue. All gas cooktops have some sort of grating to hold the pots above the flames; make sure you can move these easily for cleaning. With electronic ignition, gas cooktops and ovens do not have pilot lights, so the risks of extinguished pilot lights are no longer an issue.

Gas ovens are often not as well insulated as self-cleaning electric ovens, so they may heat your kitchen space more. If you broil often, make sure the broiler is located in the main oven compartment, and not in a separate, lower compartment. This eliminates bending and allows for greater broiling capacity.

Electric cooktops come in a variety of burner configurations. The traditional is the electric coil with drip plate. Solid disks are made of cast iron sealed to the cooktop. Halogen burners are underneath a glass cooktop and are heated by vacuum-sealed halogen lamps. Induction burners are also under a glass cooktop and have an electromagnetic coil that conducts electrical energy directly to the pot, requiring ferrous cookware (stainless steel, aluminum and ceramic cookware will not work). The flat ceramic tops are smooth, but may require special cleaners.

Electric ovens are conventional, convection or multi-mode. A conventional oven is the standard oven with a heating element at the bottom for baking and an element at the top for broiling. A true convection oven has no elements in the oven cavity. Instead, the baking element and a fan are located outside the cavity. The fan circulates the heated air to produce an absolutely balanced heat—you can bake as many trays of cookies as you have oven racks. A more expensive option is the multi-mode oven, which uses conventional, convection and microwave cooking.

If you entertain often, you may want to consider having two ovens, either as a double wall unit or as part of a dual range. Also popular now are professional-style ranges and cooktops. These units produce high heat and generally have larger capacities than standard units. Be aware that they also require professional-style venting.

Warming drawers are available as part of a range, or as separate units. These can be handy for dough raising, keeping courses warm or dealing with staggered meal times. If you do a great deal of wok cookery, you may also consider investing in a specialized wok burner that generates the heat necessary in the proper configuration for this style.

Gleaming, professional-grade appliances (left) are at the top of just about everyone's kitchen wish list, but the truth is most homeowners probably can't afford them. If you are financing your kitchen remodeling project with a home equity loan, however, it might be worth your time to analyze the actual cost to you of a couple of high-end luxuries once you spread out the payment and factor in the tax benefits. You may be surprised.

Professional-style gas ranges (below) have the capabilities of restaurant stoves, but have important safety features necessary for home use.

Microwave Ovens

Microwaves are now a standard kitchen appliance—both for their convenience and low price. Look for the features that you will use most often and an interior cavity that has the capacity you need. Though a space-saving microwave with integral exhaust fan installed over a range is popular, it is not necessarily a good idea. The ventilation provided is not optimal, the microwave impinges on the cooktop workspace and reaching over the cooktop to use the microwave can be hazardous—especially for children. If you are tight on counter space, an undercabinet-mounted microwave is a better idea.

Vent Fans

Vent fans and range hoods protect your kitchen surfaces and your health by exhausting the heat, steam, grease and odors produced by cooking. Local codes may apply to venting systems, so check with a building inspector or HVAC contractor. To truly be effective, vent fans must vent to the outdoors, not filter and recirculate the air.

Vent fans are rated for airflow in cubic feet per minute (cfm) and by noise level measured in sones. Look for a high flow rating with a low noise rating. Large cooktops, specialty grills and wok burners require heavy-duty ventilation systems. Vent hoods over islands need to be more powerful because of the open, rather than enclosed, setting. Down-draft and pop-up vents pull the air down to exhaust, so they also need to be more powerful. Slide-out and low-profile vents are available, though they may not be as effective.

Each vent will have specific limitations concerning size and length of ductwork; make sure your planned vent outlet is within these limits.

Build in plenty of clear swing space for appliance doors when designing your kitchen. One of the most common mistakes inexperienced designers make is to locate an island too close to a refrigerator or oven door, making it difficult to use the appliances. Try and maintain a minimum of 3 ft. of clearance for each appliance.

Universal Design ▸

Placement and configuration of appliances can make them easier to use. Wall-mounted ovens and raised dishwashers make baking and cleanup easier by eliminating bending. In addition, moving the oven away from the cooktop makes it easier for two cooks to work at the same time. Side-swinging doors on a wall-mounted oven make them even easier and safer to use. Side-by-side refrigerators also cut down on bending, and the built-in water and ice dispensers conserve energy. Avoid dangerous reaches across steaming stovetops by installing range hoods with wall- or counter-mounted controls and cooktops with front-mounted controls.

This two-oven gas range is located right in the middle of this photo, but the real reason for the picture is the pair of side-by-side refrigerators that you don't notice. Some high end appliance manufacturers offer appliance panels that can be customized to match your cabinets exactly.

Refrigerators

Buying a new refrigerator can be expensive, but running an older refrigerator can account for as much as 20% of your household electrical costs. New energy and pollution standards created over the past 20 years have helped make refrigerators much more efficient.

Refrigerators come in a number of styles and configurations. Slide-in refrigerators are the traditional style, usually 28" to 34" deep, though some may be 24" deep. Built-in refrigerators are wider than slide-ins, but only 24" deep so they are flush with base cabinets. Built-ins need space above for venting. Refrigerator and freezer configurations include top freezer, bottom freezer and side-by-side. The top freezer is more efficient,

and easier to access, but the bottom freezer puts more of the refrigerator at a usable height. Side-by-side configurations are popular because both are easily accessed, and in-door ice servers are only available in this style. The major drawback of the side-by-side is the diminished width of the refrigerator side. A platter of hors d'oeuvres, a cookie sheet or a large roasting pan often won't fit in this narrow compartment.

New freezer and refrigerator options include commercial-grade refrigerators, individual drawers that look like cabinet drawers and can be located anywhere, dual-temperature wine coolers and freestanding vertical freezer and refrigerator components that can be installed separately.

Dishwashers

Dishwashers, like refrigerators, have also become more efficient and quieter. A dishwasher that doesn't require hand rinsing before loading will also save water—enough so that using a dishwasher actually conserves water!

The key issues to consider in buying a dishwasher are the operating costs, noise reduction, cleaning power and features. Operating costs can be determined by looking at the yellow Energy Guide tag. Noise reduction measures are often directly related to price. Look for sound-absorbent insulation around the tub, behind the door, over the top and behind the access panel and toe kick. Because you won't usually be able to hear a dishwasher run through its cycles in a showroom, refer to consumer ratings magazines for sound-level comparisons. A dishwasher's cleaning power depends on how it disperses and filters water. How the water jets are aimed can be as important as how many sprayers are present.

Food Disposers

The main consideration when looking at food disposers is horsepower. Models come with $1/3$- to 1-horsepower motors, with the larger, more expensive models being quieter, carrying longer warranties and having more features. Most models are continuous feed, which means that a switch (usually on the wall, but occasionally sink or counter mounted) is flipped, the motor runs and items can be fed through the rubber gasket continuously.

People with septic systems should be aware that a disposer adds to the overall load on the septic tank. Even though disposer units say they are safe for septic tanks and some even come with enzyme sprays to help promote the bacterial action, they will still add to the amount of sludge in the tank.

A dishwasher knife drawer (above) holds your professional grade cutlery safely during cleaning.

Dishwashers (left) are available in a wide variety of sizes, including standard slide-in units, high capacity machines and also small drawer or countertop units.

Sinks & Faucets

Sinks come in numerous stock configurations, sizes and materials. The first choice to consider is the material. Stainless steel, cast iron, enameled steel, solid surface, fireclay, acrylic and resin are all standard sink materials, each with its own advantages and disadvantages. Custom sinks are available in copper, brass, soapstone, concrete and granite.

Stainless steel sinks are easy to clean, long lasting and available in every possible bowl configuration (top mounts, undermounts and apron fronts) and in every price range. The only drawbacks are that stainless steel shows water spots and the sinks can be noisy if not properly undercoated with sound-deadening material.

Cast-iron sinks are actually cast iron with a fired-on porcelain finish. These sinks are durable, attractive, and are available in a wide range of designs and colors including top mount, undermount and apron front. The only drawback of this type of sink is its hardness—you may break a few more glasses than with a stainless, solid-surface or resin sink.

Enameled steel is the inexpensive cousin to cast iron. The metal is thinner, the enamel is less durable than porcelain, and the designs available may be limited. However, if you can find a steel sink with a porcelain finish and polyester-resin backing, you will have a sink that costs and weighs less than cast iron and absorbs shock better so you have fewer broken glasses.

Solid-surface sinks are available in a number of styles, but a limited range of colors. They are most frequently found in undermount styles rather than drop-ins. This is because the majority of solid surface sinks are integrated with a solid-surface counter, where they will be attached under the countertop in a seamless installation. Solid-surface sinks are shock absorbent, stain resistant and repairable. If you should happen to stain, gouge or scorch the material, a seamless, invisible repair through sanding or patching can be made.

Fireclay is a vitreous-china product that has a strong, smooth finish and a very hard, non-marking surface. These sinks are heavy and can be expensive, but they are available in a number of apron-front designs, which has increased their popularity.

Acrylic and fiberglass sinks are inexpensive, shock-absorbing sinks that are easy to clean but might not have good longevity. Resin sinks are composites of resin, pigment and quartz or other minerals. This material does not chip, scratch, stain, crack or mar.

A visually appealing and properly functioning sink and faucet are essential if you are to maximize your enjoyment of your new kitchen.

An apron sink (above) sets a tone of casual luxury and establishes your kitchen as one of distinction. These sinks, also called farmhouse sinks, can be single or double bowl, and are either mounted beneath a countertop or tiled into a tile countertop.

This one-piece stainless steel sink (left) with backsplash eliminates seams, making it easy to clean.

Most kitchen sinks are drop-in, double bowl models that typically have a garbage disposer and dishwasher hooked up to the drain system. But supplementary sinks, such as this lovely hammered copper prep sink, are becoming increasingly popular.

Sink Styles

These days, sinks are mounted in one of two ways: they can be self-rimming (they rest on top of the countertop), or undermounted (screwed into the underside of the countertop).

Self-rimming sinks are used in any type of countertop and are the most widely available. A variation of the self-rimming sink is the tile-in sink for tile countertops.

Some, such as cast-iron, are very heavy and rely mostly on their own weight to stay put. Lighter self-rimming sinks (also called drop-ins) are fastened with clips below the countertop.

Undermount sinks are popular because of their clean lines—no part of the sink protrudes above the countertop—and because debris is less likely to accumulate between the sink and countertop. A drawback is that undermount sinks cannot be used with laminate, post-form or tile countertops.

Sinks are currently available in so many bowl configurations that it would be impossible to list all of them here. They may be single-, double- or triple-bowled, with the bowl depth and size ranging from a small bar sink to a large farm or utility sink.

When choosing a sink, remember that the primary sink should be roomy enough to wash large pots and serving pieces. A sink that is more than 9" deep should be located in a raised countertop, because reaching into such a deep sink can cause back strain.

Kitchen faucet design is a high-end exercise that is constantly evolving. Shapes and finishes change the most often.

Universal Design ▸

Sink depths of 8", 9" or 10" are becoming popular, but very tall or short users will find it difficult to reach the sink bottom comfortably. Raise or lower your sink countertop to enable the primary user to stand at the sink and easily reach the bottom without bending. Single-handle faucets are much easier to use, allowing for continuous temperature adjustment and easy on and off. Incorporating an anti-scald device makes the faucet safer for children.

Faucet Styles

Faucets also come in a dizzying array of styles, materials and features. Though many kitchen faucets come with separate hot and cold taps, the single-handle lever faucets are much easier to use. Gooseneck and pull-out faucets make pot filling easier, but make sure that your sink is deep enough to accommodate the splashing from an extra-tall gooseneck. Most faucets require little or no maintenance and will retain their finish for many years, so it is mostly a matter of finding a style that suits you and your kitchen.

Energy-Efficient & Water Saving Choices

For the sake of both environmental resources and your own budget, selecting a kitchen design that incorporates energy- and water-saving appliances is a good idea. Most of the new appliances on the market are more energy efficient than older models, but the relative quality of their performance varies. Do some comparison-shopping when it comes to appliances and you are sure to outfit your kitchen with fixtures that save energy and money.

Lighting is another way to save energy. Consider the aesthetic benefits of adding a skylight or window to your kitchen; now think of the impact that natural lighting will have on your energy budget. Less artificial light will be needed, thus lowering electric bills.

Another way to cut down on energy requirements is to use fluorescent lighting or new innovations like LED lighting in the kitchen. These products not only reduce glare better than incandescent bulbs, they also use a fraction of the energy used by incandescent bulbs and need to be replaced less frequently. Newer versions of fluorescent bulbs produce a more true-to-life light color, rather than the old buzzing overhead tubes that gave everything a greenish hue. Some local building codes require a certain percentage of a kitchen's lighting to be fluorescent, so consider the benefits before lamenting this ordinance.

Natural light, both from large windows and skylights, make this kitchen feel sunny and warm. A blend of different types of artificial lighting also means that the levels can be set to the dimmest setting to cut down on energy use.

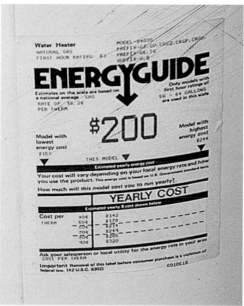

As a general rule, newer appliances are more efficient when it comes to energy and water consumption. For example, this dishwasher has a feature that allows the user to wash only one of the racks, using less water and energy when smaller loads are being cleaned.

Energy usage labels can be found on most major appliances you'll encounter at the appliance store. More energy efficient models may qualify for a rebate from your local public utility company. Ask the sales staff for information on these programs.

Flooring

Your kitchen floor is more than just a surface—it also helps to create the room's style by adding color, texture, and personality. You can use flooring to complement your countertops and cabinets, or create a point of contrast. Using different types of flooring can help define task and traffic areas, giving a large kitchen floor a bit more style. Flooring choices can help the kitchen flow into other rooms or create more visible boundaries.

Almost any material can and has been used as kitchen flooring, and with new processes of factory lamination, many inexpensive and easy-to-install options are available. The only floor covering that is truly not suited to kitchen use is carpeting. Non-slip area rugs, however, are a good way to add color, texture, and help break up a large expanse of one material. Different flooring options have different merits, especially in the kitchen. It pays to think carefully about what you want, because the cost and labor involved in flooring projects mean you won't soon want to change it.

Kitchen floors should be water and moisture resistant and very easy to clean. If given a choice some homeowners prefer a floor that conceals spills. This cork floor, when treated with a durable water resistant finish, has the added advantages of an on-trend appearance and a soft feel underfoot.

A traditional hardwood floor with genuine Oriental rugs makes a beautiful design statement in any room. High quality carpets resist staining and a well-applied finish will offer more than adequate protection for hardwood in a kitchen situation.

Green Design ▸

A number of choices are available in flooring if you desire an environmentally friendly option. The old standby, linoleum, is an excellent choice made from linseed oil, fabric backing, and cork or wood dust.

Cork is harvested from cork oak trees every 9 to 15 years. The trees can grow for up to 250 years. Because of this, cork plantations are home to diverse wildlife populations.

Bamboo is a renewable resource. It is harvested every 3 to 5 years, with the rootstock left to produce another crop.

In terms of outgassing, linoleum and ceramic tile are the safest, though some ceramic tile sealers may be problematic. Cork and bamboo are generally laminated to a substrate, or, in the case of bamboo, many layers of bamboo are glued together. These glues should be safe for everyone except the most chemically sensitive.

Vinyl Flooring

Vinyl flooring, also known as "resilient flooring," is a versatile, flexible surface. Vinyl flooring is available in both sheets and tiles, in thicknesses ranging from 1/16" to 1/8". Sheets come in 6' wide or 12' wide rolls, with either a felt or a polyvinyl chloride (PVC) backing, depending on the type of installation. Tiles typically come in 12" squares and are available with or without self-adhesive backing.

Installation is easy. Sheet vinyl with felt backing is glued to the floor using the full-spread method, meaning the entire project area is covered with adhesive. PVC-backed sheet vinyl is glued only along the edges (perimeter-bond method). Tiles are the easiest to install, but because tile floors have a lot of seams, they're less suitable for high-moisture areas. All vinyl flooring must be installed over a smooth underlayment.

Sheet vinyl is priced per square yard, while tile is priced per square foot. Cost for either style is comparable to carpet and less expensive than ceramic tile or hardwood. Prices vary based on the percentage of vinyl in the material, the thickness of the product and the complexity of the pattern.

Resilient sheet vinyl has long been a kitchen standard. It is available in hundreds of colors and patterns at flooring distributors and design centers.

Slate floor tiles in irregular shapes and sizes create a unique and rustic look for kitchens.

Tile

Tile is a hard, durable, versatile material that's available in a wide variety of sizes, patterns, shapes and colors. This all-purpose flooring is an excellent choice for high-traffic and high-moisture areas.

Common floor tiles include unglazed quarry tile, glazed ceramic tile and porcelain mosaic tile. As an alternative to traditional ceramic tiles, natural stone tiles are available in several materials, including marble, slate and granite. Stone tile is similar to ceramic tile. It is available as cut square shapes or irregular pieces. Techniques for setting are the same as for ceramic tile, but stone tiles must always be sealed. Thicknesses for most floor tiles range from 3⁄16" to 3⁄4".

In general, tile is more expensive than other types of floor coverings, with natural stone tile ranking as the most expensive. While tile is more time-consuming to install than other materials, it offers the most flexibility of design.

Floor preparation is critical to the success of a tile installation. All floors that support tile must be stiff and flat to prevent cracking in the tile surface. Tile is installed following a grid-pattern layout and adhered to the floor with thin-set mortar. The gaps between individual tiles are filled with grout, which should be sealed periodically to prevent staining.

Porcelain floor tile or any stone floor tile is a good design match for a natural stone countertop.

Wood Flooring

Wood floors are resilient and durable, yet they still look warm and elegant. They hold up well in high-traffic areas. Traditional solid wood planks are the most common type of wood flooring, but there's a growing selection of plywood-backed and synthetic-laminate products (also called laminated wood) that are well suited for do-it-yourself installation. Oak and maple are the most common wood species available, and size options include narrow strips, wide planks and parquet squares. Most wood flooring has tongue-and-groove construction, which helps to provide a strong, flat surface.

In general, hardwood flooring is slightly less expensive than ceramic tile, and laminated products are typically less expensive than solid hardwood. Most types of wood flooring can be installed directly over a subfloor and sometimes over vinyl flooring. Installation of laminated wood flooring is simple. It can be glued or nailed down, or "floated" on a foam cushion. Parquet squares typically are glued down. Solid hardwood planks must be nailed to the subfloor.

The rich tones of stained wood flooring are perfect for setting off painted cabinets in the kitchen.

A herringbone pattern (left) gives this wood floor a distinctive look.

Prefinished wood flooring is available in a variety of woods and finishes. This floor is teak.

Other Flooring Options

Other flooring options available for kitchens are concrete, stone tile, cork, bamboo and linoleum.

Concrete is a low-maintenance flooring that can look sophisticated. After pouring in place, it can be dyed and scored to resemble stone or tile. Most installations include in-floor heating, though any repairs on the underfloor heating system may require replacing the entire floor.

Cork is available in a variety of colors and patterns, many of which use cork's natural brown shadings. Cork provides comfort because it because it "gives" slightly and has noise-reducing properties.

Cork flooring is available in sheets, tiles or planks for floating installations.

Though bamboo is actually a grass, it is harder than oak. It does not take stain uniformly, so it is available only in its natural hues. Thin bamboo strips are laminated and milled into planks for floating or bonded installation.

Linoleum is made from linseed oil, fabric backing, and cork or wood dust. It continues to be a popular option in Europe and is an excellent choice for people with chemical sensitivities. Available in many colors and styles, it resembles vinyl resilient flooring and is available in sheets or tiles.

Resilient vinyl tile, which is closely associated with diners and church basements, comes in a multitude of colors and patterns, is very inexpensive, and is relatively easy to install. It scuffs and scratches easily, however.

Cork flooring is easy on the feet because it is resilient. Sold in tiles or "planks" it is available in many shades of natural brown and may be unfinished or prefinished. The prefinished products are less likely to cause problems.

Lighting

Designers divide light sources into four basic types: task, accent, ambient and decorative. Each type has an important function when it comes to lighting your kitchen.

Task Lighting

Task lighting is lighting directed at a specific area to aid in illuminating the job at hand. Basically, it helps you see what you are doing. But task lighting also helps define and emphasize working spaces. In a kitchen, you have numerous areas where specific task lighting is necessary—the sink, cooktop, countertop and other food prep areas, the dining area, and desk or study area.

Begin by putting an overhead fixture, recessed light or track lights over the sink. Most range hoods have a lighting option—if you don't have a range hood, consider adding one for proper ventilation and lighting. Add pendants or spotlights over an island to brighten this valuable space. Don't use just one fixture, however, because this can create distracting shadows. To eliminate shadows, use cross lighting. Cross lighting is the use of two or more light sources directed at a space from different angles. Using a dimmer switch on these fixtures allows you to switch from bright lighting for prep work to subdued lighting for dining. Add strip lights under cabinets to shorten the distance light has to travel and reduce the number of shadows. Use pendants with chrome-bottomed bulbs over the breakfast table for a softly lit eating space. A small clip-on or desktop halogen light illuminates a desk or study area.

Kitchen lighting is a combination of natural light that enters through windows and skylights, overhead "ambient" light that fills the whole room, task lighting that is concentrated on an activity area, and accent lighting that exists mostly to look pretty.

Accent Lighting

Accent lighting is basically lighting for emphasis rather than lighting for a task. Careful accent lighting draws attention to an object or a space. For kitchens, this might be lighting a display of antique plates or focusing a spotlight on an alcove that holds a flowering plant.

Shadows are as important as the lighted spaces when using accent lights. Tight beams of light from small spotlights are ideal for accent lighting. Directing light from below gives bold, dramatic shadows. Lighting small objects from the side creates large shadows. You may want to light architectural features—accent lights can bring out the details of a rough brick chimney or a textured plaster wall.

Accent light fixtures are not the center of attention, so they should be small and inconspicuous. Small, inexpensive, low-voltage recessed fixtures are perfect for ceilings and cabinets. For glass-front cabinets, in-cabinet lighting rather than external spotlighting is necessary to prevent glare off the glass fronts.

Ambient Lighting

Ambient lighting is the diffuse light that illuminates a room from several sources and sets the minimum level of lighting. This layer is considered last in designing because the task and accent layers of lighting will provide some ambient light. The ambient layer provides a background by gently lighting areas not illuminated by specific task and accent lights, reducing the eye-straining contrast between brightly lit task areas and dim, unlit surroundings. If your kitchen needs more ambient light, above-cabinet or cove lighting are excellent options.

Decorative Lighting

Decorative lighting is lighting simply to show off the beauty of light. Decorative lighting in a kitchen may be candles or a string of paper lanterns. This type of light is not meant to be the only source of light in the room—creating too great a contrast between light and dark diminishes the decorative impact.

A pendant light or chandelier can be suspended from the ceiling at a relatively low height so it provides focused overhead light for a kitchenette or island. The only drawback to this strategy is that if you choose to relocate the table you'll need to move, or at least raise, the light.

Lighting is well coordinated in this kitchen (above): Recessed canister lights provide basic navigational light for times when the kitchen is not in use. The decorative pendant lights focus on the eat-in island and work areas, and the stovetop area is serviced by task lights in the vent hood. And finally, mirrored glass in frames bounces ambient light back onto the countertop prep area.

Artistic light fixtures (left) can be every bit as important as wall art or room color when it comes to creating a unique design effect. The high-tech stainless steel fixtures seen here have an important role in establishing the almost futuristic tone of this kitchen.

Light Sources

In addition to the layers of lighting design, it is important to consider light sources. Many city codes require a certain percentage of energy-efficient bright fluorescent lighting in a kitchen. Until recently, fluorescent bulbs cast what is called cool light and produced poor color rendering. The older tubes produced an excess of green and yellow light, which meant everything illuminated looked slightly green. New, color-corrected fluorescent tubes do not have this problem.

The other common light bulb is the incandescent—the standard globe with metal filament that looks very much like what Thomas Edison invented. The light produced by incandescent bulbs is a much warmer light, with more reds and yellows. This warmer light is perceived as being cozier and more inviting.

The latest in lighting is the use of halogen, compact fluorescent (CFL) and light-emitting-diode (LED) bulbs. Of these, halogen has the longest track record, but CFL and LED have the brightest futures because of their low heat loss and high efficiency.

Daylight is also an important light source in the kitchen. If you are contemplating a complete kitchen remodel, make sure you consider adding sources of daylight in the form of skylights, clerestories, larger windows or greenhouse windows. Daylight can provide excellent ambient light, but it can also be harsh and create glaring bright spots on highly polished surfaces, so be sure to consider light-diffusing window shades, too.

Lots of natural light floods this kitchen. When the sun goes down, low-voltage cable lights and recessed lights supply task and accent lighting.

Pendant lighting defines the peninsula in this kitchen. Recessed lights provide task lighting without interrupting the look of the paneled ceiling.

Universal Design ▶

Add as much natural light as you can to your kitchen to diminish the need for lighting during the day, and lower your energy usage.

Fluorescent bulbs are more energy efficient and have much longer life than incandescent bulbs. Remember that they need to be disposed of properly—they contain traces of hazardous substances that can be recycled for future use. Xenon bulbs have a longer life expectancy than halogen bulbs and provide the same type light.

Using dimmer switches saves energy by allowing you to select the appropriate level of light for the occasion. Of course, turning the lights off when not in use will save energy and prolong the life of the bulbs.

A combination of light sources is the norm in most kitchens, so it is unavoidable that the type of light and the way things look will change according to time of day and season.

Color & Materials

If you're tired of the colors and materials—or have found that they just don't work, it's easy to give a fresh face to the kitchen.

But before choosing a new color scheme or material palette, start with your current kitchen and analyze where it's gone wrong. Often the surface materials that are the most economical or trendy are not the most durable options. Make a note if your existing materials have not performed or lasted well by withstanding the heat of hot pans or the heavy traffic of a busy home. Choose a more durable, lasting material for your kitchen's next incarnation, and you will have learned a valuable lesson.

As for color, people frequently shy away from bold hues because they fear that they'll get tired of their choice or it will make the room look smaller. In a kitchen, where so much active time is spent, this notion may have some truth to it. But whether we notice it or not, color and lighting have a deep effect on our state-of-mind and while there are countless theories on which colors work best for different scenarios, a single piece of advice reigns supreme: Always select a color that you like. Don't go for moss green walls because it's fashionable, if that shade has always made you a bit queasy. Don't avoid yellow because a scientist once said it made people irritable. If you are drawn to a color, use it liberally and it should please you to see it every day.

Because cabinet, floor and appliance colors are more difficult to change than paint on the walls, it is important to factor these materials first when making your color choices. Be aware that vivid colors can impart their hue to neutral surfaces; a hot pink wall will give a rosy glow when reflected on neighboring white cabinets. Whichever color you choose, begin by painting a 2 × 2-foot sample swatch on the wall and living with it for a couple days to see how it works in different lighting conditions.

Kitchen Painting Tips ▸

Use a quality kitchen and bath paint, and quality brushes and rollers. You may balk at paying $25 to $45 per gallon for better quality paint, but good paint spreads more easily, covers more evenly, and is more durable than less expensive paint. A poor quality roller will leave a trail of fuzzy bumps regardless of the paint quality.

Avoid textured paint surfaces in a kitchen. Even with proper ventilation, a certain amount of cooking grease and spatter will be floating around your kitchen. Semi-gloss paint surfaces are easiest to clean. Matte and textured surfaces are more difficult to clean and "hold" more dust—making your kitchen appear dingy.

Lighting Effects ▸

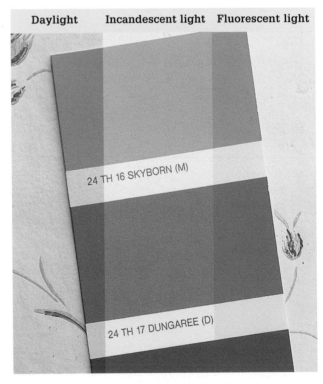

Daylight   Incandescent light   Fluorescent light

24 TH 16 SKYBORN (M)

24 TH 17 DUNGAREE (D)

Lighting affects our perception of color. Make sure you view your selections in daylight as well as under artificial lighting.

This kitchen uses bold colors and a contrasting palette of materials to give it style and personality.

Even muted colors can make a dramatic design statement when they are used in a contrasting fashion. By selectively repeating the colors, as with the pendant light fixtures and cabinet doors seen here, the effect is intensified.

Designing Your New Kitchen

On average, kitchens are remodeled every ten to fifteen years—significantly more time than the average period between remodels in any other room in the home. This is due primarily to the expense of remodeling such a fully outfitted space but also to the longevity of most kitchen components. What this means, however, is that you should take time to design and plan, not just for now but for a decade from now, before you begin a kitchen remodel.

The kitchen is such a condensed working space with so many surface, fixture and appliance options to consider. All these layers may make a kitchen update or remodeling project seem a daunting task. But if you break it down into individual parts, it becomes much easier. This chapter introduces you to some of the initial things to consider when remodeling a kitchen. Function and style are two of the biggest priorities but it's also important to take time to think about special considerations that may be uniquely yours: Do you need to plan for young children in the future? What about an aging relative who may join your household? You'll need to come up with a design that can accommodate those needs as well as your own special kitchen considerations, like how you like to cook or where you prefer to dine.

A crucial first step toward your future satisfaction is to carefully evaluate your present kitchen and determine what problems it has and what features are lacking. Creating a new kitchen that simply puts a new face on old problems may make you feel better for the moment, but it's ultimately a waste of time. If you take the time now to determine what features are necessary and appropriate for your new kitchen, this effort will pay big dividends in the end.

In This Chapter
- Assessing Your Current Kitchen
- Kitchen Remodeling Strategies
- Design Standards

Assessing Your Current Kitchen

Your motives for remodeling your kitchen probably fall into one of two categories: efficiency or appearance. In other words, either your kitchen is inconvenient for your family to use, or you just don't like the way it looks. Or maybe it's both dysfunctional and ugly. A logical place to start, then, is by documenting the elements that need improvement.

Begin by simply taking the time to observe how you now use your kitchen. Keep a notepad handy and jot down any major or minor problems and annoyances that prevent you from being as efficient or as comfortable as you'd like to be when cooking or eating. Also consider how your kitchen is used for special occasions and what issues arise at those times. Don't forget to make note of the positives. If you love having that window over your kitchen sink or the skinny cabinet next to the stove, jot those observations down as well.

Once you have documented the problems with your kitchen, give your imagination permission to roam. Don't worry about money yet. This is your dream kitchen, after all, and there will be plenty of time to bring your fantasies down to earth as you begin the planning stages. Now is the time to consider every possibility. Look at friends' kitchens, at magazine kitchens and at model kitchens. When looking at photographs like the ones included in this book, look at both the overall effect and the individual components. Don't let an odd color scheme scare you away from a faucet that you love. Use a file folder to collect pictures of kitchens or items you like. When it comes down to business, you'll have a refined idea of what you're looking for.

If your kitchen needs remodeling, you will know it. The trick in coming up with a workable design for your space is to get past the "Ick" factor and really examine what you have to work with. When you assess your cabinets, you may notice immediately that they are very dark and outdated in appearance. But go past that and ask yourself if they are laid out efficiently. Imagine them as brand new cabinets in the same arrangement, and then try and think of ways you could improve the layout. Whether it's with cabinets or countertops or lighting or appliances, consider the components of your kitchen as generic elements.

It's okay to hang onto elements you love. Even if your favorite pullout shelf or work table or stool doesn't immediately appear to go with the new elements you hope to introduce, as the owner of the kitchen you're allowed to hang onto the things you're used to working with.

Special Considerations

If you're going through the trouble of remodeling your kitchen—and the remodel is not solely for resale value—consider making room for some of your own interests and idiosyncrasies. A pull out recycling center with bins for separating different categories is always a smart idea. A built-in beer refrigerator with a custom tap is great for a home-brew enthusiast. A pull out shelf custom-sized to display a selection of

tea is perfectly located next to the kettle. Another, perhaps more practical, investment is the careful measurement of counter heights and seat heights to ergonomically suit your personal needs. Finally, consider how your kitchen will be used over the next five to twenty years. The needs of a family with young children are much different than the needs of empty nesters.

Kitchen Remodeling Strategies

Kitchen remodeling projects come in many levels, based largely on how much the room's layout will be changed. To determine how much to change, ask yourself a few questions. Do you have enough space to prepare meals? How far apart are the refrigerator, range and sink from one another? Are there efficient and convenient pathways through the kitchen—or are other people always crossing your path as you work? Is there an adequate dining area or does it block the flow of traffic through the room?

If you've identified the problems with your layout or floor plan, ask yourself if they can be corrected simply by rearranging your existing kitchen. If not, explore how you might address them, perhaps by adding or moving doors, redirecting traffic or expanding the kitchen.

If your current needs are few, or you simply want a new look in your kitchen, you'll probably plan a relatively inexpensive cosmetic makeover, in which you simply redo the surfaces and make only minor changes to the layout and floor plan. This level is popular because the cost is relatively low and many homeowners can complete most of the work themselves.

On the other hand, if you would like to move the refrigerator over a few feet or put the sink closer to the range, you're thinking of a more involved project. Rearranging the whole kitchen is still more complex, and if you're knocking out an interior wall to expand the kitchen into an adjacent room you're looking at a very major project indeed. The most involved, and expensive, kitchen remodeling projects aren't really remodeling at all. Adding an addition, be it a small bump-out or a whole new wing, is a very involved project that will probably require professional help and a massive budget.

Before and After: Reshuffling the appliances was the key move in opening up this kitchen floorplan without sacrificing counter space. Important decorative touches included replacing the overhead light in the ceiling fan with discreet recessed lights and a pair of ceiling-hung pendants. New granite countertops, stainless steel appliances, updated fixtures and lighter wood cabinets round out the decorative improvements.

Before and After: The passthrough at one end of this kitchen, at first blush, appears to be a design impediment that interrupts traffic flow and fulfills no critical function. But by removing the wall between the galley kitchen and the hallway, this kitchen designer was able to preserve the architectural character of the room and actually turn a strange detail into a successful design focal point.

Changing the Layout

With this option, you'll retain the same basic floor space as the existing kitchen, but will change the positions of the appliances, fixtures and eating areas to create a more efficient floor plan. This level of remodeling includes most elements of a cosmetic makeover—installing new surfaces and upgrading appliances and fixtures—but may also require the work of a carpenter, electrician and plumber. Homeowners with ample do-it-yourself experience might choose to do most of this work themselves.

Redirecting Traffic

In a slightly more complicated scenario, you might find it necessary to change the layout more radically in order to redirect traffic moving through the kitchen. Often this means adding or moving a doorway, as well as redesigning the basic kitchen layout. Unless you are a very experienced do-it-yourselfer, much of this work will require the help of a carpenter and other subcontractors. At this fairly extensive level of remodeling, many homeowners also take the opportunity to add new windows, patio doors or skylights.

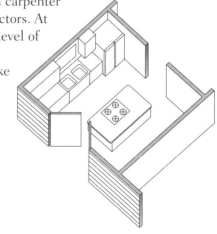

Expanding Inward

If your present kitchen just isn't large enough to accommodate your needs, one option is to extend the space by borrowing space from adjacent rooms. This generally means that interior partition walls will need to be removed or moved, which is work for an experienced home construction carpenter. This level of remodeling often includes significant rearrangement of the appliances and cabinets, as well as the installation of new windows, doors or skylights. In a major remodeling project of this kind, many homeowners may want to hire professional contractors for some of the work.

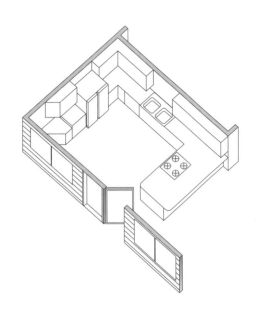

Before and After: An efficient layout is worth preserving when you redesign a kitchen. In the remodel seen here, the designer was able to retain the same work triangle while giving a dramatic facelift to the cabinets and countertops. The net effect is a kitchen that works the same, but feels brand new.

Expanding Outward

This is the Cadillac of kitchen remodeling possibilities—as big as it gets. If you find more space essential and can't expand inward into adjoining rooms, then the last option is to build an addition onto your home. This ambitious undertaking requires the aid of virtually the same collection of professionals it takes to build a home from scratch: architects and engineers, excavation and concrete contractors, construction and finish carpenters, plumbers and electricians. At this level, some homeowners choose to hire a general contractor to manage the project.

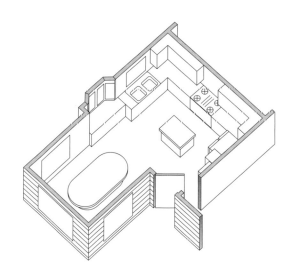

Before and After: This kitchen remodel is not as extensive as the photos suggest. The only structural change to the room was to create a recess in the wall for the new refrigerator so it no longer obstructs the doorway. Otherwise, the major changes are fresh paint, new countertops and new wall and floor surfaces: all fairly cosmetic. The new appliances also go a long way toward updating the look.

Design Standards

While you may imagine that the answer to every cramped kitchen is to knock down walls and add more space, that's often not the easiest or best solution. One alternative to tearing down the walls, is to add more windows for added light. An extra door, or even a pass-through window—from the kitchen to an adjacent room—can also help make the space feel more airy. In short, the cramped feeling may only be one of perception.

Most kitchens fall into one of four categories: Galley, L-shaped, U-shaped and Open Plan. Whether they are small or large, old or new, these floor plans have proven to be popular models for efficient kitchens, though that doesn't mean they'll necessarily be the most efficient for your needs.

Galley: In small homes or city apartments, the galley kitchen is a space-saving choice that is ideal for one or two users. The components may all be lined up along one wall or divided between two parallel walls. For this floor plan to work best, the central galley space should be large enough to allow for all appliances to be open at the same time, with enough space remaining for someone to walk through the middle.

L-shape: This corner kitchen layout can feel roomier than it is in reality, because of the L-shape floor plan. However, the two "arms" might also create an awkward workstation, with little room to set items down mid-way through a meal. Consider taking advantage of the lost central space with a counter-height dining table that can double as a prep station or even a freestanding central island.

U-shape: This layout takes the benefits of a galley kitchen—space-saving solution plus accessibility for one user—and adds a third wall to create the ultimate triangular floor plan. In a compact space, placing the sink at the far end with the refrigerator and range on opposing walls creates a simple workstation. On a larger scale, a sizable island can anchor the center of the room and provide more storage.

Open Plan: Whether the kitchen is located in the middle of a larger great room or off to one side, an open plan layout works best with the addition of a central island or a dividing counter of some type. Perfect for family kitchens or entertaining spaces where the cooks can easily visit with guests, it's important for this floor plan to be well organized so that all necessities are close at hand.

Whichever layout plan you opt for, the most fundamental principle that you don't want to violate is to maintain plenty of free area between appliances, sinks and other elements of the work triangle. In a galley kitchen like the one seen here, the corridor between kitchen walls should be at least 4 ft. wide, and preferably wider.

Common Kitchen Layouts

Galley

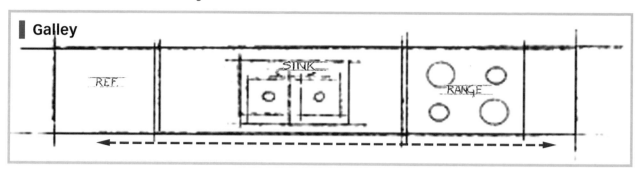

U-Shape

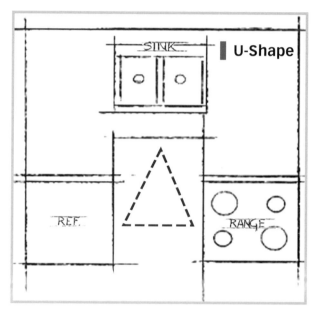

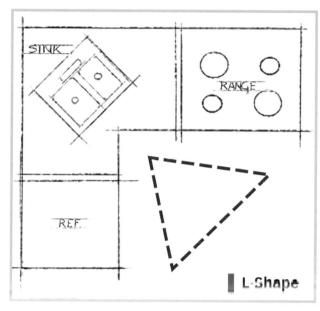

L-Shape

Open Plan

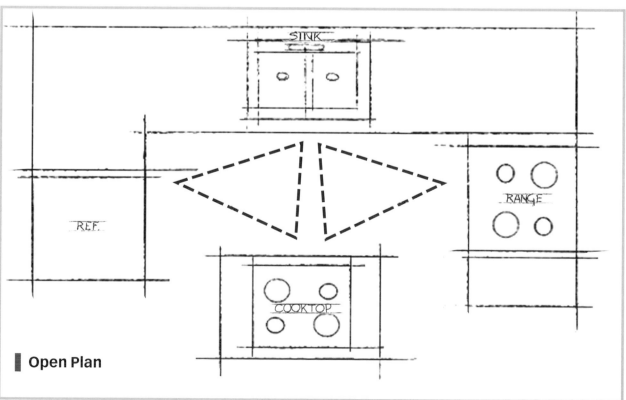

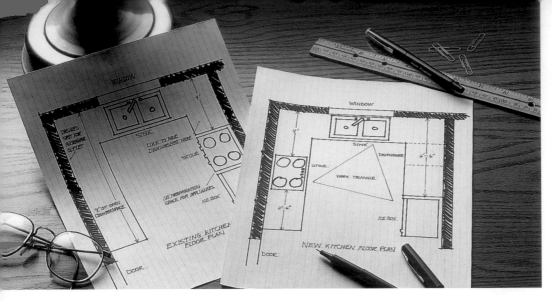

The work triangle is a layout concept that lets you develop a convenient arrangement of the range, sink and refrigerator in the kitchen.

Whether you are doing the work yourself or hiring others, once you have a good idea of the features you want in your new kitchen, it's time to create detailed plan drawings. Good planning drawings will help you in several phases of the planning process:

- Selecting cabinets and appliances to fit your kitchen layout.
- Soliciting accurate work bids when negotiating with plumbers, electricians and other subcontractors.
- Obtaining a building permit at your local Building Inspections office.
- Scheduling the stages of a remodeling project.
- Evaluating the work of contractors. If a carpenter or cabinetmaker fails to meet your expectations, your plan drawings serve as proof that the contractor did not complete the work as agreed.

Codes & Standards

Creating plans for a kitchen can seem like an overwhelming challenge, but fortunately there are guidelines available to help you. Some of these guidelines are legal regulations specified by your local Building Code and must be followed exactly. Most codes have very specific rules for basic construction, as well as for plumbing and electrical installations.

Another set of guidelines, known as standards, are informal recommendations developed over time by kitchen designers, cabinetmakers and appliance manufacturers. These design standards suggest parameters for good kitchen layout, and following them helps ensure that your kitchen is comfortable and convenient to use.

Guidelines for Layout

The goal of any kitchen layout is to make the cook's work easier and, where possible, to allow other people to enjoy the same space without getting in the way. Understanding the accepted design standards can help you determine whether your present layout is sufficient or if your kitchen needs a more radical layout change or expansion.

Work triangle & traffic patterns. A classic kitchen design concept, the work triangle theory proposes that the sink, range and refrigerator be arranged in a triangular layout according to the following guidelines:
- Position of the triangle should be such that traffic flow will not disrupt the main functions of the kitchen.
- Total distance between the corners of the triangle should be no more than 26 ft. and no less than 12 ft.
- Each side of the triangle should be between 4 and 9 ft. in length.

If two people frequently work in the kitchen simultaneously, the layout should include two work triangles. In a two-triangle kitchen, the triangles may share one side, but they should not cross one another.

Don't fret too much if you can't make the triangle layout work perfectly. Some kitchens, for example, may have four workstations instead of three, and others may not have enough space to accommodate the classic triangle.

For general traffic design, it is recommended to leave 4-ft. "corridors" between all stationary items for walking comfort. Some designers will allow this standard to be reduced to 3 feet in smaller kitchens.

Industry Standards

Standard Appliance Dimensions

Appliance	Standard Dimensions (width)	Minimum Countertop space	Comments
Refrigerator	30" to 36"	15" on latch side	12 cu. ft. for family of four; 2 cu. ft. for each additional person
Sink	27" single 36" double	24" on one side 18" on other side	Minimum of 3" of countertop space between sink and edge of base cabinet
Range	30", 36"	15" on one side 9" on other side	
Cooktop	30", 36", 42" 48"	15" on one side 9" on other side	If a window is positioned above a cooking appliance, the bottom edge of the window casing must be at least 24" above the cooking surface
Wall oven	24", 27", 30"	15" on either side	Oven bottom should be between 24" and 48" above the floor
Microwave	19", 24", 30"	15" on either side	When built in, place low in wall cabinets or just under counter

Eating Surface Standards

Height of Eating Surface	30"	36"	42"
Min. width for each seated diner	30"	24"	24"
Min. depth for each seated diner	19"	15"	12"
Minimum knee space	19"	15"	12"

Cabinet Standards

Recommended Minimum For Size of Kitchen

	Less than 150 sq. ft.	More than 150 sq. ft.
Base cabinets	13 lin. ft.	16 lin. ft.
Wall cabinets	12 lin. ft.	15.5 lin. ft.
Roll-out shelving	10 lin. ft.	13.75 lin. ft.

Shown cutaway for clarity

Maximum height 80"

12"

Minimum 18"

Sink

80"

44"

36"

24"

36" min.

3½" min.

15"

3" min.

24"

30"

Dimensions and positions of cabinets follow accepted design standards, as shown here.

The sizes of base cabinets and wall cabinets are fairly uniform among manufacturers, and unless you have them custom-built in unusual sizes, they will conform to the following standards:

- **Base cabinets:** height—34½"; depth—23" to 24"; width—9" to 48", in 3" increments.
- **Wall cabinets:** height—12", 15", 18", 24", 30", 33", 42"; depth—12"; width—24", 30", 33", 36", 42", 48".
- **Oven cabinets:** height—84", 96"; depth—24"; width—27", 30", 33".
- **Utility cabinets:** height—84"; depth—12", 24"; width—18", 24", 36".

Not every manufacturer will offer all these sizes and styles, so it's a good idea to obtain product catalogs when planning the layout of cabinets. Some other tips:

- Use functional corner cabinets rather than "blind" cabinets that provide no access to the corner area.
- Include at least five storage/organizing units, such as swing-out pantry units, appliance garages and specialized drawers or shelves.

Eating areas. Kitchen tabletops and countertops used for dining are generally positioned 30", 36", or 42" above the floor, and the recommended space for each person varies according to the height of the surface.

Islands. A kitchen island should be positioned so there is at least 36" of clear space between the edges of its countertop and surrounding walls or cabinets

Guidelines for Basic Construction

Plans for a major remodeling project that involves moving or adding walls, or building a new room addition must accurately show the locations and dimensions of the new walls and all doors and windows. This will allow the construction carpenter to give you an accurate bid on the work and will allow him to obtain the necessary building permits. If you will be moving walls or adding windows or doors, you must identify load-bearing walls and provide appropriate support during removal and rebuilding.

Windows

Most Building Codes require that kitchens have at least one window, with at least 10 sq. ft. of glass area. Some local Building Codes, however, will allow windowless kitchens, so long as they have proper venting. Kitchen designers recommend that kitchens have windows, doors or skylights that together have a total glass surface area equal to at least 25% of the total floor area.

Doors

Exterior entry doors should be at least 3 ft. wide and 6½ ft. high. Interior passage doors between rooms must be at least 2½ ft. wide. A kitchen must have at least two points of entry, arranged so traffic patterns don't intrude on work areas.

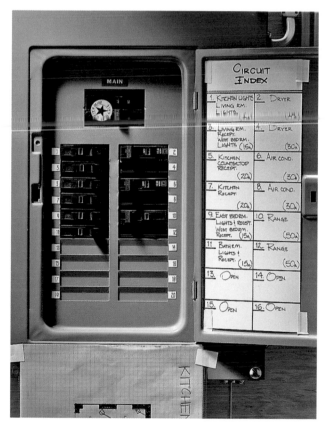

Examine your circuit breaker panel. It may have an index that identifies circuits serving the kitchen. If your service panel has open slots, an electrician can add additional kitchen circuits relatively easily. If your service panel is full, he may have to install a new service panel at additional cost.

Guidelines for Electrical Service & Lighting

Nearly any kitchen-remodeling project will require some upgrading of the electrical service. While your old kitchen may be served by a single 120 volt circuit, it's not uncommon for a large modern kitchen to require as many as seven individual circuits. And in a few cases, the extra demands of the new kitchen may require that the main electrical service for your entire house be upgraded by an electrician. By comparing the electrical service in your present kitchen with the requirements described below, you'll get an idea of how extensive your electrical service improvements will need to be. Your plan drawings should indicate the locations of all the outlets, lighting fixtures and electrical appliances in your new kitchen.

The National Electric Code requires the following for kitchens:

- Two small-appliance circuits (120-volt, 20-amp) to supply power for the refrigerator and plug-in countertop appliances.
- Wall outlets spaced no more than 12 ft. apart.
- Countertop outlets spaced no more than 4 ft. apart.
- GFCI (ground-fault circuit interrupter), protected receptacles installed in any general use outlet, whether above counter or at floor level.
- Dedicated circuits for each major appliance. Install a 20-amp, 120-volt circuit for a built-in microwave, a 15-amp circuit for the dishwasher and food disposer. An electrical range, cooktop or wall oven requires a dedicated 50-amp, 240-volt circuit.

The Electric Code only requires that a kitchen have some form of lighting controlled by a wall switch, but kitchen designers have additional recommendations:

- A general lighting circuit (120-volt, 15-amp) that operates independently from plug-in outlets.
- Plentiful task lighting, usually mounted under wall cabinets or soffits, to illuminate each work area.
- Decorative lighting fixtures to highlight attractive cabinets or other features of the kitchen.

Guidelines for Plumbing

If your new kitchen layout changes the location of the sink, or if you are planning to add an additional sink or dishwasher, the water supply and drain pipes will need to be upgraded. Your plan drawings should indicate these intended changes.

Extending plumbing lines for a new kitchen is often fairly easy and surprisingly inexpensive, but there are some exceptions you should note:

Old pipes. If your present plumbing is more than 25 years old, there is a good chance the plumber will recommend replacing these pipes before installing the kitchen fixtures. Depending on circumstances, this can be an expensive proposition, but if you're faced with this decision, we strongly urge you to take a deep breath and do what the plumber suggests. Those corroded old pipes will need to be replaced someday, and this work is easier and cheaper if you're already in the process of remodeling the kitchen.

Outdated systems. Older plumbing systems may have drain trap and vent arrangements that violate modern Code requirements. If your plumber needs to run all-new vent pipes, this will increase the costs.

Island sinks. If your new kitchen will include an island sink, your plumber will need to run vent pipes beneath the floor. For this reason, plumbing an island sink is more expensive than plumbing a wall sink.

Guidelines for Heating, Ventilation & Air-conditioning

Your plan drawings should also show the locations of heating/air-conditioning registers or fixtures in your proposed kitchen. If you're planning a cosmetic make-over or a simple layout change, there is a pretty good chance you can get by with the same registers, radiators or heaters found in

Code books can help you understand the structural, electrical and plumbing requirements for kitchens. In addition to the formal Code books, which are written for professional tradesmen, there are many Code handbooks available that are written for homeowners. Bookstores and libraries carry both the formal Code books and Code handbooks.

your present kitchen. But if your new kitchen will be substantially larger than it is now, or if the ratio of wall space filled by glass windows and doors will be greater, it's possible that you'll need to expand its heating and cooling capacity.

Increasing your kitchen's heating and cooling can be as simple as extending ducts by a few feet, or as complicated as installing a new furnace. When installing a large room addition, for instance, you may learn that the present furnace is too small to adequately heat the increased floor space of your home.

How do you determine what your kitchen needs in the way of expanded heating and cooling? Unless you happen to be a mechanical engineer, you'll need to consult a professional to evaluate your heating/ventilation/air-conditioning (HVAC) system. The Code requirements for room heating are quite simple, but the methods used to calculate required energy needs of a room are fairly complex.

The Building Code requires simply that a room must be able to sustain a temperature of 70°F, measured at a point 3 ft. above the floor. HVAC contractors use a complicated formula to calculate the most efficient way to meet this Code requirement. You can make this estimation more accurate by providing the following information:

- The exact dimensions of your kitchen.
- The thickness and amount of insulation in the walls.
- The number of doors and windows, including their size and their energy ratings.
- The total square footage of your house.
- The heating and cooling capacity of your furnace and central air-conditioner, measured in BTUs. This information, usually printed on the unit's access panel, will help the HVAC contractor determine if the system can adequately serve your new kitchen.

Finally, your cooktop should be equipped with an electric vent hood to exhaust cooking fumes and moisture from the kitchen. The volume of air moved by a vent fan is restricted by Code, so you should always check with a Building Inspector before selecting a vent hood.

Metal ductwork for the vent hood must be run through an exterior wall or through the ceiling. If your cooktop is located in an island cabinet, a special island vent fan is necessary.

Vent hoods are required by some local codes on all ranges and cooktops. The vent fan exhausts cooking fumes and moisture to the outdoors.

Planning Your Remodeling Project

Now that we've presented all the ideas, inspiration, design considerations and appliance options you could ever want in your dream kitchen, it's time to start thinking about taking action. In this chapter, we'll cover all the practical elements of a remodel, from determining a budget to finding a contractor to drawing an accurate floor plan.

This chapter also contains practical planning information on budgeting and scheduling your kitchen project. Many people hire contractors for some or all of the work, and if you follow this path, you'll find plenty of information on the following pages to help you find an expert you can trust, as well as advice on how to best supervise the creation of your new kitchen.

The chapter also includes the first step-by-step project in the book: Creating Floor Plans and Elevation Drawings. If you are considering changing the layout of your kitchen in any way, you'll want to map out your options accurately to confirm a successful work triangle and traffic pattern. You'll also want to measure some of your ideas on paper to make sure everything fits before you purchase new materials or start tearing out existing cabinets. Like any successful endeavor, a good remodel requires lots of planning and strict adherence to a few practical considerations.

In This Chapter

- Creating Plans & Drawings
- Budgeting & Financing Your Project
- Working with Contractors
- Practical Tips

Creating Plans & Drawings

Now the fun starts. Armed with a vision of the features you want to include in your new kitchen and equipped with an understanding of the code requirements and design standards, you're ready to put pencil to paper and begin to develop plan drawings—the next important step in transforming your dream kitchen into reality.

The key to success when developing plan drawings is to take as much time as you need and to remain flexible. A professional kitchen designer might take 30 to 80 hours to come up with precise floor plans and elevation drawings, so it's not unreasonable to allow yourself several weeks if you're doing this work yourself. You will almost certainly revise your plans several times before you settle on a layout that feels right to you. And it's not uncommon for kitchen plans to undergo changes as you make decisions about appliances and other materials. As you begin to research the price of cabinets and appliances and receive bids from contractors, you may well decide that it's prudent to scale back for the sake of your bank account, and these changes may require you to revise your plan drawings.

The process of creating finished plans for a kitchen project takes time and is done in three phases. First, you'll be drawing a floorplan of your present kitchen, providing a reference on which to base your new design. Next, you'll be experimenting with various layout options to find a design that best suits your needs, a process that can take several days, or even weeks. Finally, you'll be creating precise, finished floorplans and elevation drawings, which you will use when you begin interviewing contractors to do the work.

A floorplan is a scaled drawing made from an overhead perspective, showing the exact room dimensions, as well as the location of windows, doors, cabinets, appliances, electrical and plumbing fixtures. Elevation drawings are plans depicting a wall surface as if viewed from the side. For clarity, use an architectural template to show the position of appliances and fixtures in your kitchen plans. These templates are available at drafting and office supply stores, or you can photocopy the examples on pages 108 to 109. Carpenters, electricians, plumbers and other contractors will understand exactly what you want if your plan drawings speak their language.

Once you've completed floor plans and elevation drawings of your kitchen-to-be, you're ready to begin choosing the appliances, cabinets and other materials for your new kitchen. Create a detailed shopping list that includes dimensions and specifications for each item you'll be buying.

Now would be a good time to enlist the aid of an interior designer to help you select colors and patterns for flooring, countertops and wall materials. Many installation contractors can also help you with design decisions.

Detailed Plan Drawings

Whether you are doing the work yourself or hiring others, once you have a good idea of the features you want in your new kitchen, it's time to create detailed plan drawings. Good plan drawings will help you in several phases of the planning process:

- Selecting cabinets and appliances to fit your kitchen layout.
- Soliciting accurate work bids when negotiating with plumbers, electricians and other subcontractors.
- Obtaining a building permit at your local Building Inspections office.
- Scheduling the stages of a remodeling project.
- Evaluating the work of contractors. If a carpenter or cabinetmaker fails to meet your expectations, your plan drawings serve as proof that the contractor did not complete the work as agreed.

Most kitchen remodeling projects should have a plan drawing. A fully developed drawing includes elevations and floorplans (you'll need these to get your construction permit) and any other visual details that are of use, such as the style of the cabinets and the sizes of the new appliances you plan to buy. Lighting and plumbing illustrations also are helpful.

Literature from manufacturers provides key information that you'll need for planning and for making your plan drawings. Stock cabinetry suppliers, in particular, produce very useful materials that you can use to identify and represent precisely the exact size and style of cabinets you want.

Creating Kitchen Plans ▸

Although some homeowners have the artist's eye needed to draw accurate plans, others find this difficult, if not impossible. If you fall into the latter category, don't be afraid to seek help. Home centers and cabinet manufacturers often have designers on staff who can help you draw up plans if you agree to buy materials from them. In addition, there are computer software programs that can help you develop accurate plans that can be printed out. And, of course, there are professional kitchen designers and architects who specialize in creating kitchen plans.

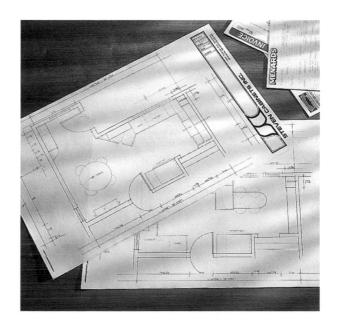

How to Create Floor Plans & Elevation Drawings

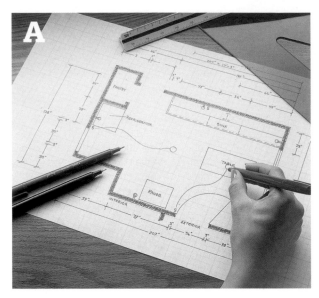

Measure each wall in your kitchen as it now exists. Take accurate measurements of the position and size of every feature, including doors, windows, cabinets, countertops and appliances. Also note the locations of all light fixtures and electrical outlets. Using graph paper, create a scaled floor plan of your present kitchen, using a scale of ½" equals 1 ft. Indicate doors, windows, interior and exterior walls. Add the cabinets, appliances and countertops, electrical outlets and lights, plumbing fixtures and HVAC registers and fixtures. In the margins, mark the exact dimensions of all elements.

Using tracing paper overlaid on your kitchen drawing, begin sketching possible layouts for your new kitchen, again using a scale of ½" equals 1 ft. As you develop your kitchen plan, refer often to your wish list of kitchen features and the kitchen standards and Code requirements listed earlier in this section. The goal is to create a kitchen that meets all your needs with the minimum possible impact on the present kitchen, because this will reduce the overall cost of your project.

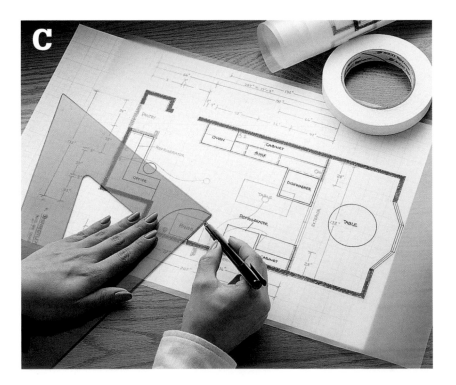

If simple rearrangement of kitchen elements doesn't do the trick, explore the possibility of expanding your kitchen, either by enlarging the kitchen into an adjoining room, or by building a room addition. A kitchen designer or architect can help with this task.

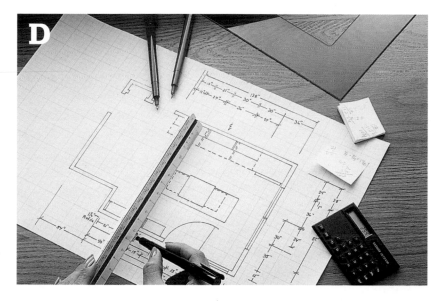

Once you settle on a layout, use graph paper to draw a very detailed floor plan of your new kitchen. Use dotted lines to fill in the base cabinets and appliances, and solid lines to show the wall cabinets and countertops. (For straight runs of cabinets, leave a margin of about 3" to allow for adjustments during cabinet installation.) In the margins around the wall outline, indicate dimensions of kitchen elements and the distances between them.

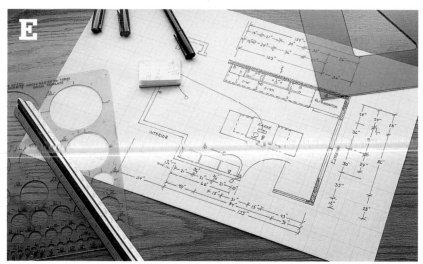

Use colored pencils to mark the locations of plumbing fixtures, electrical outlets and lighting fixtures and the heating registers, radiators or fixtures.

Draw a detailed, precise front elevation for each wall of your kitchen, using a scale of ½" equals 1 ft. Mark the vertical and horizontal measurements of all features, including doors, windows, wood moldings, cabinets, countertops, appliances and soffits. Draw a side elevation of each wall of the kitchen, complete with all measurements. When satisfied with the elevation drawings, add the locations for plumbing pipes, electrical outlets and lighting fixtures. Create close-up detail drawings of problem spots, such as the areas where appliances butt against window frames.

Create Your Drawings

Use the icons shown here and ¼-in. graph paper to create drawings for your new kitchen. Use a scale of ½ in.= 1 ft. (1 square = 6 in.) when drawing your plans; the icons are drawn to match this scale.

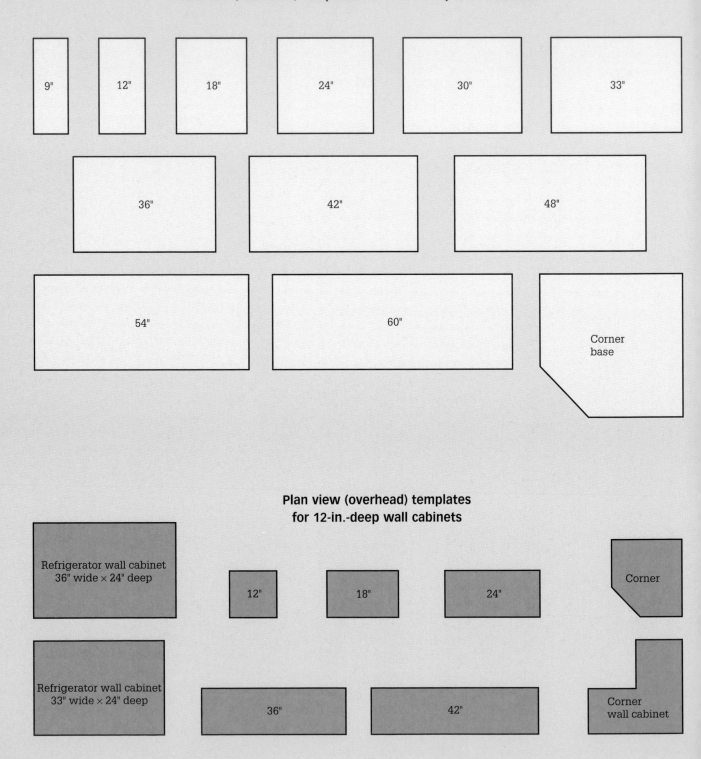

Plan view (overhead) templates for 24-in.-deep base cabinets

9" 12" 18" 24" 30" 33"

36" 42" 48"

54" 60" Corner base

Plan view (overhead) templates for 12-in.-deep wall cabinets

Refrigerator wall cabinet 36" wide × 24" deep

12" 18" 24" Corner

Refrigerator wall cabinet 33" wide × 24" deep

36" 42" Corner wall cabinet

Basic construction symbols (not to scale)

Wall with insulation

Exterior door

Interior door

Folding door

Patio door

Double-hung window

Bay window

Skylight

SKY

Stairway

Range/cooktop, 30" wide

WO

Oven, 27" wide

DW

Dishwasher, 24" wide

R

Refrigerator, 32" wide

Electrical symbols

120-volt GFCI outlet	**GFCI**	Range outlet	**R**
Single-pole switch	**S**	Three-way switch	**S₃**

Single-pole switch **S**   Three-way switch **S$_3$**

Vent fan **F**   Thermostat **T**

Telephone outlet   Incandescent ceiling fixture

Wall-mounted light fixture   Recessed light fixture **R**

Fluorescent light fixture

Track light fixture

Double-bowl sink

Single-bowl sink

Utility sink

GD

Garbage disposer

MW

Built-in microwave

R

Refrigerator, 36" wide

TC

Compactor, 15" wide

Budgeting & Financing Your Project

Any successful kitchen remodel starts with dreams and becomes reality. Which means that at some point, after you've spent time wishing and dreaming, you'll have to figure out where reality lies for you. Dream kitchens can be expensive—very expensive, in some cases. But before you panic, take a deep breath and read this chapter. You'll discover many practical ways to control costs and reduce the financial sting of remodeling.

Although you probably have an idea of how much you'd like to spend on your dream kitchen, you're likely to find that the figure is too small to cover everything you want. To avoid disappointment later, you might as well know up front: when budgeting for a kitchen remodel, you need to be prepared to pay a bit more than you've planned and be willing to settle for a bit less than you've dreamed. Compromise is inevitable in the remodeling process, but with perseverance and a bit of luck, you can spend reasonably and still end up with a beautiful new kitchen that you'll love to use.

Determining a budget depends primarily on the extent of remodeling needed in your kitchen. When budgeting for a kitchen remodel, you must also consider how much an updated kitchen will add to the value of your home. Kitchen remodels have the highest rate of return over every other room in the home, so that you can expect to recoup up to 80 or 90 percent of your investment in added real estate value. Another thing to consider when shopping for a loan to finance a kitchen renovation is that if you choose to take out a home equity loan, the interest may be tax deductible.

Whatever your projected budget, comparison-shopping can help keep you within your budget. Be sure to get three to four estimates for any work you hire out, and ask that the estimates be broken down by materials and labor costs. The same goes for appliances, a simple online search can help you determine the lowest rates for standard appliances, which will often be honored by any subsequent seller you find. A visit to your local supplier allows you to touch and feel the products before buying. Be sure to quote the lowest going-rate for the same model and style, to see if they can match it.

As a guide, here are a few of the projected prices for standard kitchen appliances and fixtures in brand-new condition. This does not account for top-of-the-line imported models available at the luxury end of the spectrum or bargain-basement discontinued models at the lowest end.

Dream kitchens, even modest ones like this, can be shockingly expensive. Realistic decision making, comparison shopping and strict budgeting can feel like they're dampening your dream kitchen at times, but they are an important aspect of turning your dreams into a real kitchen.

Budgeting

Establishing a budget is an important step in the remodeling process, and it involves more than determining how much money you have, or want, to spend. Additional factors, including the current value of your home and how long you plan to stay there, should have bearing on your budgeting decisions because they will help you set a sensible budget goal.

Setting a Budget Goal

How much should you spend on your kitchen project? Real estate professionals offer the following rough guidelines, based on the market value of your home before the remodel, and the complexity of your project.

- For a full, down to the wall studs kitchen remodeling job with a general contractor and all new materials and fixtures, plan to spend 10% to 20% of your home's value ($15,000 to $30,000 for a $150,000 home).
- For a full remodel that includes an addition to your house, plan to spend up to 35% of your home's value ($52,500 for a $150,000 home).
- For a simple cosmetic makeover, plan to spend at least 2% of your home's value ($3,000 for a $150,000 home).

Do these sound like huge sums of money? There are good reasons to invest in a new kitchen. A remodeled kitchen is one of the few home improvements that translates directly into a higher market value for your home. Even if you plan to sell in the near future, you'll enjoy the improvements until that time, and the kitchen's new look may help make the sale when the time comes. However, it's probably wise to scale back on the project if you plan to sell immediately.

If you'll be keeping your home for many years, the investment risk of the project lies in your enjoyment of the new kitchen. But with thoughtful planning and careful selection of appliances and materials, you're sure to get a great return on your investment over the years.

While it may be best to pay for a remodel with disposable income—that is, accumulated savings—there are several legitimate ways to pay for an improvement project, and even more ways to reduce and manage the cost of a new kitchen.

Major appliances are likely to account for a big percentage of your total kitchen remodeling budget. But unlike other aspects of the project, you have a great ability to control the costs of appliances by choosing inexpensive but dependable models. Consider, however, that expensive, high-end ranges and refrigerators are likely to last longer, both functionally and stylistically.

Appliance Costs

Side-by-Side Refrigerator: $900 - $5,000
Self-cleaning Range: $800 - $2,000
Gas Cooktop: $400 - $6,000
Convection Oven: $1,000 - $4,000
Range Hood: $100 - $2,500
Dishwasher: $200 - $1,500
Double basin sink: $300 - $2,000
Faucet with Sprayer: $100 - $400

Estimating Costs

Begin your budgeting process by estimating the cost of your ideal kitchen, as you've envisioned it so far, including appliances, countertops, cabinets, flooring, lighting and miscellaneous materials. Note that the cost figures for products and services can involve guesswork; minimize it by checking the prices in appliance stores and building centers, and ask contractors about their rates. Also add any additional labor charges you expect, such as interior design, cleanup help and trash hauling.

Finally, total all your costs, then add a 10% to 20% contingency fund to the total. The contingency fund is essential: few remodeling projects come in exactly on budget, and it's difficult to list every expense at this stage, so keep your estimates on the high side to avoid any unpleasant surprises.

Use Your Rough Estimate

Don't panic when you see the total; your first rough estimate is simply a starting point. In addition, it can help you answer some crucial questions:

- Is your rough estimate within the recommended ratio of your home's market value? If it exceeds the range shown above, look for ways to reduce your budget.
- Should you do the work yourself, or hire a contractor? The elements with the highest labor cost offer the greatest potential savings if you do the work yourself. In most cases, however, there are reasons why labor costs are high, so you should consider doing work yourself only if you're experienced and confident that you can successfully complete the job.
- Are you getting accurate bids? If a contractor submits a bid that's much higher or lower than the ranges shown, ask why (see Working with Contractors, page 114).

Reducing Costs

At this point you should have a rough idea of how much your dream kitchen will cost. Are you already over your budget? If so, don't worry; the first estimate usually exceeds the budget. That's why you're figuring costs before you get started—it allows you to make carefully planned cutbacks now, which may save you from having to make drastic ones later. There are several ways to begin lowering your remodeling costs.

Comparison-Shop for Materials

If your heart is set on premium-quality materials, do some homework to make sure you're getting the best price you can. If the best price is still too high, bear in mind that good-quality materials can be just as serviceable as top-of-the-line luxury products.

Although contractors and subcontractors will purchase appliances and materials for you, this service isn't free; they typically take a markup on every item they buy. It's often cheaper to research and purchase the materials yourself.

Comparison-Shop for Contractors

While cost shouldn't be your first consideration when looking for a contractor, it's an important one for most people. If you want to reduce your total labor expense, it's better to cut back on service rather than on the contractor's experience and abilities.

Regardless of the contractor's reputation or how much he or she charges, always check references. Whenever possible, talk to several recent customers and visit some completed job sites. As the saying goes, "The best predictor of future success is past performance."

Do Some Work Yourself

Since labor is often the most expensive element of a remodeling project, you may be able to save money by doing parts of the job yourself. However, tackle only those tasks that you're confident you can complete successfully.

Bargain hunting is a very practical way to control remodeling costs that many homeowners actually enjoy (but many others despise). Do bear in mind this simple bit of advice however: Don't buy junk.

Financing Options

Once you've reduced the cost estimate to a realistic amount, it's time to consider where the money will come from. The following are six of the most common methods of financing a major remodeling project. Some methods of financing involve considerable paperwork that can take several weeks to process, so the sooner you start, the better.

Out-of-Pocket Funds

The ideal way to pay for a remodeling project is to use accumulated savings. The advantage of this method is that you don't have to pay any loan interest, which can mean a savings of thousands of dollars. For example, when you borrow $25,000 at 10% interest and pay it off over 10 years, you actually end up paying over $39,000—the cost of the loan plus over $14,000 in interest. Although paying out-of-pocket is cheaper in the long run, it has one significant drawback: If the actual costs far exceed your estimates, you could end up in a pay-as-you-go situation, and the project would take a lot longer to complete. A sizable kitchen remodel could easily take many months to complete if you're paying for it by squeezing a little bit from each paycheck.

Revolving Credit

If you're thinking of using credit cards to pay the bills for your new kitchen, think again. Unless it's absolutely unavoidable, resist all temptations to pull out the plastic when remodeling your kitchen. The interest rates on credit cards, which typically range from 12% to 25%, are far higher than other financing options. This will add thousands of dollars to the cost of your project, and none of the interest is tax deductible.

Government-Backed Loans

There are a number of programs that you may be able to turn to for help through the FHA (Federal Housing Administration). To find qualified lenders, contact your local HUD (Housing & Urban Development) field office. The interest rates and payback schedules for these government-backed loans are about the same as conventional mortgages, but obtaining them often has income-based eligibility requirements.

Mortgage Refinancing

Converting an old mortgage to a new loan is a common way to finance a new kitchen. This option is especially advisable if current interest rates are 1% or more below the rate of your old mortgage, and you have a sizable amount of equity in your home. Refinancing is also a good choice if you're doing a costly project that will add considerably to the market value of your home. One potential benefit of refinancing your current mortgage is that you may be able to take a tax deduction on the interest you pay on the loan. Ask a mortgage company or bank about the current tax laws regarding mortgage loans; then consult your tax advisor.

Home Equity Loans

If you prefer not to refinance your existing mortgage, you can opt to borrow money against your home equity—the difference between your home's market value and the amount you owe on your mortgage. For example, if your home is worth $150,000 and your remaining mortgage balance is $100,000, you have $50,000 in home equity; you can use much of this money to serve as collateral for a loan. Find out the outstanding balance on your mortgage by calling your lender. There are two types of home equity loans. The first is a simple second mortgage, in which you borrow a lump sum at a fixed interest rate and pay it back in regular installments over a period of 15 years or more. The second is an equity line of credit. Equity credit lines operate like revolving credit card accounts, in which you borrow money when you need it and pay interest on the outstanding balance. The interest rates on these loans vary with the market rates, so your payments may change from month to month. Like credit cards, equity credit accounts can be dangerous if you aren't a disciplined borrower.

Home Improvement Loans

This is the standard, everyday bank loan—the same type of loan you would use to buy a car. Any full-service bank or credit union can process a home improvement loan. The advantage of a home improvement loan is that it can be processed very quickly, no appraisal is needed and little paperwork is involved, other than a quick computerized credit check. The drawback is that the interest rates are generally 2% to 5% higher than the current rates for home equity loans. Since home improvement loans are generally secured by your home, the interest may be tax deductible. Ask your lender about the tax laws specific to your loan.

Working with Contractors

When it comes to hiring professionals for help with home improvements, few homeowners have done it enough to become experts. Many people dread this part of the process; it puts them on edge because they're afraid they'll be taken advantage of. Although general awareness and careful scrutiny are important, finding the best professionals for your project is primarily a matter of asking the right questions. Before any work starts, it's essential that both parties know exactly what is to be done and how much money is involved.

Depending on the size of your kitchen remodel, you may be hiring professionals from several different fields, such as designers, carpenters, plumbers and flooring installers. Some hiring decisions will simply be based on your budget or on your skills as a do-it-yourselfer.

Start by identifying the kind of help you need—then ask around for referrals of reputable contractors. If you're managing the job yourself, you'll need to interview with many different subcontractors to find the best person for each job. On the other hand, if you hire a general contractor, the rest of the hiring will be done for you, so finding the right person for that job is critical.

To start the search for a contractor, first check with your county building department for a listing or association of recommended companies. The building department will also be able to help you check the background and license status of any contractor you are considering.

Here are some other ways to find a contractor:

- Ask friends and neighbors for recommendations. Consider remodels you've seen around town or friends that have completed successful renovations. Be sure to find out how the project ended—hopefully everyone was pleased with the final results.
- Check out online referral services.
- Flip through local publications for kitchens that you like or jobs that seem similar to your project. Newspapers and magazines will often credit the contractors, architects and designers who worked on the featured projects. Read the captions or turn to the back of the magazine for names and contact information.

Hiring a Pro is often the single decision that preve DIY remodeling project from turning into a disaster. any phase of the process, you can find qualified professional help.

Professional Service Providers for Kitchen Remodeling

Design Professionals

Designers specialize in turning your rough ideas into working plans or blueprints for actual construction. They work under different professional labels and generally command substantial fees for their time. Kitchen designers specialize in planning kitchen spaces. As a group, they offer a wide range of services, from helping you choose colors to acting as general contractors. There are many kitchen design firms out there as well as individuals, and it's important to find the right one for your project. See Resources (page 282) for more information. Kitchen designers charge their fees in a variety of ways. Some charge a flat fee, others charge hourly. Depending on what kind of help they give you, designers may charge a percentage of the project materials or the total project cost. Using a designer often results in a close working relationship, so be sure to interview several candidates before hiring one.

Design/Build Firms

Design/Build Firms are companies that offer a complete remodeling package in one service. They have their own designers and contractors who work together to complete the project from the first stages of drawing the plans to the final finish construction and decorating. In most cases, you'll pay one fee for this "turnkey" service.

General Contractors

General contractors are professional remodeling managers who hire, schedule, coordinate and supervise the activities of all the other professionals working on a remodeling project. General contractors can make a large, complicated job much easier for you, since they'll hire and schedule the subcontractors and serve as the liaison between you and the other workers. However, this convenience comes at a price—either a flat fee or a percentage of the budget. A reputable general contractor typically charges 10% to 20% of the total construction cost. Also, many general contractors will only take on projects with a relatively high total cost ($10,000 and up).

Building & Installation Professionals

These tradespeople provide the actual hands-on labor needed to complete your kitchen remodel. If you manage the project yourself, you'll need to hire and supervise them directly.

CARPENTERS handle many different building tasks, such as tearing down walls, adding beams and partitions, and framing new walls, windows and doors. Many carpenters will do both the rough carpentry and the finish work, including installing cabinets, trim and some countertops and flooring.

PLUMBERS plan and route the water supply and the drain, waste and vent pipes from the existing lines to the new fixtures. In some areas, plumbers also make gas connections for a range, oven or cooktop, and they may hook up appliances, like dishwashers, food disposers and refrigerator icemakers. However, if you buy a large appliance, such as a dishwasher or refrigerator, the installation may be included in the delivery cost.

HVAC (Heating, Ventilation and Air Conditioning) CONTRACTORS route duct work for forced-air heating and air-conditioning systems and cooktop hoods, and they add new heating and air-conditioning registers.

BOILER CONTRACTORS are needed if you have an older home with a steam heating system or a hydronically (hot water) heated home. A boiler contractor will install new radiators and pipe runs if your project includes a heated room addition.

ELECTRICIANS install wiring, circuits, outlets and lighting fixtures. They add electric baseboard heaters and hard-wired large appliances, such as electric ranges. They can also upgrade your old wiring and electrical circuits.

DRYWALL INSTALLERS hang, tape and finish drywall so it's smooth and ready for paint or wallpaper. Some homeowners choose to install the drywall themselves, then hire a professional to tape and finish it. Some drywall installers also texture walls and ceilings or do painting and wallpapering.

PAINTERS AND WALLPAPER HANGERS complete new wall surfaces. Some also stain and finish wood surfaces.

FLOORING INSTALLERS remove existing flooring and subfloors, prepare underlayment, and install new flooring. Many installers specialize in only one type of flooring.

TILE INSTALLERS (or tile setters) install tile of all types for floors, walls and countertops.

CUSTOM CABINETMAKERS design and build tailor-made kitchen cabinets and install them.

GENERAL LABORERS do unskilled manual labor, such as demolition, cleanup, delivering and moving building supplies. If you have teenage children, you may wish to enlist their help, or you can hire college students to help out.

Once you've selected a few good candidates, ask for license information and a list of references. You can check their professional background with either your building department or an online reference-checking service. You'll want to verify the validity of the contractor's license, and confirm that they have the type of license needed to complete your job—there are dozens of license types for various construction skills. Make sure the contractor is properly insured and bonded. And check for existing liens, outstanding disputes or other legal action taken against the contractor.

Having confirmed their credibility, you'll want to check your potential contractor's references to verify craftsmanship, reliability, and working hours. Ask as many questions as you need about the working relationship between these prior clients and their contractor, since their experience will likely be a template for yours.

A good rule of thumb is to ask for bids from three potential contractors. In addition to asking for a bid, which outlines fees and schedule estimates, request a meeting to walk through your kitchen and brainstorm ideas for your remodel. Don't worry too much if you're not interested in incorporating all of their concepts into your new kitchen, it's simply a good way to experience how each contractor works. It's important to choose a contractor that you can easily communicate with, as well as trust.

Stay organized when working with contractors. Make copies of everything, especially contracts and work orders, so there is no confusion. If it begins to look like you'll be working with three or more separate tradesmen, it's a good time to look into hiring a manager or general contractor for a larger project.

How to work with a Contractor

After choosing a contractor, focus on the contract. Keep in mind that estimated budgets and projected timelines from the bid are usually just that, optimistic approximations. The most important way to protect against unforeseen problems is to get everything in writing, either in the initial contract or in signed change orders or riders added to the contract.

An agreement meant to protect both you and the contractor, a contract should include the following:

- A detailed description of the job and materials. If the contractor is installing cabinets, for example, it's important that the extent of the labor and materials is outlined. Make sure that it states which parts of the job you'll be doing yourself. Any plans that you and the contractor have agreed upon should also be signed and dated.

- The financial requirements. A contract should include the total price—broken down by labor and materials—a payment schedule, and whether there is a cancellation penalty. On any home improvement job, you should expect to make a down payment of approximately ten percent of the total contract price and warranties.
- The contractor is generally responsible for procuring any building permits needed. You'll also want to ask for signed warranties from the contractor on labor and materials, as well as the original warranties on any new products purchased.
- A schedule of work. The contract should clearly state a start date and an approximate end date, rather than an estimated length of time required. Otherwise the ten days agreed to complete a project may be spread out over many months.
- Special requests. Be sure to get any oral agreements in writing if they are important to you. For example, you could include a line stating that the contractor must remove and dispose of old materials before completion.

Sample Remodeling Contract (minimal)

Payment Schedule:
Amounts and due dates should be indicated. (Terms may vary between contractors.) Your interim payment is a good time to make sure your contractor is on schedule. Be sure to retain at least 15% (preferably 30%) for the final payment, which will be made only after you're satisfied that the job is truly complete.

Change Orders:
Specify how any changes will be treated. Misunderstandings can be avoided if the contract requires a quote (or a close estimate) in advance for every task not included in the original contract.

Insurance:
Your contractor should carry both Worker's Compensation and liability insurance for all workers used on your project.

Classic Carpentry Incorporated
222 Oakland Lane
Somewhere, IL 55344

April 14, 2006

John and Jane Smith
4116 Anystreet
Big City, State 12345

Kitchen Remodeling Proposal

Classic Carpentry Inc. (CCI) herein submits a quotation for carpentry labor and building materials (as specified in the attached drawings and specifications) to remodel the kitchen at 4116 Anystreet.

Total Price: **$5, 414.00**

Terms: Initial Payment - $1, 353.50 (25%) upon acceptance of proposal.
         Interim Payment - $2,707.00 (50%) upon installation and taping of drywall.
         Final Payment - $1,353,50 (25%) upon completion of specified work.

Any changes to this proposal price shall be made in writing, and signed by both CCI and the homeowner. Any price increase shall be agreed upon between the parties before additional work is actually done.

Homeowner agrees to pull and post necessary building permits.

Duration of this project is expected to be five weeks from start to completion. If proposal is accepted by April 17, 2000, and demolition by owner is complete, CCI agrees to begin work on or before Monday, April 27 and expects to be completed by May 29, 2000. CCI shall not be liable for delays due to circumstances beyond its control, including strikes, unavailability of materials, or delays caused by weather.

CCI is licensed, bonded, and insured, and warrants all materials and labor for 24 months following date of completion.

Proposal submitted by:_____ Date:_____

Proposal accepted by:_____ Date:_____

                              _____ Date:_____

Warranties:
Labor and materials are often guaranteed for one year by contractors, but some products and materials may be guaranteed for longer by the manufacturer.

Your best defense against surprise bills and extended completion dates is to repeatedly make sure that you and your contractor are on the same page. You've already learned about budgets and timelines as well as how to create floor plans and elevation drawings. Have that information on hand throughout the project, and your contractor will know that you are part of the team, rather than just a client. The worst mistake a homeowner can make in any type of renovation is to blindly follow a team of contractors. Be a part of the planning and decision-making process from the very beginning and stay in the loop. That way, if the gray-green granite you've chosen isn't available, your countertop installer won't make the decision on your behalf to use the gray instead.

However, the reason to hire a professional is that you need an expert opinion. Even if you're hiring a professional for just a small part of your project, be sure to hand the reins over as much as necessary. Despite the fact that this is your dream kitchen, a contractor usually has a bit more experience in making that dream come true.

Practical Tips

There are plenty of practical things to consider before starting a kitchen remodel, but some of the most important involve timing and preparation. In short, the more planning you can do before even touching a tool, the better you will be able to handle the inevitable setbacks. As long as you make sure that it doesn't coincide with major holidays or extended houseguests, a do-it-yourself kitchen remodel doesn't have to take over your life.

The first tip is to be generous when creating a timeline. You never know when ordered parts will be delayed or paint will take twice as long to dry as you estimated. For the most part, the simplest remodel can be completed within a week with more extensive remodels—that involve new cabinets, floors and professionally installed countertops—taking up to three months to complete. Even if it's a small-scale project, be prepared to not have access to your kitchen while work is being done, since even paint fumes can disrupt daily life for a day or two. One smart solution is to create a temporary kitchen elsewhere in your home where you can plug in a coffee maker or microwave, or even a mini refrigerator.

Another thing to consider is the need for permits from your local building authority. Familiarize yourself with local codes before you alter anything electrical or structural. For plumbing projects, you'll want to look into the requirements in your area or determine the need for a new line before you get started. As for changes that involve ventilation, you'll want to refer to some of the Building Code and guidelines we've included earlier in the book.

The most important lesson of any DIY project is to know when to call in the professionals. While many of the how-to projects in this book are simply completed by someone with little construction experience, some projects will be more involved than they first appear. For instance, replacing a resilient tile floor may seem like an easy enough project, but the plot thickens when the subfloor is revealed to be in terrible shape and must be torn out and rebuilt. Another time to call in expert assistance is when plumbing or electrical systems are more than 20 years old—though wires and pipes are meant to last over 50 years, some conditions will cause them to deteriorate making it tricky to remove them safely. And while many builder hobbyists can pull off the replacement of upper cabinets with the help of a friend, there are plenty of us who would require a team of carpenters to help hang and install new cabinets.

The how-to lessons in this book have been carefully broken down into step-by-step manuals for each project. Whether you need assistance or have lots of experience at DIY home improvement, the right tools and smart safety precautions make it possible for anyone to achieve dream-kitchen status.

Flextime: Your Little Secret ▸

For added security, it's a good idea to add at least 25% more time to your best guess when determining the overall schedule for your remodeling project. Building in a few flex days as a safeguard against unforeseen problems is also a good idea. However, keep this information to yourself.

If contractors know that your schedule is padded, they may feel free to bump your project for a day or two to squeeze in a smaller rush job for another client. To ensure that your contractors stay on schedule, mark your flex days "cleanup" or "out of town"—don't tell them you've built some extra time into the schedule.

Like successful stand-up comedy, successful kitchen remodeling requires impeccable timing. Dedicate a calendar to the projects and be sure to keep it updated. Planning the timing is the only way to keep the amount of time you'll be without a functioning kitchen to a bare minimum, and it will let contractors and tradespeople work more efficiently.

Talk to Building Inspectors ▸

Although building inspectors aren't paid consultants, they can be an excellent design and planning resource. They are your community's field representatives, and their job is to inspect the work done on your project to ensure that it meets building code requirements.

As experts in their respective fields, the building inspector, electrical inspector and plumbing inspector can give you sound advice on designing your kitchen. Not all inspectors have the time or the willingness to answer a lot of design questions, so make your questions short and specific, and be sure to describe your situation clearly. Also ask if the inspections office provides a pamphlet that summarizes the local code requirements for kitchens.

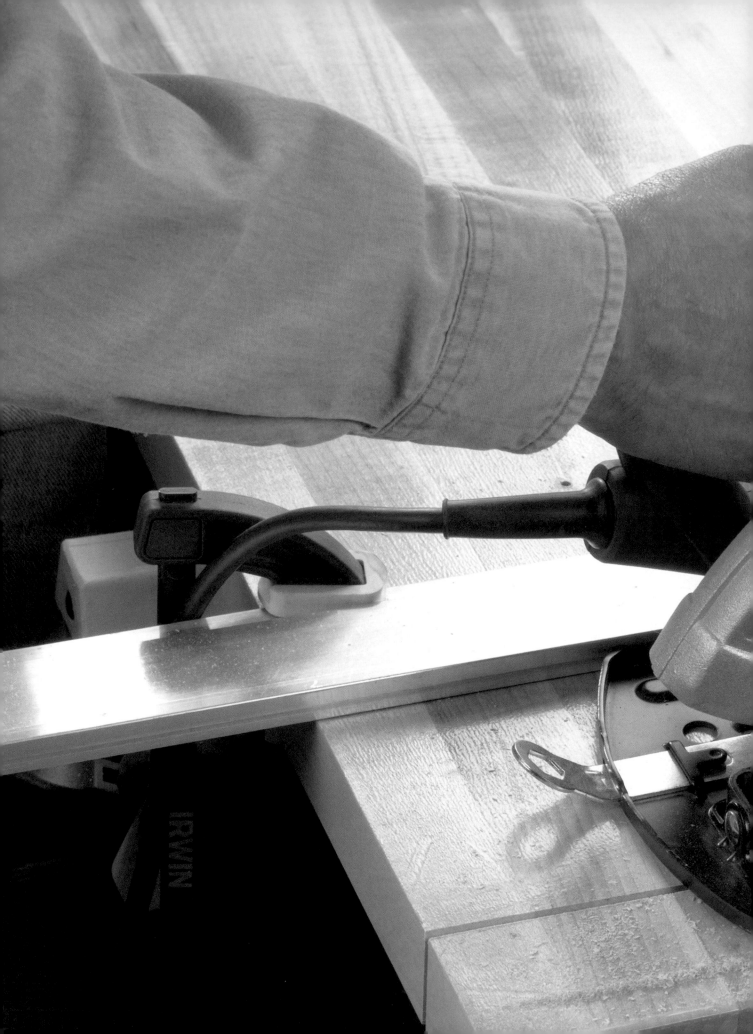

Kitchen Projects

Kitchen Cabinets

Years ago the built-in kitchen cabinet was relatively rare. Food was stored in pantries and in freestanding cupboards, such as Hoosiers, now considered antiques. Plates and silver resided in chests or in boxes stacked on open shelves. Today you rarely see a kitchen that doesn't dwell in the shadow of large banks of built-in cabinets that span from floor to ceiling. But just as the kitchen furnishings have evolved, the cabinets themselves continue to change, mostly to reflect changes in style and design. It is also true that many cabinets installed in the last 20 or 30 years were, simply put, cheap.

If your cabinets are dated or marred (or just plain ugly), but still structurally sound, consider painting or refacing them and replacing the cabinet doors. In this chapter, you'll find information on how to perform these easiest of cabinet updates and make a dramatic change to the look and feel of your kitchen.

In many cases, the unavoidable conclusion you'll draw when you evaluate your cabinets is that it is time for them to go. Though installing cabinets yourself may seem like a daunting task, it actually is made up of several easy to moderately difficult do-it-yourself steps. We cover each step with clear directions and photographs in this chapter. You may want to modify the cabinets you have to be more usable or accessible. The section on pull-down and pop-up shelves shows you how to install these convenient amenities.

Also covered in this chapter is information on cabinet styles and features, factors to consider for design and layout of new cabinet installations, and issues of universal design and green design.

In This Chapter

- Cabinet Updates
- Painting Cabinets
- Refacing Cabinets
- Removing Trim & Old Cabinets
- Preparing for New Cabinets
- Installing Cabinets
- Creating a Kitchen Island

Cabinet Updates

Customize your kitchen storage with swing-up, glide-out and pull-down shelves. Incorporate heavy-duty, swing-up shelves to bring base-cabinet items like stand mixers to the countertop. Build your own full-extension, glide-out shelves to divide larger spaces into two or more shelves and reduce bending and reaching for wheelchair users and people with back problems. Choose pull-down shelf accessories to bring upper-cabinet items like spices within reach. When purchasing specialized hardware accessories, check load ratings, locking mechanisms, arc swings and clearance heights to be sure they can support the items you want to store and they will fit in the intended location.

Installing Swing-up Shelves

Swing-up shelves are perfect for storing heavy appliances beneath the counter. Most swing arms are sold without the shelf surface, which must be purchased separately and cut to fit.

Take accurate measurements of your cabinet's interior dimensions, noting any objects that protrude into the interior. Purchase a swing-up unit that is compatible with your cabinetry. Frameless cabinets often have fully concealed hinges that can interfere with swing mechanisms. Framed cabinets have a front perimeter face frame and may have hinges that interfere with lifting hardware.

Refer to the manufacturer's recommendations for the proper length of the shelf to ensure it will fit into the cabinet when the assembly is locked down and the door is closed. Cut the shelf from ¾"-thick plywood, MDF or melamine-coated particleboard. If the shelf is bare wood, finish all sides with a washable paint or varnish. For melamine-coated board, cover the cut edges with melamine tape to prevent water from damaging the wood core.

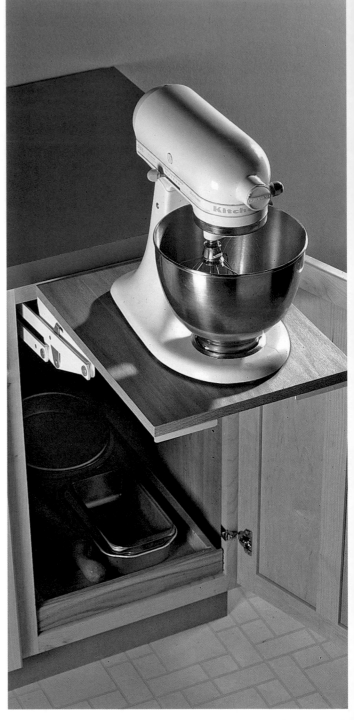

Swing-up shelves are used most often to store stand mixers and other heavier small appliances so they're always at the ready.

Tools & Materials Circular saw ▪ Tape measure ▪ Screwdriver ▪ Shelving ▪ 1 × 3 lumber ▪ #8 machine screws.

How to Install a Swing-up Shelf

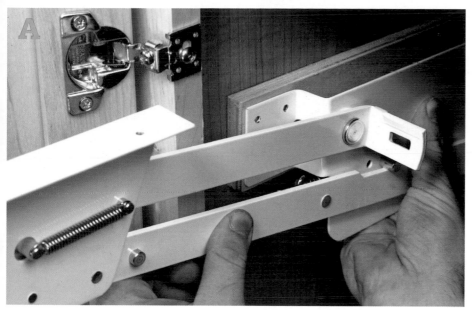

Carefully trigger the locking mechanism on each swing arm and set the arm in its fully extended position. Hold each arm against the inside face of the cabinet side and make sure the arm will clear the door hinge and/or the cabinet face frame. If the arms do not clear, you'll need to use wood spacers to allow the arms to clear the hinges or frames by at least ½". In most cases, one 1 × 3 spacer for each arm will provide enough clearance. Cut the spacers so they match the length of the mounting plate on the swing arms.

Mark the locations of the swing arm mounting plates onto the inside cabinet faces. Mount a swing arm on each side of the cabinet opening, using screws.

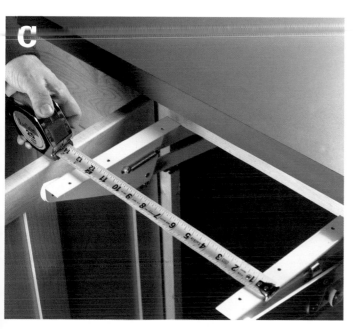

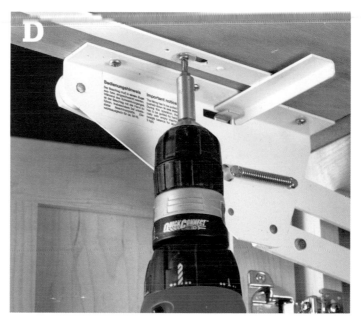

Unlock and rotate both swing arms so they are fully extended. Determine the width of the shelf by measuring across the swing arms, parallel to the countertop, and finding the distance between the outer edges of the shelf-mounting flanges (on the ends of the swing arms). Attach the shelf to the shelf-mounting flanges using #8 machine screws. Follow the manufacturer's instructions for shelf placement.

Fasten each locking bar to the bottom shelf face with the provided screws and plastic spacers to ensure the bars will slide smoothly. Test the locking bars' operation with the shelf in the extended and retracted positions, and make any necessary adjustments.

Installing Glide-out Shelves

Glide-out shelves make getting to the back of a base cabinet much easier. This project gives you directions for building the shelves and installing them. Before installing the shelves, carefully measure the items to be stored to truly customize your storage space.

To determine the proper size for the glide-out shelves, measure the inside dimensions of the cabinet and subtract the distance that hinges and face frames protrude into the interior of the cabinet. Then subtract 1" from the width for the two slides and tracks (½" each).

Tools & Materials

Jig saw ▪ Router ▪ Hammer ▪ Clamps ▪ Drill ▪ Nail set ▪ Circular saw ▪ Straightedge ▪ Sander ▪ Level ▪ Screwdriver ▪ 4d finish nails ▪ Drawer guides (2) ▪ Finishing materials ▪ 1¼" utility screws ▪ Wood glue.

Glide-out shelves improve access to deep cabinets and are often cited in universal design standards.

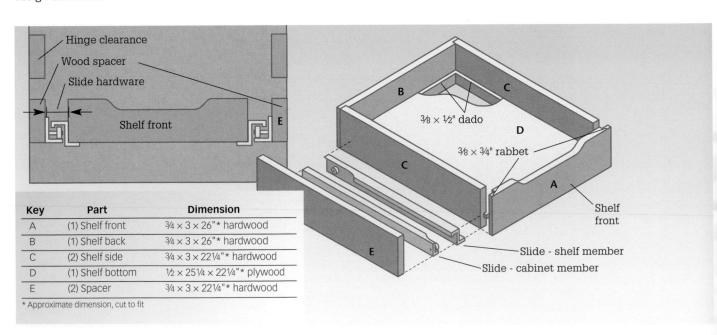

Key	Part	Dimension
A	(1) Shelf front	¾ × 3 × 26"* hardwood
B	(1) Shelf back	¾ × 3 × 26"* hardwood
C	(2) Shelf side	¾ × 3 × 22¼"* hardwood
D	(1) Shelf bottom	½ × 25¼ × 22¼"* plywood
E	(2) Spacer	¾ × 3 × 22¼"* hardwood

* Approximate dimension, cut to fit

How to Build & Install a Glide-out Shelf

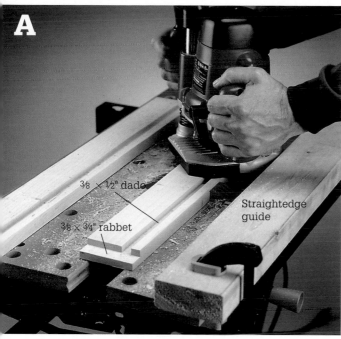

A

$\frac{3}{8} \times \frac{1}{2}"$ dado

$\frac{3}{8} \times \frac{3}{4}"$ rabbet

Straightedge guide

Rout a $\frac{3}{8}$"-deep × $\frac{1}{2}$"-wide dado into the front, back and side panels, $\frac{1}{2}$" up from the bottom edges, using a router straightedge guide. Also cut a $\frac{3}{8}$"-deep × $\frac{3}{4}$"-wide rabbet across the inside face of each end of the front and back pieces.

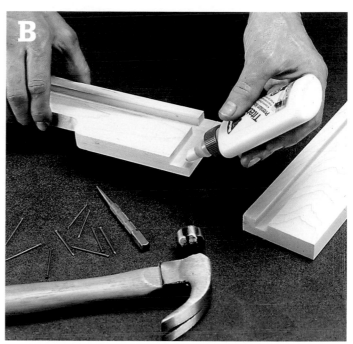

B

Spread glue onto the rabbets of the shelf fronts and attach the sides using three 4d finish nails to hold each joint. Countersink the nails with a nail set. Slide the bottom panels into the dado grooves, then glue and nail the back pieces in place. Clamp the shelves square, and allow the glue to dry.

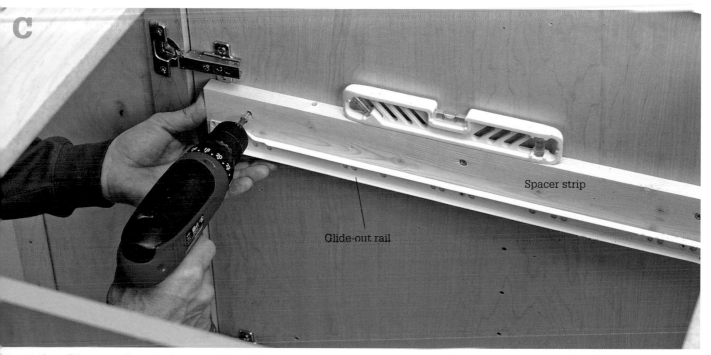

C

Spacer strip

Glide-out rail

Mount the glide-out rails to the bottom edges of the 1 × 3 spacer strips. Then, attach the spacers to the interior walls of the cabinet with 1¼" wallboard screws. Use a level to ensure the rails are installed properly. Screw a sliding rail to each side of the shelves, making sure that the bottom edges of the rails are flush against the bottom edges of the shelves. Install each shelf by aligning its sliding rails with the glides inside the cabinet and pushing it in completely. The rails will automatically lock into place.

Installing Pull-down Shelves

A pull-down shelf makes wall cabinets more user friendly by bringing all the contents down to eye level. Because of the space taken up by the mechanism and the shelf boxes, this is not a good project for a narrow cabinet.

Before you begin this project, hold each swing arm assembly against the inside face of the cabinet side and make sure both arms will clear the door hinge and the cabinet face frame. If the arms do not clear, add custom wood spacers of plywood or solid lumber that are at least as large as the swing arm mounting plates.

Follow the manufacturer's specifications for the box dimensions, which will be based on the size of your cabinet. If the boxes are bare wood, lightly sand the edges and finish all sides with a highly washable paint or a clear varnish, such as polyurethane. For melamine-coated board, cover the cut edges with melamine tape, to keep water from damaging the wood core.

Note: The springs that help raise the arms are strong and may make it difficult to lower empty shelves. When the shelves are loaded, the weight of the items makes it easier to move the shelf.

A pull-down shelf is essentially the opposite of a swing-up shelf (page 124). Mounted in an upper wall cabinet, a pull-down shelf can be drawn out of the cabinet and lowered so the user can reach the contents more easily.

Tools & Materials

Tape measure ▪ Pencil ▪ Circular saw ▪ Drill ▪ Awl ▪ Hacksaw ▪ Allen wrench ▪ Swing-up shelf kit & hardware ▪ ½" mdf ▪ Fasteners & finishing materials for shelf boxes ▪ #8 pan-head screws ▪ Coarse-thread drywall screws ▪ Lumber for custom spacers.

Shopping Tips ▸

- Specialty hardware catalogs carry pull-down shelf hardware.

- Check that the capacity of the mechanism you are purchasing matches the items you will be storing on the shelf.

How to Install a Pull-down Shelf

Use the shelf manufacturer's paper template to determine the general positions of the swing arms, then fasten the wood spacers to the inside faces of the cabinets with coarse-thread wallboard screws. The screws should not go completely through the cabinet side.

Use the template as a reference for marking the location of the swing arm mounting plates with a scratch awl. Drill a pilot hole at each mark. Fasten the swing arms to the custom spacers or cabinet sides with #8 panhead screws (inset). The screws should not go completely through the cabinet side.

Build two shelf boxes from ½" MDF. Install the boxes between the sides of the shelf unit, using the predrilled holes in the side pieces. Secure the boxes with #8 pan-head screws. Because the lower box can be installed in only one position, install it first. Then, find the desired position for the upper box, and secure it in place. Slide the lower handle through the holes in the side pieces.

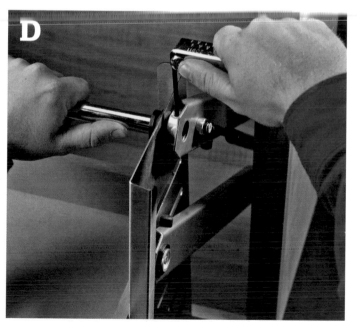

Cut the upper handle to length. With the assistance of a helper, position the box unit in front of the cabinet, rotate the lower arms downward, and secure them to the side pieces using the bolts, washers and nuts provided. Insert the top handle. Lower the upper arms one at a time, and insert the handle end into the arm. Secure the handle with the two setscrews in each arm, using an Allen wrench.

Painting Cabinets

If your kitchen cabinets are in good shape structurally and you are happy with their configuration but not their appearance, a coat of paint may be all it takes to update your kitchen in a dramatic way. You can brighten dark wood, freshen up previously painted cabinet surfaces, or create a new look with faux finish techniques. Any wood, metal or previously painted cabinets can be painted.

As with any painting project, your final results depend on careful and thorough preparation and use of high-quality products. Remove doors, drawers and all hardware so you can paint the surfaces in a flat position, eliminating many drips and sags.

Choose a high-quality enamel paint in either satin, low-luster or semi-gloss finish. A high gloss finish will highlight surface defects and create glare. Latex paint is suitable for this project. Using an alkyd (oil-based) paint may result in a smoother finish with fewer brush marks, but the cleanup is more involved and the fumes may require that you wear a respirator.

Cabinets with matte surfaces in good condition need only be washed with trisodium phosphate (TSP) or another appropriate detergent for preparation. But if the surface is smooth or glossy, as when varnished or painted with a gloss enamel, you'll need to sand and/or chemically degloss before you apply paint. An undercoat of primer improves adhesion and reduces stain-through. If the previous paint was dark or a highly saturated color, or bare wood has been exposed, an undercoat is also necessary. Do not spot-prime because the top coat will not cover evenly in those areas. Avoid applying two layers of top coat, but if you do, make sure to sand or degloss the first coat to get good adhesion of the second coat.

If you are also changing hardware, determine whether you will be using the same screw holes. If not, fill the existing holes with wood putty before sanding.

Painted cabinets are re-emerging as a popular design element in kitchens. Bright paint adds liveliness and fun, while more neutral tones are soothing and let other kitchen elements have the spotlight.

How to Paint Cabinets

Remove doors and drawers. Wash all surfaces to be painted with TSP or other degreaser. Scrape off any loose paint. Sand or chemically degloss all surfaces. Wipe away sanding dust and prime varnished surfaces, dark colors or bare wood with primer.

Remove shelves, when possible, to create access for painting cabinet interiors. Paint the cabinet backs first, followed by the tops, sides and then the bottoms. Paint the face frames last (so you won't need to reach over them when painting the interior).

Paint both sides of doors beginning with the interior surfaces. With raised panel doors, paint the panel inserts first, then the horizontal rails. Paint the vertical stiles last.

Refacing cabinets usually involves replacing the doors and drawer fronts, and applying new self-adhesive wood veneer over the face frames and exposed cabinet sides.

Refacing Cabinets

Refacing cabinets is not as popular an exercise as it once was, but if you want to retain your cabinets in their existing configuration, while upgrading with new doors, it is a good compromise solution. The easy part of refacing, for most homeowners, is switching out old door and drawer fronts for new ones. Simply bring your old door and drawer dimensions to a cabinet shop, select a style, and you should be able to get your new kitchen in just a few weeks. If your new wood doors and drawers don't match the old cabinet sides and face frames (a likely situation) you can either paint the cabinets (see pages 130 to 131) or you can cover the old cabinets with new wood veneer that matches the door and drawer fronts. Replacing hinges and hardware completes the update. Flat panel doors on frameless cabinets can be reveneered as well.

Tools & Materials
Utility knife ▪ Straightedge ▪ Combination square ▪ Handsaw ▪ Drill ▪ Cordless screwdriver ▪ Wallcovering roller ▪ Paint scraper ▪ Refacing kit ▪ Stain and polyurethane finish (for unfinished refacing materials) ▪ Cabinet hardware ▪ 100- and 150-grit sandpaper.

Shopping Tips ▸

- Find refacing kits on the Internet or at woodworking stores.

- Refacing kits, doors and drawers are available in a wide range of styles and quality levels.

How to Reface Cabinets

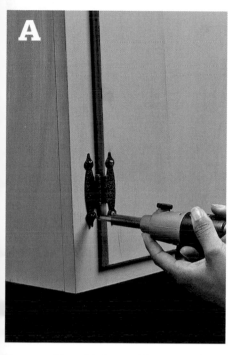

Remove the old doors, hinges, catches, and other hardware. Paint interior of cabinets, if desired.

Scrape any loose or peeling finish. Fill holes and chips with wood patching compound, let it dry, and then lightly sand the cabinet sides, faces and edges with 150-grit sandpaper.

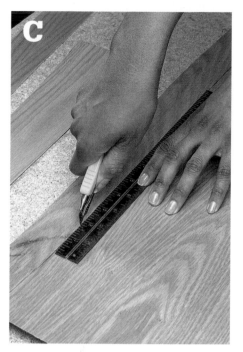

Lay self-adhesive veneer flat on a smooth surface. Measure each surface to be covered, and add ¼" for overlap. Cut veneer pieces with a utility knife and straightedge.

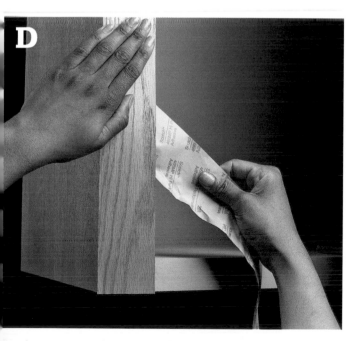

Apply veneer to the vertical frame members first. Peel veneer backing off to reveal one corner of adhesive. Align veneer and press lightly to adhere corner. Gradually remove the backing, and smooth out air bubbles with fingertips. Trim excess veneer with a utility knife.

Apply veneer to the horizontal frame members, overlapping the vertical frame member. Trim overlapping veneer with a utility knife, using a straightedge as a guide. Apply veneer to the cabinet sides and trim off overhanging material with a utility knife.

(continued next page)

How to Reface Cabinets (continued)

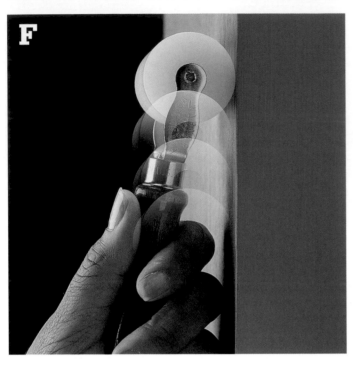

Set the veneer by rolling the entire surface with a wallcovering roller or J-roller.

Stain the new doors and drawer fronts, if they are unfinished. Stain unfinished veneer to match. Apply three coats of polyurethane finish, sanding lightly with 150-grit sandpaper between coats.

Lock a combination square at the 2" mark. Use the square to position hinges an equal distance from top and bottom of the door. Use a finish nail or awl to mark screw locations.

Drill pilot holes and attach the hinges with screws. Mount knobs, handles and catches. A cordless screwdriver speeds up this job.

Attach the cabinet doors to the cabinet face frames. Make sure doors overlap openings by an equal amount on all sides (for overlay doors). Allow ⅛" gap between doors that cover a single opening.

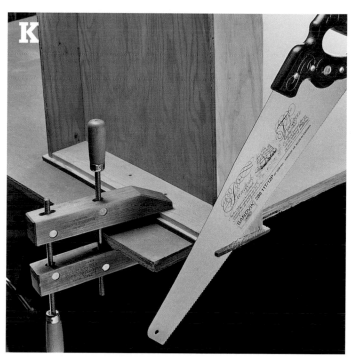

Saw off all overhanging edges of existing solid (one-piece) drawer fronts. If the drawer fronts are two-piece (consisting of a false front and a drawer front), remove the screws and discard the old drawer front.

Attach new drawer fronts by drilling pilot holes and driving screws through the inside of the drawer into each drawer front. Normally, drawer fronts overlap drawers by an equal margin on all sides.

Attach fixed drawer fronts on sink and cooktop cabinets by cutting wood blocks to span the drawer openings. Place the blocks across the openings inside the cabinets. Drive screws through the wood blocks and into the fixed fronts.

Removing Trim & Old Cabinets

Old cabinets can be salvaged fairly easily if they are modular units that were installed with screws, and some custom built-in cabinets can be removed in one piece. If you're not planning to salvage the cabinets (they can be donated to charitable organizations that process building materials) they should be cut into pieces or otherwise broken down and discarded. If you're demolishing your old cabinets, the main danger is causing collateral damage in the room, especially to the plumbing, so work with care.

Tools&Materials Pry bar ▪ Putty knife
▪ Cordless screwdriver ▪ Reciprocating saw ▪ Hammer
▪ Eye protection.

Remove trim moldings at the edges and tops of the cabinets with a flat pry bar or putty knife.

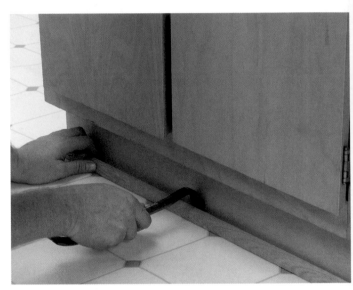

Remove base shoe from cabinet base if the molding is attached to the floor.

Remove baseboards and other trim moldings with a pry bar. Protect wall surfaces with scraps of wood. Label the trim boards on the back side so you can replace them correctly.

Remove valances above cabinets. Some valances are attached to the cabinets or soffits with screws. Others are nailed and must be pried loose.

How to Remove Cabinets

Remove doors and drawers to make it easier to get at interior spaces. You may need to scrape away old paint to expose hinge screws.

At the backs of cabinets, remove any screws holding the cabinet to the wall. Cabinets can be removed as a group, or can be disassembled.

Detach individual cabinets by removing screws that hold face frames together.

Countertops are usually not salvageable. Cut them into manageable pieces with a reciprocating saw, or take them apart piece by piece with a hammer and pry bar.

Preparing for New Cabinets

Installing new cabinets is easiest if the kitchen is completely empty. Disconnect the plumbing and wiring, and temporarily remove the appliances. To remove old cabinets and countertops, see pages 136 to 137. If the new kitchen requires plumbing or electrical changes, now is the time to have this work done. If the kitchen flooring is to be replaced, finish it before beginning layout and installation of cabinets.

Cabinets must be installed plumb and level. Using a level as a guide, draw reference lines on the walls to indicate cabinet location. If the kitchen floor is uneven, find the highest point of the floor area that will be covered by base cabinets. Measure up from this point to draw reference lines.

Stud finder

Filled-in low area

The first step in cabinet prep is to establish level reference lines to mark cabinet height and locate and mark wall studs.

Stud locations

1 × 3
ledger

Reference
line

How to Prepare Walls

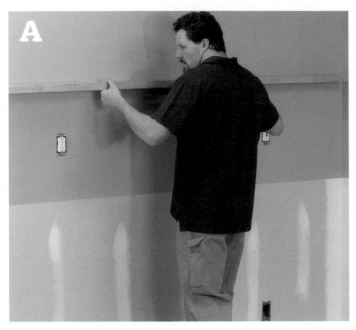

Find high and low spots on wall surfaces, using a long, straight 2 × 4. Sand down any high spots.

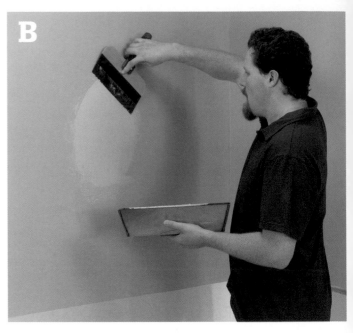

Fill in low spots of wall by applying wallboard compound with a taping knife. Let the compound dry, and then sand it lightly.

Locate and mark wall studs, using an electronic stud finder. Cabinets normally will be hung by driving screws into the studs through the back of the cabinets.

Find the highest point along the floor that will be covered by base cabinets. Place a level on a long, straight 2 × 4, and move the board across the floor to determine if the floor is uneven. Mark the wall at the high point.

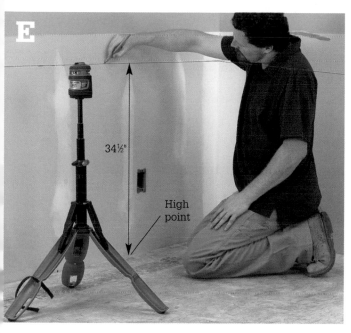

Measure up 34½" from the high-point mark (for standard cabinets). Use a level (a laser level is perfect) to mark a reference line on walls. Base cabinets will be installed with top edges flush against this line.

Measure up 84" from the high-point mark and draw a second reference line. Wall cabinets will be installed with their top edges flush against this line.

Measure down 30" from the wall-cabinet reference line and draw another level line where the bottoms of the cabinets will be. Temporary ledgers will be installed against this line.

Install 1 × 3 temporary ledgers with top edges flush against the reference lines. Attach ledgers with 2½" wallboard screws driven into every other wall stud. Mark stud locations on ledgers. Cabinets will rest temporarily on ledgers during installation (the ledgers alone will not support them, however).

Installing Cabinets

Cabinets must be firmly anchored to wall studs, and they must be plumb and level when installed. The best way to ensure this is by attaching a ledger board to the wall to assist in the installation. As a general rule, install the upper cabinets first so your access is not impeded by the base cabinets. (Although some pros prefer to install the base cabinets first so they can be used to support the uppers during installation.) It's also best to begin in a corner and work outward from there.

Tools & Materials
Handscrew clamps ▪ Level ▪ Hammer ▪ Utility knife ▪ Nail set ▪ Stepladder ▪ Drill ▪ Counterbore drill bit ▪ Cordless screwdriver ▪ Jig saw ▪ Cabinets ▪ Trim molding ▪ Toe-kick molding ▪ Filler strips ▪ Valance ▪ 6d finish nails ▪ Finish washers ▪ #10 × 4" wood screws ▪ #8 × 2½" screws ▪ 3" drywall screws.

Stock cabinets are sold in boxes that are keyed to door and drawer packs (you need to buy these separately). It is important that you realize this when you are estimating your project costs at the building center (often a door pack will cost as much or more than the cabinet). Also allow plenty of time for assembling the cabinets out of the box. It can take an hour or more to put some more complex cabinets together.

▶ How to Fit a Corner Cabinet

Before installation, test-fit corner and adjoining cabinets to make sure doors and handles do not interfere with each other. If necessary, increase the clearance by pulling the corner cabinet away from the side wall by no more than 4". To maintain even spacing between the edges of the doors and the cabinet corner, cut a filler strip and attach it to the corner cabinet or the adjoining cabinet. Filler strips should be made from material that matches the cabinet doors and face frames.

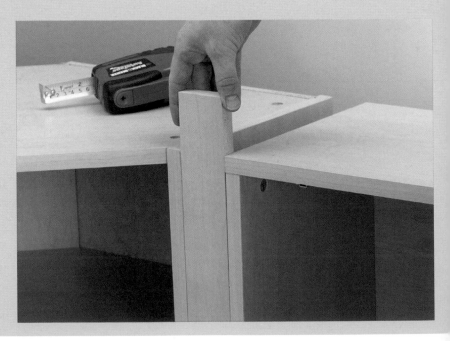

How to Install Wall Cabinets

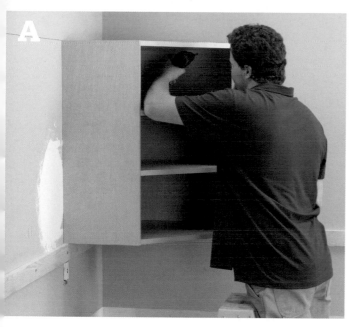

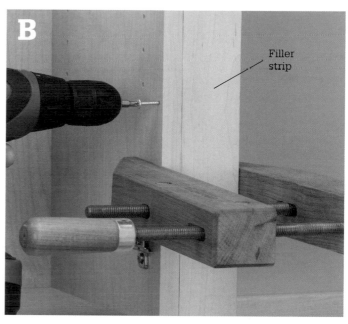

Position a corner upper cabinet on a ledger (see page 141) and hold it in place, making sure it is resting cleanly on the ledger. Drill 3/16" pilot holes into the wall studs through the hanging strips at the top, rear of cabinet. Attach the cabinet to the wall with 2½" screws. Do not tighten fully until all cabinets are hung.

Attach a filler strip to the front edge of the cabinet, if needed (see page 142). Clamp the filler in place, and drill counterbored pilot holes through the cabinet face frame, near hinge locations. Attach filler to cabinet with 2½" cabinet screws or flathead wood screws.

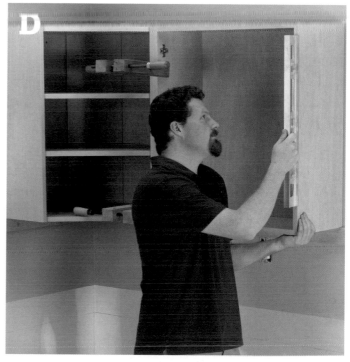

Position the adjoining cabinet on the ledger, tight against the corner cabinet or filler strip. Clamp the corner cabinet and the adjoining cabinet together at the top and bottom. Handscrew clamps will not damage wood face frames.

Check the front cabinet edges or face frames for plumb. Drill 3/16" pilot holes into wall studs through hanging strips in rear of cabinet. Attach cabinet with 2½" screws. Do not tighten wall screws fully until all cabinets are hung.

(continued next page)

How to Install Wall Cabinets (continued)

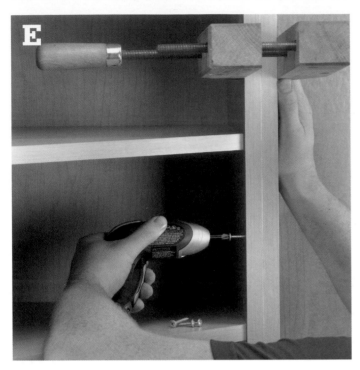

Attach the corner cabinet to the adjoining cabinet. From inside corner cabinet, drill pilot holes through face frame. Join cabinets with sheet-metal screws.

Position and attach each additional cabinet. Clamp frames together, and drill counterbored pilot holes through side of face frame. Join cabinets with wood screws. Drill ³⁄₁₆" pilot holes in hanging strips, and attach cabinet to studs with wood screws.

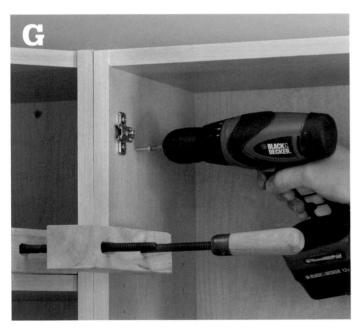

Join frameless cabinets with #8 × 1¼" panhead wood screws or wood screws with decorative washers. Each pair of cabinets should be joined by at least four screws.

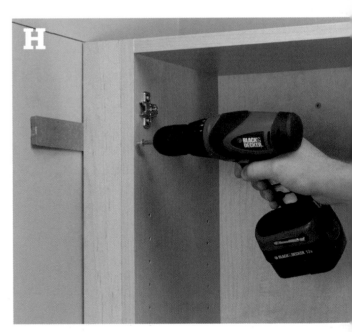

Fill gaps between the cabinet and wall or neighboring appliance with a filler strip. Cut the filler strip to fit the space, then wedge wood shims between the filler and the wall to create a friction fit that holds it in place temporarily. Drill counterbored pilot holes through the side of the cabinet (or the edge of the face frame) and attach filler with screws.

Remove the temporary ledger. Check the cabinet run for plumb, and adjust if necessary by placing wood shims behind cabinet, near stud locations. Tighten wall screws completely. Cut off shims with utility knife.

Use trim moldings to cover any gaps between cabinets and walls. Stain moldings to match cabinet finish.

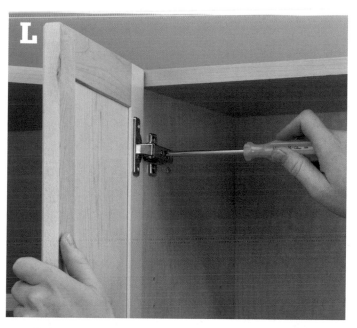

Attach decorative valance above sink. Clamp valance to edge of cabinet frames, and drill counterbored pilot holes through cabinet frames into end of valance. Attach with sheet-metal screws.

Install the cabinet doors. If necessary, adjust the hinges so that the doors are straight and plumb.

How to Install Base Cabinets

Begin the installation with a corner cabinet. Draw plumb lines that intersect the 34½" reference line (measured from the high point of the floor—see page 141) at the locations for the cabinet sides.

Place cabinet in corner. Make sure the cabinet is plumb and level. If necessary, adjust by driving wood shims under cabinet base. Be careful not to damage flooring. Drill ³⁄₁₆" pilot holes through the hanging strip and into wall studs. Tack the cabinet to the wall with wood screws or wallboard screws.

Clamp the adjoining cabinet to the corner cabinet. Make sure the new cabinet is plumb, then drill counterbored pilot holes through the cabinet sides or the face frame and filler strip. Screw the cabinets together. Drill ³⁄₁₆" pilot holes through hanging strips and into wall studs. Tack the cabinets loosely to the wall studs with wood screws or wallboard screws.

Use a jig saw to cut any cabinet openings needed in the cabinet backs (for example, in the sink base seen here) for plumbing, wiring or heating ducts.

Position and attach additional cabinets, making sure the frames are aligned and the cabinet tops are level. Clamp cabinets together, then attach the face frames or cabinet sides with screws driven into pilot holes. Tack the cabinets to the wall studs, but don't drive screws too tight—you may need to make adjustments once the entire bank is installed.

Make sure all cabinets are level. If necessary, adjust by driving shims underneath cabinets. Place shims behind the cabinets near stud locations to fill any gaps. Tighten wall screws. Cut off shims with utility knife.

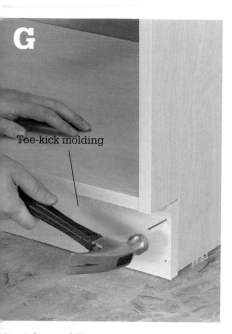

Toe-kick molding

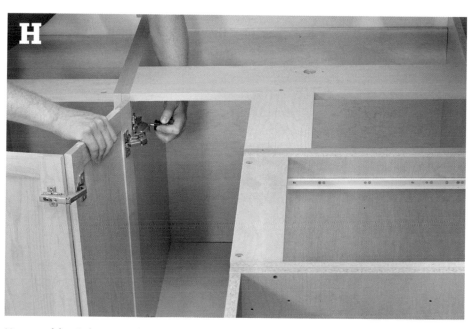

Use trim moldings to cover gaps between the cabinets and the wall or floor. The toe-kick area is often covered with a strip of wood finished to match the cabinets or painted black.

Hang cabinet doors and mount drawer fronts then test to make sure they close smoothly and the doors fit evenly and flush. Self-closing cabinet hinges (by far the most common type installed today) have adjustment screws that allow you to make minor changes to the hardware to correct any problems.

Two base cabinets arranged back-to-back make a sturdy kitchen island base that's easy to install. When made with the same style cabinets and countertops as the rest of the kitchen, the island is a perfect match.

Creating a Kitchen Island

Kitchen islands can be created using a whole range of methods, from repurposing an old table to fine, custom woodworking. But perhaps the easiest (and most failsafe) way to add the conveniences and conviviality of a kitchen island is to make one from stock base cabinets. The cabinets and countertops don't have to match your kitchen cabinetry, but that is certainly an option you should consider. When designing and positioning your new island, be sure to maintain a minimum distance of 3 ft. between the island and other cabinets (4 ft. or more is better).

Tools & Materials Marker
▪ Drill/driver ▪ 2 × 4 cleats ▪ Pneumatic nailer and 2" finish nails or hammer and 6d finish nails
▪ 2 base cabinets (approx. 36" wide × 24" deep)
▪ Countertop ▪ Wallboard screws.

How to Create a Stock-cabinet Island

Set two base cabinets back-to-back in position on the floor and outline the cabinet corners onto the flooring. Remove the cabinets and draw a new outline inside the one you just created to allow for the thickness of the cabinet sides (usually ¾").

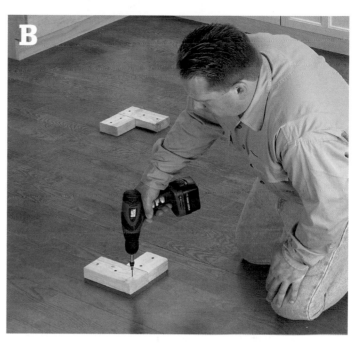

Cut 2 × 4 cleats to fit inside the inner outline to provide nailing surfaces for the cabinets. Attach the cleats to the floor with screws or nails. TIP: Create an L-shape cleat for each inside corner.

Join the two base cabinets together by driving 1¼" wallboard screws through the nailing strips on the backs of the cabinets from each direction. Make sure the cabinet sides are flush and aligned. Lower the base cabinets over the cleats. Check the cabinets for level, and shim underneath the edges of the base if necessary.

Attach the cabinets to the floor cleats using 6d finish nails. Drill pilot holes for nails, and recess nail heads with a nail set. Make a countertop (see pages 164 to 183) and install it on top of the cabinets.

Kitchen Countertops

More than simply a work surface, a kitchen countertop can dazzle with the look-at-me pizzazz of granite, or bring together a country theme with soapstone and butcher block. There are many choices in countertops, from the less-expensive laminate and linoleum, through ceramic and stone tile, to high-end stainless, granite and marble.

Countertop options for your kitchen depend on how much you are willing to spend, whether you will be doing it yourself or contracting out, and what look you want to achieve. In this chapter we will cover available countertop options, their pluses and minuses, and give directions for those you can install yourself.

Step-by-step instructions with photographs are included for three countertop projects: post-form laminate, custom laminate and tile. Also included in this chapter is a section on metallic laminates, and how to create a tiled backsplash.

Shopping tips, universal design tips, and environmental information are also included.

In This Chapter

- Tips for Installing Countertops
- Installing a Post-form Countertop
- Installing a Butcher Block Countertop
- Building a Custom Laminate Countertop
- Creating Wood Countertop Edges
- Building a Tile Countertop
- Tiling a Backsplash

Take careful measurements of your base cabinets before ordering countertop material. Take measurements along the wall and at the front edge of the cabinets. If there is a discrepancy, use the smaller measurement if the countertop will butt against a wall or appliance on each end. Use the larger measurement if the cabinet bank is open on one end or both ends. Be sure to add length for overhang on countertops with open ends (generally, 1" overhang per end). If the countertop will butt up against an appliance, do not include any allowance for overhang (in fact, some installers recommend subtracting 1/16" to minimize contact between the countertop and the appliance).

Tips for Installing Countertops

If you are installing countertops on brand new cabinets, the best way to ensure a successful installation is to do a good job installing the cabinets. If they are level, half the countertop battle is over. If you are replacing only the countertop, the success of the new installation hinges on two critical elements: removing the old countertop without causing any damage or disruption to the cabinets; and taking careful measurements of the cabinets so you can order new countertops that fits perfectly.

If you are replacing your old countertops with the same type of material, it may be worth your time to take careful measurements of the old countertop before you remove it. On the other hand, there is nothing guaranteeing that the old countertop was

sized correctly or that the counter and cabinets haven't shifted since the original installation. The surest method is to rely on the cabinets for your measurements. But before taking them, do any minor repairs or leveling that may be required. Then, once your cabinets are level, take the measurements you'll need for ordering materials.

Tools & Materials Channel-type pliers
■ Reciprocating saw ■ Pry bar ■ Utility knife ■ Masonry chisel ■ Circular saw ■ Ball peen hammer ■ Gloves ■ Eye protection.

How to Remove an Old Countertop

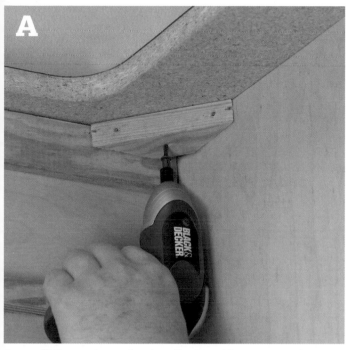

Turn off the water at the shutoff valves. Disconnect and remove plumbing fixtures and appliances. Remove any brackets or screws holding the countertop to the cabinets. Unscrew the take-up bolts at the corners of mitered countertops.

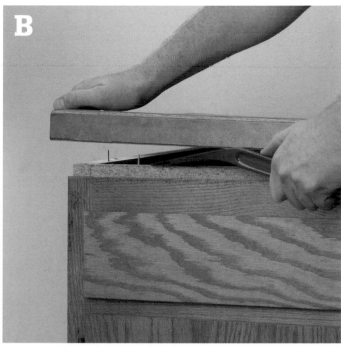

Use a utility knife to cut caulk beads along the backsplash and edge of the countertop. Remove any trim. Using a flat pry bar, try to lift the countertop away from base cabinets.

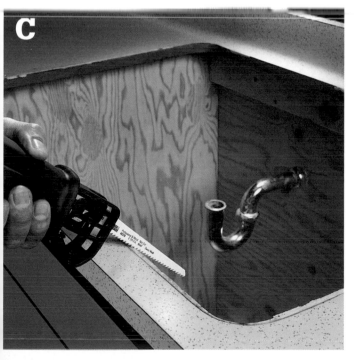

If the countertop cannot be pried up, use a reciprocating saw or jig saw with coarse wood-cutting blade to cut the countertop into pieces for removal. Be careful not to cut into base cabinets.

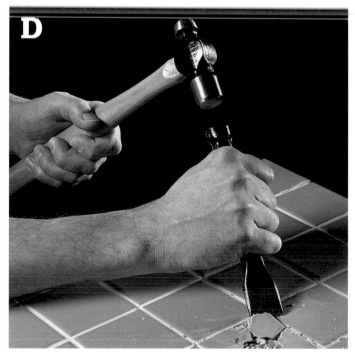

Ceramic tile: Wear eye protection. Chisel tile off with a masonry chisel to create a few tile-free cutting lines. Use a circular saw and remodelers blade to cut the countertop and substrate into pieces for removal.

Installing a Post-form Countertop

Post-form laminate countertops are available in stock and custom colors. Pre-mitered sections are available for two- or three-piece countertops that continue around corners. If the countertop has an exposed end, you will need an endcap kit that contains a preshaped strip of matching laminate. Post-form countertops have either a waterfall edge or a no-drip edge. Stock colors are typically available in 4-, 6-, 8-, 10- and 12-foot straight lengths and 6- and 8-foot mitered lengths.

Materials and tools for installing a post-form countertop include: Wood for shimming (A), take-up bolts for drawing miters together (B), household iron (C), endcap laminate to match countertop (D), endcap battens (E), file (F), adjustable wrench (G), buildup blocks (H), compass (I), fasteners (J), silicone caulk and sealer (K).

Post-form countertops are among the easiest and cheapest to install. They are a good choice for beginning DIYers, but the design and color options are fairly limited.

How to Install a Post-form Countertop

OPTION: Use a jig saw fitted with a downstroke blade to cut post-form if the saw foot must rest on the good surface of the post form. If you are unable to locate a downstroke blade, you can try applying tape over the cutting lines, but you are still likely to get tear-out from a normal upstroke jig saw blade.

Tools & Materials

Tape measure ▪ Framing square ▪ Pencil ▪ Straightedge ▪ C-clamps ▪ Hammer ▪ Level ▪ Caulking gun ▪ Jig saw ▪ Compass ▪ Adjustable wrench ▪ Belt sander ▪ Drill and spade bit ▪ Cordless screwdriver ▪ Post-form countertop ▪ Wood shims ▪ Take-up bolts ▪ Drywall screws ▪ Wire brads ▪ Endcap laminate ▪ Silicone caulk ▪ Wood glue.

Use a framing square to mark a cutting line on the bottom surface of the countertop. Cut off the countertop with a jig saw, using a clamped straight-edge as a guide.

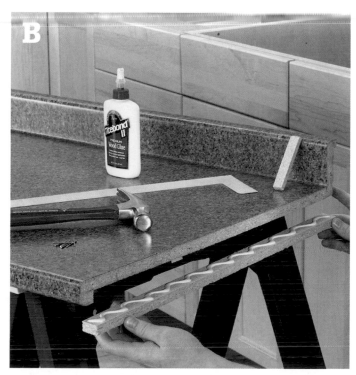

Attach the battens from the endcap kit to the edge of the countertop, using carpenter's glue and small brads. Sand out any unevenness with a belt sander.

(continued next page)

How to Install a Post-form Countertop (continued)

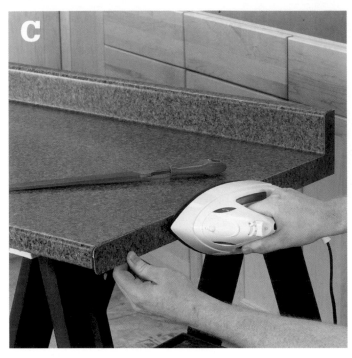

Hold the endcap laminate against the end, slightly overlapping the edges. Activate adhesive by pressing an iron set at medium heat against the endcap. Cool with a wet cloth, then file the endcap laminate flush with the edges of the countertop.

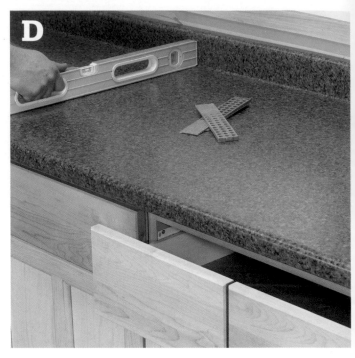

Position the countertop on base cabinets. Make sure the front edge of the countertop is parallel to the cabinet faces. Check the countertop for level. Make sure that drawers and doors open and close freely. If needed, adjust the countertop with shims.

Because walls are usually uneven, use a compass to trace the wall outline onto the backsplash. Set the compass arms to match the widest gap, then move the compass along the length of the wall to transfer the outline to the top of the backsplash. Apply painter's tape to the top edge of the backsplash, following the scribe line (inset).

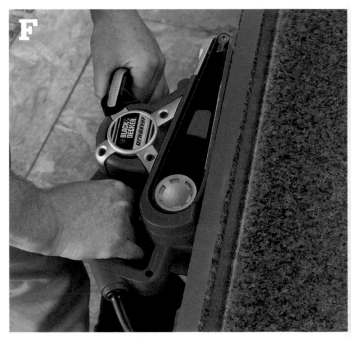

Remove the countertop. Use a belt sander to grind the backsplash to the scribe line.

Mark cutout for self-rimming sink.
Position the sink upside down on the
countertop and trace its outline. Remove
the sink and draw a cutting line 5/8" inside
the sink outline.

Drill a starter hole just inside the cutting
line. Make sink cutouts with a jig saw. Support
the cutout area from below so that the
falling cutout does not damage the cabinet.

Apply a bead of silicone caulk to the
edges of the mitered countertop sections.
Force the countertop pieces tightly
together.

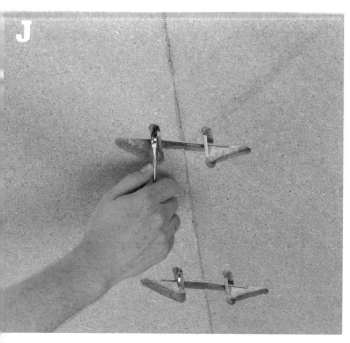

From underneath the countertop, install and tighten miter take-
up bolts. Position countertop tightly against the wall and fasten it to
the cabinets by driving wallboard screws up through corner
brackets and into the countertop. Screws should be long enough to
provide maximum holding power, but not long enough to puncture
the laminate surface.

Seal the seam between the backsplash and the wall with
silicone caulk. Smooth the bead with a wet fingertip. Wipe away
excess caulk.

Butcher block countertops are enjoying a resurgence in popularity because of their natural beauty and warm wood tones.

Installing a Butcher Block Countertop

Butcher block slabs come in a variety of woods or—since they are made up of small pieces of wood glued together—a combination of different woods. They're available most commonly in maple or oak in end grain, which is composed of vertical pieces of wood, or edge grain and face grain, made up long strips of wood. Making butcher block can be accomplished as an advanced DIY project, but it's often more cost-effective (and always faster) to purchase pieces in stock sizes and cut it down to fit your kitchen. Since butcher block is ideal for food prep areas but can be impractical near a sink or stove,

another option is to install a small section of butcher block in combination with other countertop materials.

Tools & Materials Circular saw with cutting guide ▪ Carpenters square ▪ Drill and bits ▪ Bolt connector hardware ▪ Caulk gun and silicone adhesive ▪ Router with piloted roundover bit ▪ Wood screws with fender washers ▪ Jig saw with downstroke bit ▪ Brush and finish material.

Shopping Tips ▶

- Butcher block sold by the foot for countertop ranges from 1½" to 3" thick, although some end grain products, used mostly for chopping blocks, can be up to 5" thick. For residential kitchens, the 1½"-thick material is the most available and most affordable choice. Stock length varies but 6-foot and 12-foot slabs are common. You can also order the material with sink cutouts completed. Premade countertop is sold in the standard 25" depth, but wider versions (30" and 36") for islands are not difficult to find.

- Butcher block countertop material comes pre-sealed, but a finish of varnish or oil, such as mineral or tung oil, is recommended. Seal cut wood around sink cutouts and on trimmed edges to keep it watertight.

- A self-rimming sink is the easiest type to mount in a butcher block countertop, but undermount types can look stunning (just make sure to get a perfect seal on the end grain around the sink cutout.

- End grain vs. face grain: Traditionally, butcher block countertop surfaces were made with square sections of wood (often maple) oriented with their end grain facing upward. This orientation creates a better, more durable, knife-friendly, cutting surface. For economy, many of today's butcher block sections are edge-glued with exposed edge grain or face grain.

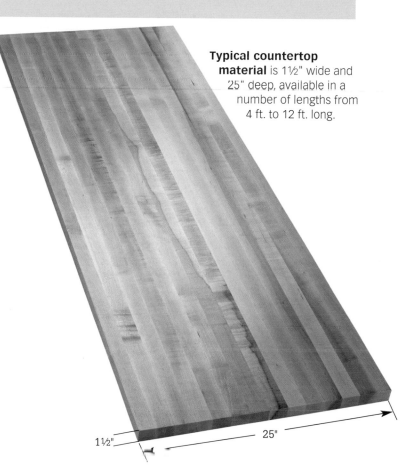

Typical countertop material is 1½" wide and 25" deep, available in a number of lengths from 4 ft. to 12 ft. long.

1½"   25"

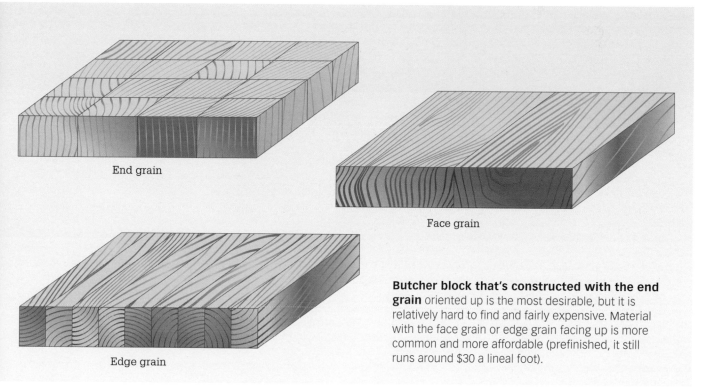

End grain

Face grain

Edge grain

Butcher block that's constructed with the end grain oriented up is the most desirable, but it is relatively hard to find and fairly expensive. Material with the face grain or edge grain facing up is more common and more affordable (prefinished, it still runs around $30 a lineal foot).

How to Install a Butcher Block Countertop

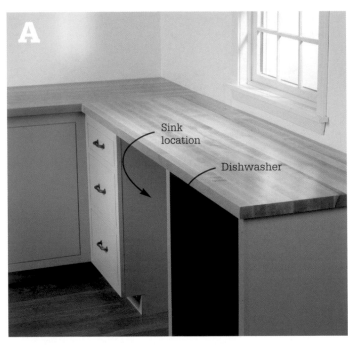

Before beginning installation, allow the butcher block to acclimate to your home's moisture level for a couple days. Wood contracts and expands with moisture and humidity, so it may have warped or expanded during transport. Place it level on the cabinet tops and let it sit until it's settled.

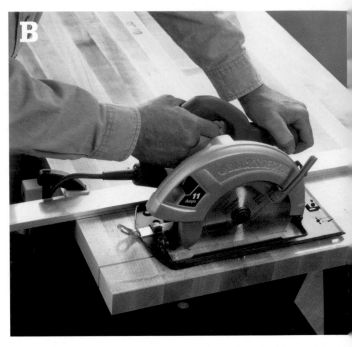

Measure your countertop area, adding 1" to the base cabinet depth to allow for overhang. Using a circular saw, cut the piece to size if needed. Butcher block with pre-cut miter corners and cutouts for kitchens are available, but if you're cutting the piece yourself, be sure to apply finish to each new raw edge.

Butcher block should be attached using wood screws that allow for some movement. Mark three points in a line on the underside of the countertop, spacing rows of drilling points at 12-inch intervals.

Drill pilot holes for screws at drilling points. Stick tape to the bit 1" from the point to create a depth stop.

Drill corresponding holes in the cabinet base that are slotted or at least ⅜" larger than the screws you are using. When driven with a washer under the screw hand, screws will be able to move slightly with the wood.

35mm Forstner bit

Bolt connectors,
(See Resources, p. 283)

Bolt driver bit

TIP: In most cases butcher block countertops are not mitered at corners as some other countertop types are. Instead, they are butted at the corners. You also may need to join two in-line pieces with a butt joint. In both instances, use connector fittings.

Make butt joints between countertop sections. Lay the two sections of countertop to be joined upside down on a flat worksurface in their correct orientation. Mark drilling points for connector holes. Drill the holes with a Forstner bit.

With the countertop sections roughly in position on the cabinets and flipped right-side up, apply a bead of silicone adhesive near the top of one mating edge.

From below, insert the connector bolt so the two heads are flat in the holes and then tighten the bolt with the driver bit (supplied with bolt hardware) to draw the two sections of countertop together. Do not overtighten.

(continued next page)

How to Install a Butcher Block Countertop (continued)

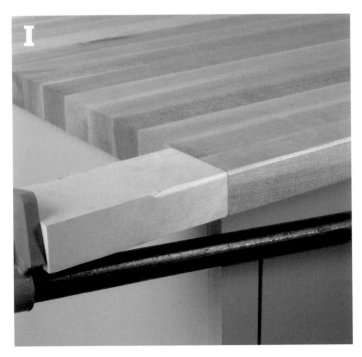

Clamp a piece of scrapwood to the end of the countertop so the tops are flush. The scrapwood prevents the router bit from rounding over the corner when the edge of the countertop is profiled.

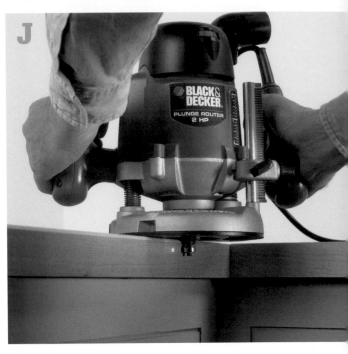

Pull the countertop section away from the wall a few inches and make a roundover cut along the front edges with a piloted roundover bit.

Attach the countertop to the cabinet mounting strips by driving screws up through the cabinet strips and into the countertop. The screws should be ¼" shorter than the distance from the bottom of the mounting strips to the top of the countertop. Use 1" fender washers with the screws and snug them up, but do not overtighten. Because of the counterbores and the washers, the countertop will be able to move slightly as it expands and contracts.

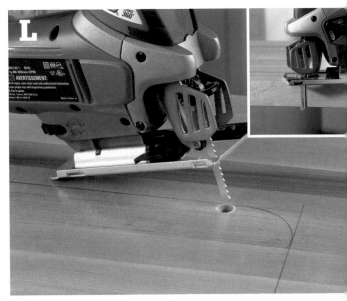

If installing a sink in your countertop, start by outlining the sink in correct position as recommended in the installation material from the sink manufacturer. Mount a downstroke blade into jig saw (inset photo) and drill a starter hole just inside the sink outline. Make the cutout, taking care to stay just inside the cutting line. If you are installing an undermount sink, smooth the cuts up to the line with a power sander.

OPTION: If you're installing an undermount sink, mark a centerpoint for drilling a hole to accommodate the faucet body, following the recommendations of the faucet manufacturer. A 1⅜"-dia. hole is fairly standard.

Seal the edges of the sink opening with a varnish as instructed by the butcher block manufacturer or by coating it generously with pure mineral oil or tung oil for a natural finish. Let sit for 15 minutes then wipe off the excess with a clean, lint-free cloth. Let dry for 48 hours. Repeat six times, letting dry thoroughly between coats.

Add backsplash of your choice and caulk between the new countertop and the backsplash area with clear silicone caulk.

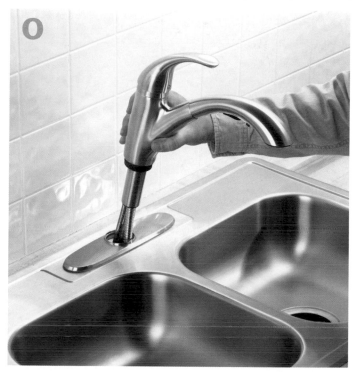

Install the faucet and sink and make the water supply and drain hook-ups (see pages 202 to 205).

Fabricating your own custom countertop from particleboard and plastic laminate is not exactly an easy DIY project, but it gives you unlimited options and the results can be very satisfying.

Building a Custom Laminate Countertop

Building your own custom laminate countertop using sheets of plastic laminate and particleboard offers two advantages: the countertop you get will be less expensive than a custom-ordered countertop, and it will allow you more options in terms of colors and edge treatments. A countertop made with laminates also can be tailored to fit any space, unlike premade countertop material that is a standard width (usually 25").

Laminate commonly is sold in 8-ft. or 12-ft. lengths that are about ¹⁄₂₀" thick. In width, they range from 30"strips to 48" sheets. The 30" strips are sized specifically for countertops, allowing for a 25"-wide countertop, a 1½" wide front edge strip and a short backsplash.

The plastic laminate is bonded to the particleboard or MDF substrate with contact cement (although most professional installers use products that are available only to the trades). Water-base contact cement is nonflammable and nontoxic, but solvent-base contact cement (which requires a respirator and is highly flammable) creates a much stronger, more durable bond.

Tools&Materials
Tape measure ▪ Framing square ▪ Straightedge ▪ Scoring tool ▪ Paint roller ▪ 3-way clamps ▪ Caulk gun ▪ J-roller ▪ Miter saw ▪ Scribing compass ▪ Circular saw ▪ Screwdriver ▪ Belt sander ▪ File ▪ Router ▪ ¾" particleboard ▪ Sheet laminate ▪ Contact cement and thinner ▪ Wood glue ▪ Drywall screws.

Tips for Working with Laminate ▶

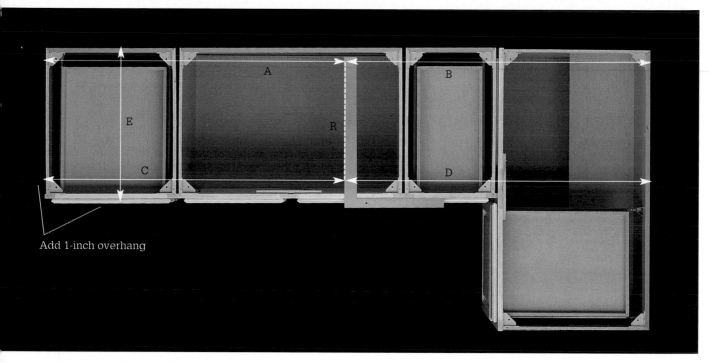

Add 1-inch overhang

Measure along tops of base cabinets to determine the size of the countertop. If wall corners are not square, use a framing square to establish a reference line (R) near the middle of the base cabinets, perpendicular to the front of the cabinets. Take four measurements (A, B, C, D) from the reference line to the cabinet ends. Allow for overhangs by adding 1" to the length for each exposed end, and 1" to the width (E).

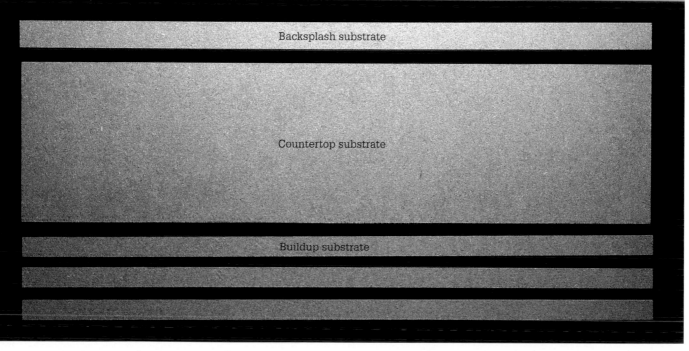

Backsplash substrate

Countertop substrate

Buildup substrate

Lay out cutting lines on the particleboard so you can rip-cut the substrate and build-up strips to size, using a framing square to establish a reference line. Cut core to size using a circular saw with clamped straightedge as a guide. Cut 4" strips of particleboard for backsplash, and for joint support where sections of countertop core are butted together. Cut 3" strips for edge buildups.

How to Build a Custom Laminate Countertop

Join the countertop substrate pieces on the bottom side. Attach a 4" particleboard joint support across the seam, using carpenter's glue and 1¼" wallboard screws.

Attach 3"-wide edge buildup strips to the bottom of the countertop, using 1¼" wallboard screws. Fill any gaps on the outside edges with latex wood patch, and then sand the edges with a belt sander.

To determine the size of the laminate top, measure countertop substrate. Laminate seams should not overlap substrate. Add ½" trimming margin to both the length and width of each piece. Measure laminate needed for face and edges of backsplash, and for exposed edges of countertop substrate. Add ½" to each measurement.

Cut laminate by scoring and breaking it. Draw a cutting line, then etch along the line with a utility knife or other sharp cutting tool. Use a straightedge as a guide. Two passes of scoring tool will help laminate break cleanly.

OPTION: Some laminate installers prefer to cut laminate with special snips that resemble avaiator snips. Available from laminate suppliers, the snips arc faster than scoring and snapping, and less likely to cause cracks or tears in the material. You'll still need to square the cut edges with a trimmer or router.

Bend laminate toward the scored linc until the shoct breaks cleanly. For better control on narrow pieces, clamp a straightedge along scored line before bending laminate. Wear gloves to avoid being cut by sharp edges.

Create tight-piloted seams with plastic laminate by using a router and a straight bit to trim edges that will butt together. Measure from cutting edge of the bit to edge of the router baseplate (A). Place laminate on scrap wood and align edges. To guide the router, clamp a straightedge on the laminate at distance A plus ¼", parallel to laminate edge. Trim laminate.

(continued next page)

How to Build a Custom Laminate Countertop (continued)

Apply laminate to sides of countertop first. Using a paint roller, apply two coats of contact cement to the edge of the countertop and one coat to back of laminate. Let cement dry according to manufacturer's directions. Position laminate carefully, then press against edge of countertop. Bond with J-roller.

Use a router and flush-cutting bit to trim edge strip flush with top and bottom surfaces of countertop substrate. At edges where router cannot reach, trim excess laminate with a file. Apply laminate to remaining edges, and trim with router.

Test-fit laminate top on countertop substrate. Check that laminate overhangs all edges. At seam locations, draw a reference line on core where laminate edges will butt together. Remove laminate. Make sure all surfaces are free of dust, then apply one coat of contact cement to back of laminate and two coats to substrate. Place spacers made of ¼"-thick scrap wood at 6" intervals across countertop core. Because contact cement bonds instantly, spacers allow laminate to be positioned accurately over core without bonding. Align laminate with seam reference line. Beginning at one end, remove spacers and press laminate to countertop core.

Apply contact cement to remaining substrate and next piece of laminate. Let cement dry, then position laminate on spacers, and carefully align butt seam. Beginning at seam edge, remove spacers and press laminate to the countertop substrate.

Roll the entire surface with a J-roller to bond the laminate to the substrate. Clean off any excess contact cement with a soft cloth and mineral spirits.

Flush cutting bit

Remove excess laminate with a router and flush-cutting bit. At edges where router cannot reach, trim excess laminate with a file. Countertop is now ready for final trimming with bevel-cutting bit.

(continued next page)

How to Build a Custom Laminate Countertop (continued)

Finish-trim the edges with router and 15° bevel-cutting bit. Set bit depth so that the bevel edge is cut only on top laminate layer. Bit should not cut into vertical edge surface.

TIP: File all edges smooth. Use downward file strokes to avoid chipping the laminate.

Cut 1¼"-wide strips of ¼" plywood to form an overhanging scribing strip for the backsplash. Attach to the top and sides of the backsplash substrate with glue and wallboard screws. Cut laminate pieces and apply to exposed sides, top and front of backsplash. Trim each piece as it is applied.

Test-fit the countertop and backsplash. Because your walls may be uneven, use a compass to trace the wall outline onto the backsplash scribing strip. Use a belt sander to grind backsplash to scribe line (see page 156).

Apply a bead of silicone caulk to the bottom edge of the backsplash.

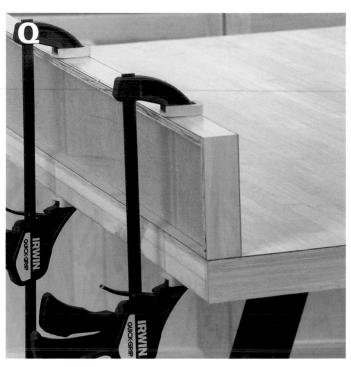

Position the backsplash on the countertop, and clamp it into place with bar clamps. Wipe away excess caulk, and let dry completely.

Screw 2" wallboard screws through the countertop and into the backsplash core. Make sure screw heads are countersunk completely for a tight fit against the base cabinet. Install countertops.

Creating Wood Countertop Edges

For an elegant added touch on a laminate countertop, use hard wood edges and shape them with a router. Rout the edges before attaching the backsplash to the countertop. Wood caps can also be added to the top edge of the backsplash. A simple edge is best for easy cleaning.

Tools & Materials Hammer
■ Nail set ■ Belt sander with 120-grit sanding belt ■ 3-way clamps ■ Router ■ 1 × 2 hardwood strips ■ Wood glue ■ Finish nails.

Incorporating hardwood into the countertop edging presents a wealth of attractive and very durable solutions for the nosing of a plastic laminate countertop.

How to Build Solid Hardwood Edges

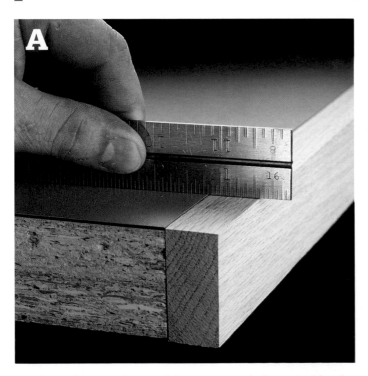

Apply laminate to the top of the countertop before attaching the edge strip. Attach the edge strip flush with the surface of the laminate, using wood glue and finish nails.

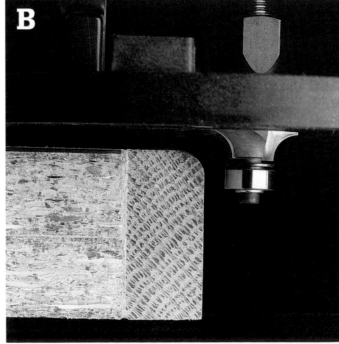

Mold the top and bottom edges of the strip with a router and profiling bit, if desired. Stain and finish the wood as desired.

How to Build Coved Hardwood Edges

Cut 1 × 2 hardwood strips to fit the edges of the countertop. Sand the strips smooth. Miter-cut the inside and outside corners.

Attach edge strips to the countertop with wood glue and 3-way clamps. Drill pilot holes, then attach strip with finish nails. Recess nail heads with a nail set or, use a pneumatic finish nailer with 2" nails.

Sand the edge strips flush with the top surface of the countertop, using a belt sander and 120-grit sandpaper.

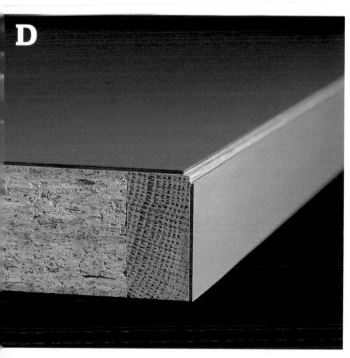

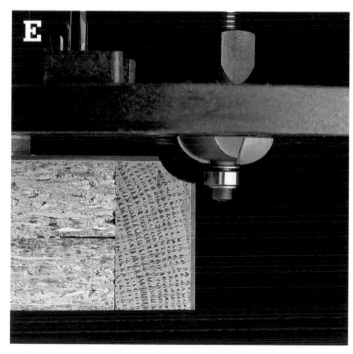

Apply laminate to the edge and top of the countertop after the hardwood edge has been sanded flush.

Cut cove edge with a router and cove bit with ball-bearing pilot. Smooth cove with 220-grit sandpaper. Stain and finish exposed wood as desired.

Ceramic or porcelain makes a durable countertop that is heat-resistant and relatively easy for a DIYer to create. By using larger tiles, you minimize the grout lines (and the cleaning that goes with them).

Building a Tile Countertop

Ceramic and porcelain tile remain popular choices for countertops and backsplashes for a number of reasons: It's available in a vast range of sizes, styles and colors; it's durable and repairable; and some tile—not all—is reasonably priced. With careful planning, tile is also easy to install, making a custom countertop a good do-it-yourself project.

The best tile for most countertops is glazed ceramic or porcelain floor tile. Glazed tile is better than unglazed because of its stain resistance, and floor tile is better than wall tile because it's thicker and more durable.

While glazing protects tile from stains, the grout between tiles is still vulnerable because it's so porous. To minimize staining, use a grout that contains a latex additive, or mix the grout using a liquid latex additive. After the grout cures fully, apply a quality grout sealer, and reapply the sealer once a year thereafter. Choosing larger tiles reduces the number of grout lines. Although the selection is a bit limited, if you choose 13" × 13" floor tile, you can span from the front to the back edge of the countertop with a single seam.

The countertop in this project has a substrate of ¾" exterior-grade plywood that's cut to fit and fastened to the cabinets. The plywood is covered with a layer of plastic (for a moisture barrier) and a layer of ½"-thick cementboard. Cementboard is an effective backer for tile because it won't break down if water gets through the tile layer. The tile is adhered to the cementboard with thin-set adhesive. The overall thickness of the finished countertop is about 1½". If you want a thicker countertop, you can fasten an additional layer of plywood (of any thickness) beneath the substrate. Two layers of ¾" exterior-grade plywood without cementboard is also an acceptable substrate.

You can purchase tiles made specifically to serves as backsplashes and front edging. While the color and texture may match, these tiles usually come in only one length, making it difficult to get your grout lines to align with the field tiles. You can solve this problem by cutting your own edging and backsplash tiles from field tiles (see step J, page 179).

> **Tools&Materials** Tape measure ▪ Circular saw ▪ Drill ▪ Utility knife ▪ Straightedge ▪ Stapler ▪ Drywall knife ▪ Framing square ▪ Notched trowel ▪ Tile cutter ▪ Carpeted 2 × 4 ▪ Mallet ▪ Rubber grout float ▪ Sponge ▪ Foam brush ▪ Caulk gun ▪ Ceramic tile ▪ Tile spacers ▪ ¾" exterior-grade (CDX) plywood ▪ 4-mil polyethylene sheeting ▪ Packing tape ▪ ½" cementboard ▪ 1¼" galvanized deck screws ▪ Fiberglass mesh tape ▪ Thin-set mortar ▪ Grout with latex additive ▪ Silicone caulk ▪ Silicone grout sealer.

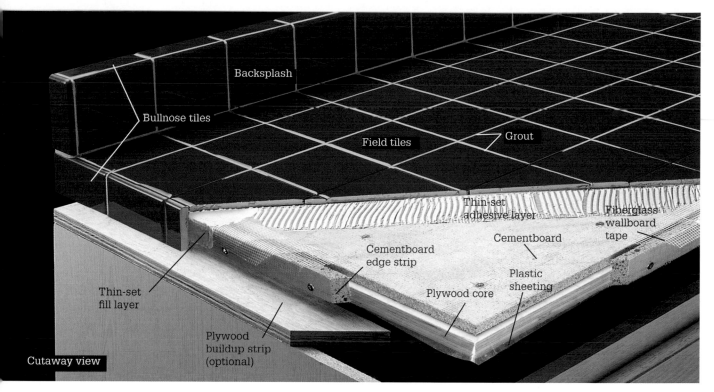

Backsplash

Bullnose tiles

Field tiles

Grout

Thin-set adhesive layer

Fiberglass wallboard tape

Cementboard edge strip

Cementboard

Plywood core

Plastic sheeting

Thin-set fill layer

Plywood buildup strip (optional)

Cutaway view

A ceramic tile countertop made with wall tile starts with a core of ¾" exterior-grade plywood that's covered with a moisture barrier of 4-mil polyethylene sheeting. Half-inch cementboard is screwed to the plywood, and the edges are capped with cementboard and finished with fiberglass mesh tape and thin-set mortar. Tiles for edging and backsplashes may be bullnose or trimmed from the factory edges of field tiles.

Options for Backsplashes & Countertop Edges

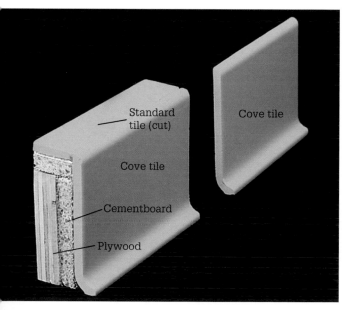

Standard tile (cut)

Cove tile

Cove tile

Cementboard

Plywood

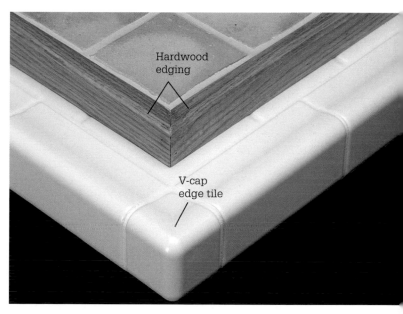

Hardwood edging

V-cap edge tile

Backsplashes can be made from cove tile attached to the wall at the back of the countertop. You can use the tile alone or build a shelf-type backsplash, using the same construction as for the countertop. Attach the plywood backsplash to the plywood core of the countertop. Wrap the front face and all edges of the plywood backsplash with cementboard before laying tile.

Edge options include V-cap edge tile and hardwood strip edging. V-cap tiles have raised and rounded corners that create a ridge around the countertop perimeter—good for containing spills and water. V-cap tiles must be cut with a tile saw. Hardwood strips should be prefinished with at least three coats of polyurethane finish. Attach the strips to the plywood core so the top of the wood will be flush with the faces of the tiles.

Tips for Laying Out Tile ▶

- **You can lay tile over a laminate countertop** that's square, level and structurally sound. Use a belt sander with 60- or 80-grit sandpaper to rough up the surface before setting the tiles. The laminate cannot have a no-drip edge. If you're using a new substrate and need to remove your existing countertop, make sure the base cabinets are level front to back, side to side and with adjoining cabinets. Unscrew a cabinet from the wall and use shims on the floor or against the wall to level it, if necessary.

- **Installing battens along the front edge of the countertop** helps ensure the first row of tile is perfectly straight. For V-cap tiles, fasten a 1 × 2 batten along the reference line, using screws. The first row of field tile is placed against this batten. For bullnose tiles, fasten a batten that's the same thickness as the edging tile, plus ⅛" for mortar thickness, to the face of the countertop so the top is flush with the top of the counter. The bullnose tiles are aligned with the outside edge of the batten. For wood edge trim, fasten a 1 × 2 batten to the face of the countertop so the top edge is above the top of the counter. The tiles are installed against the batten.

- **Before installing any tile, lay out the tiles in a dry run** using spacers. If your counter is L-shaped, start at the corner and work outward. Otherwise, start the layout at a sink to ensure equal-sized cuts on both sides of the sink. If necessary, shift your starting point so you don't end up cutting very narrow tile segments.

13 × 13" tile   12 × 12" tile   6 × 6" tile   5 × 5" tile   Mosaic tile

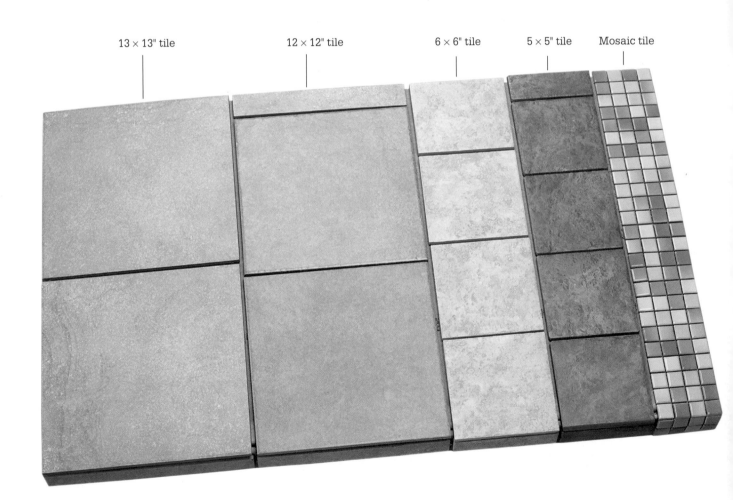

The bigger the tile the fewer the grout lines. If you want a standard 25"-deep countertop, the only way to get there without cutting tiles is to use mosaic strips or 1" tile. With 13 × 13" tile, you need to trim 1" off the back tile but have only one grout line front to back. As you decrease tiles the number of grout lines increases.

How to Build a Tile Countertop

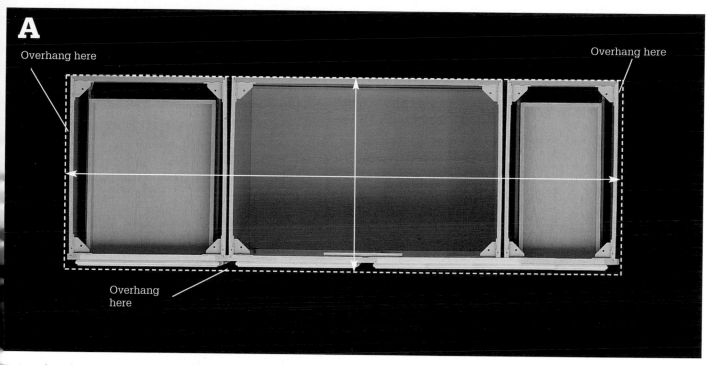

Determine the size of the plywood substrate by measuring across the top of the cabinets. The finished top should overhang the drawer fronts by at least ¼". Be sure to account for the thickness of the cementboard, adhesive and tile when deciding how large to make the overhang. Cut the substrate to size from ¾" plywood, using a circular saw. Also make any cutouts for sinks and other fixtures.

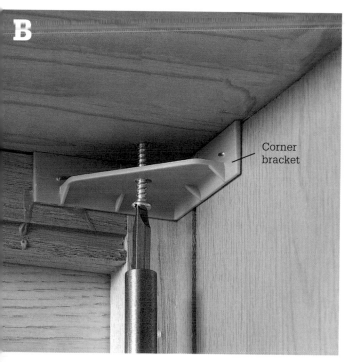

Set the plywood substrate on top of the cabinets, and attach it with screws driven through the cabinet corner brackets. The screws should not be long enough to go through the top of the substrate.

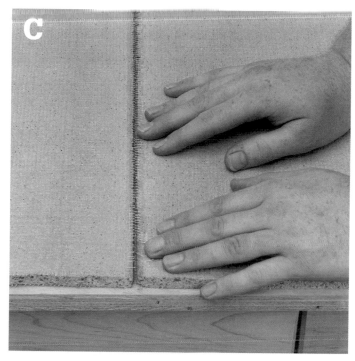

Cut pieces of cementboard to size, then mark and make the cutout for the sink. Dry-fit them on the plywood core with the rough sides of the panels facing up. Leave a ⅛" gap between the cementboard sheets and a ¼" gap along the perimeter.

(continued next page)

How to Build a Tile Countertop (continued)

Option: Cut cementboard using a straightedge and utility knife or a cementboard cutter with a carbide tip. Hold the straightedge along the cutting line, and score the board several times with the knife. Bend the piece backward to break it along the scored line. Back-cut to finish.

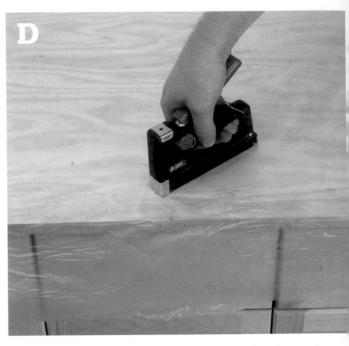

Lay the 4-mil plastic moisture barrier over the plywood substrate, draping it over the edges. Tack it in place with a few staples. Overlap seams in the plastic by 6", and seal them with packing tape.

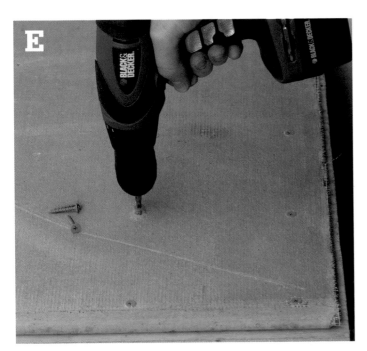

Lay the cementboard pieces rough-side up on the plywood and attach them with cementboard screws driven every 6". Drill pilot holes using a masonry bit, and make sure all screw heads are flush with the surface. Wrap the countertop edges with 1¼"-wide cementboard strips, and attach them to the core with cementboard screws.

Tape all cementboard joints with fiberglass mesh tape. Apply three layers of tape along the front edge where the horizontal cementboard sheets meet the cementboard edging.

Fill all gaps and cover all of the tape with a layer of thin-set mortar. Feather out the mortar with a drywall knife to create a smooth, flat surface.

Determine the required width of your edge tiles. Lay a field tile onto the tile base so it overhangs the front edge by ½" or so. Then, hold a metal rule up to the underside of the tile and measure the distance from the tile to the bottom of the subbase. Your edge tiles should be cut to this width (the gap for the grout line will cause the edge tile to extend past the subbase, concealing it completely)

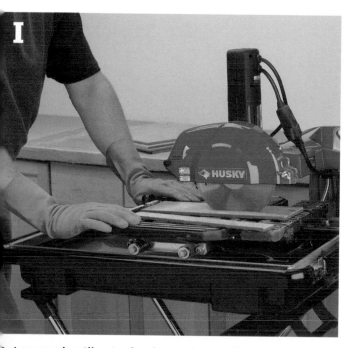

Cut your edge tiles to the determined width, using a tile saw. It's worth renting a quality wet saw for tile if you don't own one. Floor tile is thick and difficult to cut with a hand cutter (especially porcelain tiles).

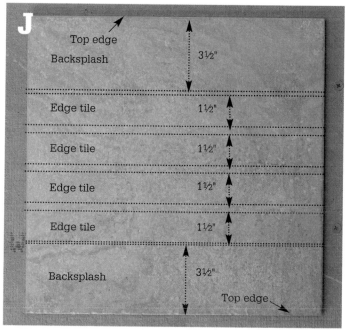

Cut tiles for the backsplash. The backsplash tiles (3½" wide in our project) should be cut with a factory edge on each tile that will be oriented upward when they're installed. You can make efficient use of your tiles by cutting edge tiles from the center area of the tiles you cut to make the backsplash.

(continued next page)

Dry-fit tiles on the countertop to find the layout that works best. Once the layout is established, make marks along the vertical and horizontal rows. Draw reference lines through the marks and use a framing square to make sure the lines are perpendicular.

▶ Variation: Laying Out with Small Floor Tiles and Bullnose Edging

Lay out tiles and spacers in a dry run. Adjust starting lines, if necessary. If using battens, lay the field tile flush with the battens, then apply edge tile. Otherwise, install the edging first. If the countertop has an inside corner, start there by installing a ready-made inside corner or cutting a 45° miter in edge tile to make your own inside corner.

Place the first row of field tile against the edge tile, separating the tile with spacers. Lay out the remaining rows of tile. Adjust starting lines if necessary to create a layout using the least number of cut tiles.

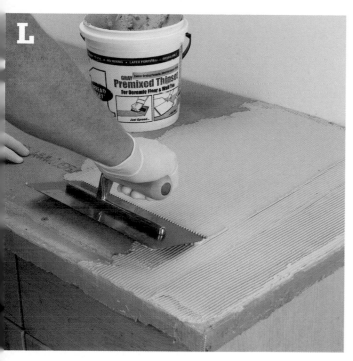

Use a ³⁄₈" square notched trowel to apply a layer of thinset adhesive to the cementboard. Apply enough for two or three tiles, starting at one end. Hold the trowel at roughly a 30-degree angle and try not to overwork the adhesive or remove too much.

Set the first tile into the adhesive. Hold a piece of the edge in tile against the countertop edge as a guide to show you exactly how much the tile should overhang the edge.

Cut all the back tiles for the layout to fit (you'll need to remove about 1" of a 13 × 13" tile) before you begin the actual installation. Set the back tiles into the thinset, maintaining the gap for groutlines created by the small spacer nubs cast into the tiles. If your tiles have no spacer nubs, see next step.

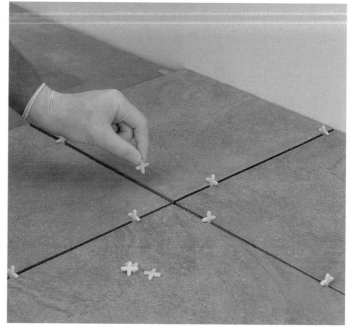

OPTION: To maintain even grout lines, some beginning tilers insert plus sign shaped plastic spacers at the joints. This is less likely to be useful with large tiles like those shown here, but it is effective. Many tiles today feature built-in spacing lugs, so the spacers are of no use. Make sure to remove the spacers before the thinset sets. If you leave them in place they will corrupt your grout lines.

(continued next page)

How to Build a Tile Countertop (continued)

VARIATION: To mark border tiles for cutting, allow space for backsplash tiles, grout and mortar by placing a tile against the back wall. Set another tile (A) on top of the last full tile in the field, then place a third tile (B) over tile A and hold it against the upright tile. Mark and cut tile A and install it with the cut edge toward the wall. Finish filling in your field tiles.

To create a support ledge for the edge tiles, prop pieces of 2 × 4 underneath the front edge of the substrate overhang, using wood scraps to prop the ledge tightly up against the substrate.

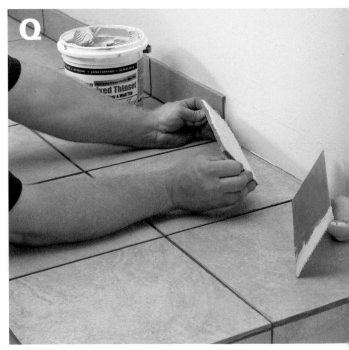

Apply a thick layer of thinset to the backside of the edge tile with your trowel. This is called "buttering" and it is easier and neater than attempting to trowel adhesive onto the countertop edge. Press the tiles into position so they are flush with the leading edges of the field tiles.

Butter each backsplash tile and press it into place, doing your best to keep all of the grout lines aligned.

Mix a batch of grout to complement the tile (keeping in mind that darker grout won't look dirty as soon as lighter grout). Apply the grout to the grout line areas with a grout float.

Let the grout dry until a light film is created on the countertop surface and then wipe the excess grout off with a sponge and warm, clean water.

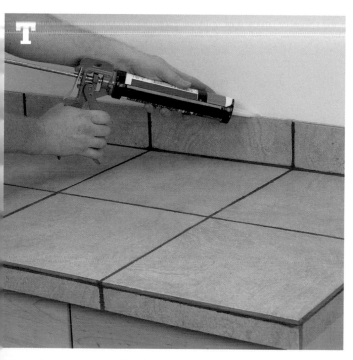

After the grout has dried (and before you use the sink, if possible) run a bead of clear silicone caulk along the joint between the backsplash and the wall. Install your sink and faucet.

Wait at least one week and then seal the grout lines with a penetrating grout sealer. This is important to do. Sealing the tiles themselves is not a good idea unless you are using unglazed tiles (a poor choice for countertops, however).

Tiling a Backsplash

There are few spaces in your home with as much potential for creativity and visual impact as the space between your kitchen countertop and cupboards. A well-designed backsplash can transform the ordinary into the extraordinary.

Tiles for the backsplash can be attached directly to wallboard or plaster and do not require backerboard. When purchasing the tile, order 10 percent extra to cover breakage and cutting. Remove switch and receptacle coverplates and install box extenders to make up for the extra thickness of the tile. Protect the countertop from scratches by covering it with a drop cloth.

Tools & Materials Level ∎ Tape measure ∎ Pencil ∎ Tile cutter ∎ Rod saw ∎ Notched trowel ∎ Rubber grout float ∎ Beating block ∎ Rubber mallet ∎ Sponge ∎ Bucket ∎ Straight 1 × 2 ∎ Wall tile ∎ Tile spacers (if needed) ∎ Bullnose trim tile ∎ Mastic tile adhesive ∎ Masking tape ∎ Grout ∎ Caulk ∎ Drop cloth ∎ Grout sealer.

Tips for Planning Tile Layouts ▸

Gather planning brochures and design catalogs to help you create decorative patterns and borders for the backsplash.

Break tiles into fragments and make a mosaic backsplash. Always use a sanded grout for joints wider than ⅛".

Add painted mural tiles to create a focal point. Mixing various tile styles adds an appealing contrast.

How to Tile a Backsplash

Make a story stick by marking a board at least half as long as the backsplash area to match the tile spacing.

Starting at the midpoint of the installation area, use the story stick to make layout marks along the wall. If an end piece is too small (less than half a tile), adjust the midpoint to give you larger, more attractive end pieces. Use a level to mark this point with a vertical reference line.

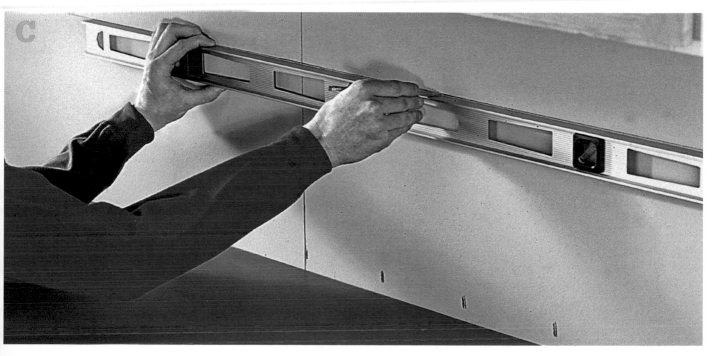

While it may appear straight, your countertop may not be level and therefore is not a reliable reference line. Run a level along the counter to find the lowest point on the countertop. Mark a point two tiles up from the low point and extend a level line across the entire work area.

(continued next page)

How to Tile a Backsplash (continued)

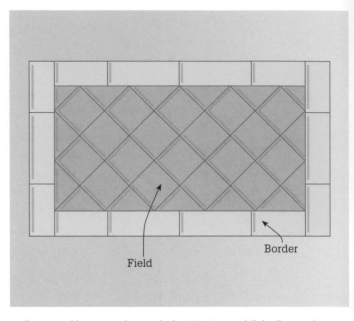

Field

Border

VARIATION: Diagonal Layout. Mark vertical and horizontal reference lines, making sure the angle is 90°. To establish diagonal layout lines, measure out equal distances from the crosspoint, then connect the points with a line. Additional layout lines can be extended from these as needed. To avoid the numerous, unattractive perimeter cuts common to diagonal layouts, try using a standard border pattern as shown. Diagonally set a field of full tiles only, then cut enough half tiles to fill out the perimeter. Finally, border the diagonal field with tiles set square to the field.

D

E

F

Apply mastic adhesive evenly to the area beneath the horizontal reference line, using a notched trowel. Comb the adhesive horizontally with the notched edge.

Starting at the vertical reference line, press tiles into the adhesive with a slight twisting motion. If the tiles are not self-spacing, use plastic spacers to maintain even grout lines. If the tiles do not hang in place, use masking tape to hold them in place until the adhesive sets.

Install a whole row along the reference line, checking occasionally to make sure the tiles are level. Continue installing tiles below the first row, trimming tiles that butt against the countertop as needed.

Apply adhesive to an area above the line and continue placing tiles, working from the center to the sides. Install trim tile, such as bullnose tile, to the edges of the rows.

When the tiles are in place, make sure they are flat and firmly embedded by laying a beating block against the tile and rapping it lightly with a mallet. Remove the spacers. Allow the mastic to dry for at least 24 hours, or as directed by the manufacturer.

Mix the grout and apply it with a rubber grout float. Spread it over the tiles, keeping the float at a low 30° angle, pressing the grout deep into the joints. Note: For grout joints ⅛" and smaller, be sure to use a non-sanded grout.

Wipe off excess grout, holding the float at a right angle to the tile, working diagonally so as not to remove grout from the joints. Clean any remaining grout from the tiles with a damp sponge, working in a circular motion. Rinse the sponge thoroughly and often.

Shape the grout joints by making slow, short passes with the sponge, shaving down any high spots; rinse the sponge frequently. Fill any voids with a fingerful of grout. When the grout has dried to a haze, buff the tile clean with a soft cloth. Apply a bead of caulk between the countertop and tiles. Reinstall any electrical fixtures you removed. After the grout has completely cured, apply a grout sealer.

Installing Fixtures & Appliances

Appliances for kitchens include refrigerators, ranges and dishwashers; fixtures include sinks, faucets, garbage disposers and ice makers. In many ways, these items define our kitchens. Essentially, they do most of the work (along with the cook, of course). The conventional thinking on purchasing appliances and fixtures is that you should buy the best quality you can afford. Although some appliance sellers may offer free installation, you can often save a significant amount of money (and thereby let yourself upgrade your purchase) by doing the installation yourself.

As long as you have a dedicated outlet in the refrigerator area, installing one is as simple as plugging it in, sliding it into the bay and making sure it is level. If your new 'fridge has an ice maker and a drinking water spigot, you'll need some basic plumbing skills to do the job yourself. But in general, installing appliances and fixtures in your kitchen is a manageable job. An exception may be made, however, when it comes to hooking up a gas range. Only professionals and very experienced do-it-yourselfers should attempt to make gas connections. The potential consequences of a mistake are far too great to risk just to free up enough money to upgrade to a stainless steel finish.

In This Chapter

- Removing Sinks & Faucets
- Installing a Drop-in Kitchen Sink
- Installing an Undermount Kitchen Sink
- Installing an Apron Sink
- Installing Faucets & Drains
- Installing a Food Disposer
- Installing Dishwashers
- Installing Refrigerators
- Installing a Hot Water Dispenser
- Installing Ranges & Cooktops
- Installing Vent Hoods

Removing Sinks & Faucets

Replacing a sink and faucet, or especially just the faucet, is a fast kitchen upgrade. The most difficult aspect of the project, aside from choosing which sink and which faucet, is the cramped working conditions under the sink.

Old fixtures often are corroded and stuck tight. It is easiest to remove the sink and faucet as one unit, rather than trying to remove the faucet mounting nuts while on your back inside the sink cabinet. Simply remove the tailpiece slip nut, the water connections and the sink mounting screws, and lift the whole unit free.

Removing an old sink or faucet can be a bit messy. Have rags and a bucket handy to catch water left in supply and drain pipes.

Turn off the water at the supply valves—if they stick, gently wiggle the handle back and forth to loosen scale deposits. A vise-style pliers around the handle will give you more leverage. If necessary, turn off the main water supply and replace the supply valves.

Tools & Materials Utility knife ■ Channel-type pliers ■ Basin wrench ■ Spud wrench ■ Hammer ■ Penetrating oil.

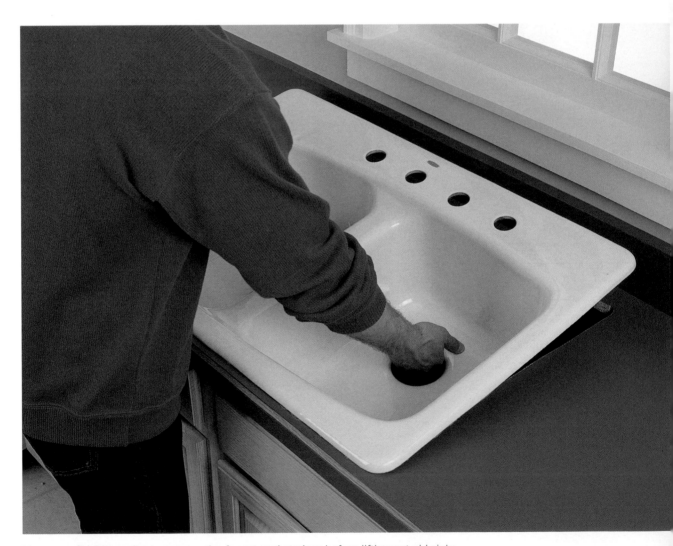

You may find it easier to remove the faucet and strainer before lifting out old sinks.

How to Remove a Sink

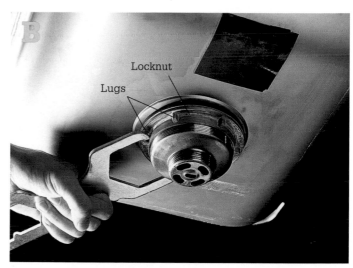

Use a utility knife to cut the caulk seal between the sink flange and the countertop. If you are not replacing the countertop, take care to avoid marring the surface.

From beneath the sink, disconnect the drain pipes at the P-tap and remove them from the sink strainer. (If your sink drain includes a garbage disposer drain line or a dishwasher drain line, see pages 212 and 214). If you plan to reuse the sink strainer on your new sink, remove it by loosening the lock nut with a spud wrench (this also may be done after the sink is removed for easier access). Disconnect the faucet supply lines and remove the sink. The faucet is easier to remove (see below) once the sink is out of the sink base.

How to Remove a Faucet

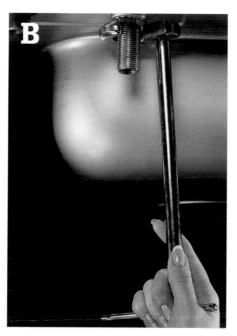

Spray penetrating oil on to the tailpiece mounting nuts and the supply tube coupling nuts. Remove the coupling nuts with a basin wrench or channel-type pliers.

Remove the tailpiece mounting nuts with a basin wrench or channel-type pliers. A basin wrench has a long handle that makes it easy to work in tight areas.

Remove faucet. Use a putty knife to clean away old plumber's putty from the surface of sink. If reusing the sink, clean the surface with mildly abrasive non-chlorine cleanser.

Drop-in sinks, also known as self-rimming sinks, have a wide sink flange that extends beyond the edges of the sink cutout. They also have a wide back flange to which the faucet is mounted directly.

Installing a Drop-In Kitchen Sink

Most drop-in, self-rimming kitchen sinks are easily installed.

Drop-in sinks for do-it-yourself installation are made from cast iron coated with enamel, stainless steel, enameled steel, acrylic, fiberglass or resin composites. Because cast-iron sinks are heavy, their weight holds them in place and they require no mounting hardware. Except for the heavy lifting, they are easy to install. Stainless steel and enameled-steel sinks weigh less than cast-iron and most require mounting brackets on the underside of the countertop. Some acrylic and resin sinks rely on silicone caulk to hold them in place.

If you are replacing a sink, but not the countertop, make sure the new sink is the same size or larger. All old silicone caulk residue must be removed with acetone or denatured alcohol, or else the new caulk will not stick.

Shopping Tips ▸

- When purchasing a sink you also need to buy strainer bodies and baskets, sink clips and a drain trap kit.
- Look for basin dividers that are lower than the sink rim—this reduces splashing.
- Drain holes in the back or to the side make for more usable space under the sink.
- When choosing a sink, make sure the predrilled openings will fit your faucet.

Tools & Materials Caulk gun ▪ Spud wrench ▪ Screwdriver ▪ Sink ▪ Sink frame ▪ Plumber's putty or silicone caulk ▪ Mounting clips ▪ Jig saw ▪ Pen or pencil.

How to Install a Self-rimming Sink

Invert the sink and trace around the edges as a reference for making the sink cutout cutting lines, which should be parallel to the outlines, but about 1" inside of them to create a 1" ledge. If your sink comes with a template for the cutout, use it.

Drill a starter hole and cut out the sink opening with a jig saw. Cut right up to the line. Because the sink flange fits over the edges of the cutout, the opening doesn't need to be perfect, but as always you should try to do a nice, neat job.

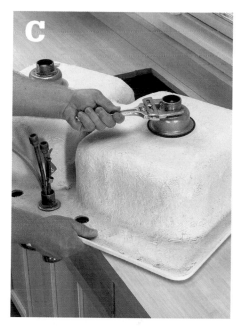

Attach as much of the plumbing as makes sense to install prior to setting the sink into the opening. Having access to the underside of the flange is a great help when it comes to attaching the faucet body, sprayer and strainer, in particular.

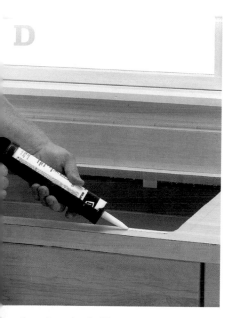

Apply a bead of silicone caulk around the edges of the sink opening. The sink flange most likely is not flat, so try and apply the caulk in the area that will make contact with the flange.

Place the sink in the opening. Try and get the sink centered right away so you don't need to move it around and disturb the caulk, which can break the seal. If you are installing a heavy cast-iron sink, it's best to leave the strainers off so you can grab onto the sink at the drain openings.

For sinks with mounting clips, tighten the clips from below using a screwdriver or wrench (depending on the type of clip your sink has). There should be at least three clips on every side. Don't overtighten the clips—this can cause the sink flange to flatten or become warped.

Installing an Undermount Sink

Undermounted sinks have become quite popular in contemporary kitchens for reasons that are both practical and aesthetic. On the aesthetic side, they look updated and sleek. Practically, they are easier to clean than rimmed sinks because you eliminate that area around the rim seal where stuff always collects.

Most sink manufacturers make sinks that are designed for undermounting, and if you don't mind paying the $100 to $200 premium, a true undermount sink is the best choice. But if your decision making is driven more by your frugal side, you can undermount a self-rimming (drop-in) stainless steel sink with little difficulty using readily available undermount clips. (Self-rimmers also come in a much wider range of styles). NOTE: You can undermount any sink you wish, including heavy cast iron models, if you support the sink from below instead of hanging it from clips.

Not all countertops are suitable for undermounting a sink. The countertop material needs to be contiguous in nature. That is, the edges that are created when you cut through it need to be of the same material as the surface. Solid-surface, granite, butcher block and concrete are good candidates for undermounting. Post-form and any laminated or tiled countertops are not. (Some new products that claim to seal countertop substrate edges around a sink opening are emerging, but are not yet proven or readily available).

If you are not able to locate solid-surface seam adhesive or undermount clips, you can use the same installation method for undermounting that is shown in the apron sink mounting project on pages 200 to 205 instead.

(see the apron sink mounting project on pages 200 to 205)

Tools & Materials
2HP or larger plunge router ▪ ½" template following router bit ▪ Roundover bit ▪ MDF or particleboard for template ▪ Jig saw ▪ Drill and bits ▪ Abrasive pads ▪ Laminate trimmer ▪ Belt sander ▪ Solid-surface scraps ▪ Solid-surface seam adhesive with applicator gun ▪ Denatured alcohol ▪ Undermount sink clip hardware ▪ Silicone caulk ▪ Pipe clamps ▪ Pad sander.

Before

After

Undermounted sinks have a sleek appearance and make cleanup easy, but they are only a good idea in countertops that have a solid construction, such as solid surfacing, stone, quartz or butcher block. Laminate and tile countertops are not compatible with undermount sinks.

▶ Amateurs and Solid-surface

Solid-surface countertop material is generally installed only by certified installers. But a simple job like mounting a non-solid-surface undermount sink can be done by a skilled amateur if you have access to adhesive and an applicator gun (without these, you can still mount a sink using the apron sink method shown on page 200.)

How to Make a Sink Cutout Template

If you are undermounting a self-rimming sink, do not use the sink template provided by the manufacturer. Instead, make your own custom router template to use with a router and pattern-following bit. The template should be sized and shaped so the cutout you make with your pattern-following bit is the same shape and about ⅛" larger than the basin opening in each direction. You can plot the cutout directly onto a piece of MDF, or make a preliminary paper or cardboard template and trace it onto the MDF.

(continued next page)

How to Make a Sink Cutout Template (continued)

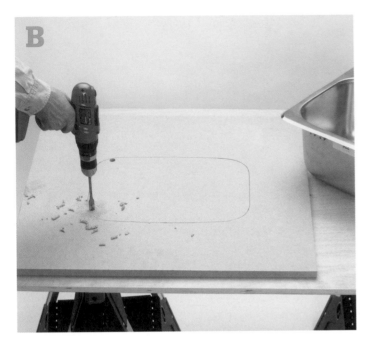

B

Drill a few starter holes just inside the template outline to create access for your jig saw blade. If the cutout has sharp radii at the corners, look for a bit or hole-cutter of the same radius and carefully drill out the corners.

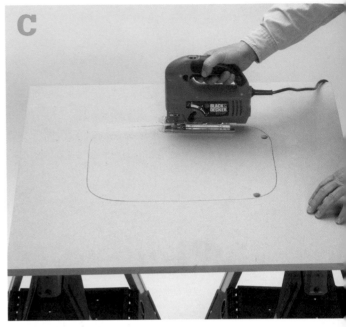

C

Connect the starter holes by cutting just inside the cutout line with a jigsaw. You can use a straightedge cutting guide for straight runs if you have little confidence in your ability to cut straight.

D

Use a belt sander or pad sander to smooth out the cutting lines and to remove material until the cutout hits the lines precisely. A drum sander attachment mounted in a power drill is useful for smoothing out rounded corners.

How to Undermount a Sink

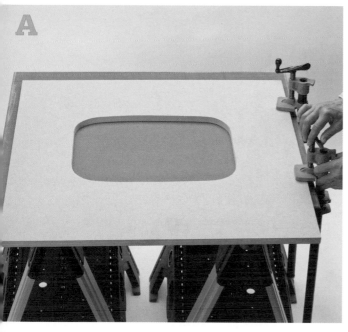

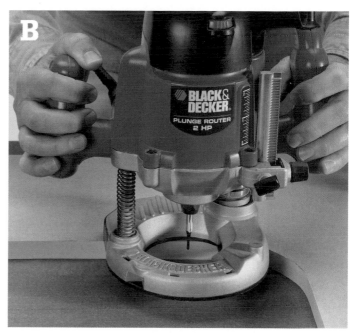

Remove the countertop from the cabinet and transport it to a work area with good light and ventilation. Set the countertop section on sawhorses and then clamp the router template (see previous page) securely so the opening is centered exactly over the planned cutout area. Make sure the router bit won't be cutting into your work area.

Chuck a two-fluted, ⅛" pattern-following bit (preferably carbide tipped) with a ½" shank into a plunge router with a minimum motor size of 2HP. Retract the bit and position the router so the bit is an inch or so away from the edge of the template. Turn the router on and let it develop to full velocity. Then, plunge the router bit into the countertop material until the bit breaks all the way through.

Pull the router bit toward the template edge until the bit sleeve contacts the edge, then slowly cut through the countertop, following the template. Pace is important here: too fast will cause chatter, too slow will cause burning or melting. Cut three continuous sides of the opening, hugging the template edge.

(continued next page)

How to Undermount a Sink (continued)

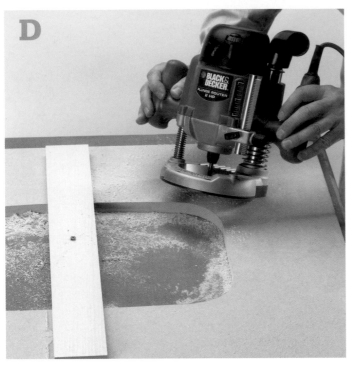

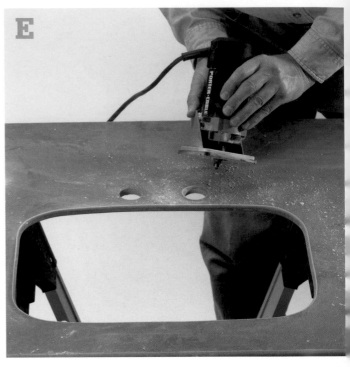

After routing three sides opening, stop routing and screw a support board to the waste piece. The ends of the support board should extend onto the template. Position the support so it is near the center, but not in the way for completing the fourth side of the cut. Then finish the cut. The support board will prevent the waste from breaking off as the cut nears completion.

If the sink outline has any chatter or the cutout is not perfectly smooth, make another pass with a straight bit before you remove the template. Remove the template and make a ⅛" roundover cut on both the top and bottom of the sink cutout. If you know exactly where your faucet hole or holes need to be, cut them with a hole saw and round over their tops and bottoms as well.

It's easier to mount the sink on the countertop before you reinstall it on the cabinet. Cut several 1 × 1" mounting blocks from the solid-surface waste cutout. You'll also need to purchase some seam adhesive to glue the mounting blocks to the underside of the countertop. After they're cut, break all the block edges with a stationary sander or by clamping a belt sander belt-side up and using it as a stationary sander (breaking the edges reduces the chance that the blocks will crack).

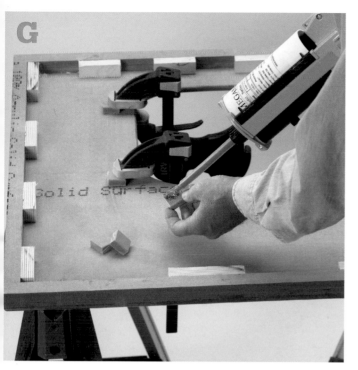

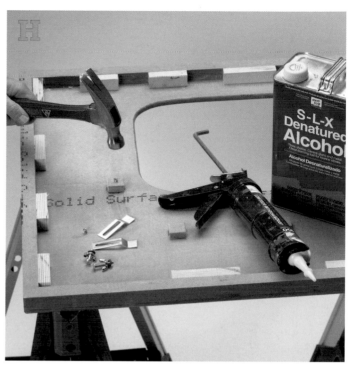

Clean the blocks and the underside of the solid-surface around the cutouts with denatured alcohol. Apply solid-surface seam adhesive to the blocks and bond them to the underside of the countertop, set back ¾" from the cutout. Install three blocks along the long sides of the cutout and two on the front-to-back sides. Clamp the blocks while the adhesive sets up.

Drill ¼" dia. × ⅜" deep pilot holes for the sink clips into each mounting block. The holes should be in the centers of the mounting blocks. Tap the brass inserts for the mounting clips into the holes in the mounting blocks.

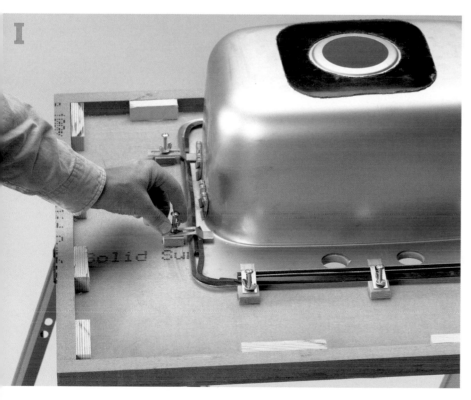

Clean the sink rim and the underside of the countertop with denatured alcohol. When the alcohol has dried, apply a bead of 100% silicone adhesive caulk to the sink rim. Carefully center the sink over the opening and press it in place. Hand-tighten the wing nuts onto the mounting nuts to secure the clips that hold the sink bowl. Replace the countertop and hook up the faucet and drain. For information on installing a kitchen faucet see pages 208 to 209.

Installing an Apron Sink

Despite their vintage look, apron sinks are relative newcomers in modern kitchen design. Also known as farmer's sinks or farmhouse sinks, they are notable for having an exposed front apron that usually projects out past the cabinets. Although they can be double bowl fixtures, most apron sinks are single bowl, and most are made from fireclay (a durable enameled porcelain). Other materials sometimes used for apron sinks include enameled cast iron, copper, stainless steel and composite. The model seen here, made by Kohler (see Resources, page 282), is a fireclay sink.

Apron sinks typically are not suspended from above as other undermount sinks are. They're just too heavy. Instead, you either attach wood ledgers to the cabinet sides to support a board that bears the sink from below, or you build a support platform that rests on the floor. Either way, the sink is not actually connected to the countertop except with caulk at the seam.

As kitchen sinks go, apron sinks are definitely on the high-end side, with most models costing over $1,000. But they possess an ability to become a focal point that makes them rather unique. Plus, they have a warm, comforting appearance that people who own them find reassuring.

Tools & Materials

Countertop material ▪ Shims ▪ Carpenter's square ▪ Jig saw ▪ Belt sander ▪ Pad sander ▪ Router or laminate trimmer ▪ Drill/driver ▪ Wood finish ▪ Brush ▪ Framing lumber ▪ Sheet stock ▪ Caulk gun ▪ Silicone adhesive ▪ Strainer ▪ Drain tailpiece.

Apron sinks, also called farmer's sinks or farmhouse sinks, can be nestled into a tiled countertop (called a tile-in) or pressed up against the underside of a solid countertop. Either way, they are gorgeous.

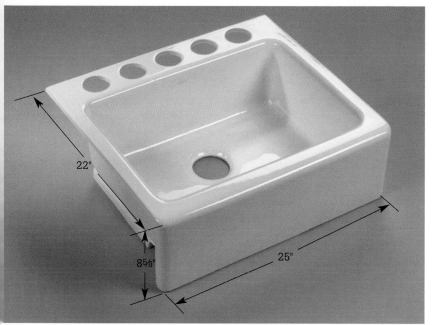

Because they are usually mounted underneath the countertop, apron sinks tend to be fairly shallow (otherwise, most people would strain their back doing dishes in them). Make sure you know the exact dimensions of your sink before ordering countertops or planning your sink installation.

Sink support for apron sinks comes from below. A typical strategy is to build a U-shaped ledger that's mounted to the walls of neighboring cabinets or supported with a post structure from below. If you're attaching the ledgers to cabinet walls, it may be necessary to reinforce them.

Some apron sinks are tiled-in to the countertop. You simply hang the sink from ledgers on the cabinet sides that create the sink opening. The faucet is mounted to the wide back flange of the sink (make sure you order a sink with the correct number of holes for your faucet). The tile, with an underlayment of cementboard, is butted against the sink, with a small gap left that is filled with caulk.

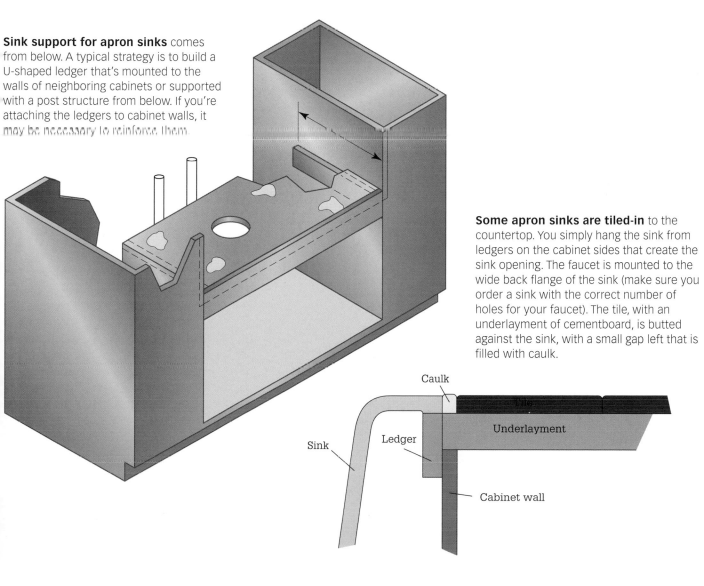

Caulk

Tile

Underlayment

Sink

Ledger

Cabinet wall

How to Install an Apron Sink in a Butcher Block Countertop

If undermounting the sink, outline the sink opening in your countertop material. Plan the opening to create an equal reveal of approximately ½" on all three sides (which basically means making the opening 1" smaller than the overall sink dimensions). For the 22 × 25" sink seen here, the opening cut into the butcher block is 24" wide and 21" deep (½" reveal in back plus ½" projection of sink in front).

Mount a downstroke blade in a jig saw (see pages 162 to 163 and be sure to read the material on working with butcher block if that is your countertop surface). Cut out the waste to form the sink opening, cutting just inside the cutting lines. Support the waste wood from below so it does not break out prematurely.

Sand up to the cutting lines with a belt sander after the waste is removed. The goal is to create a smooth, even edge.

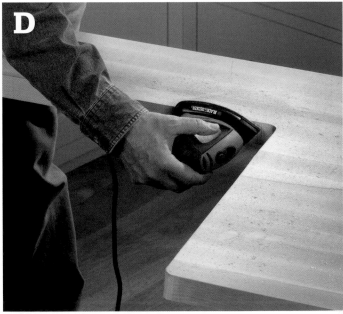

Sand into the corners of the cutout with a detail sander or, if you own one, a spindle sander (you can mount a small-diameter sanding drum in an electric drill, but be sure to practice first on some scrap wood).

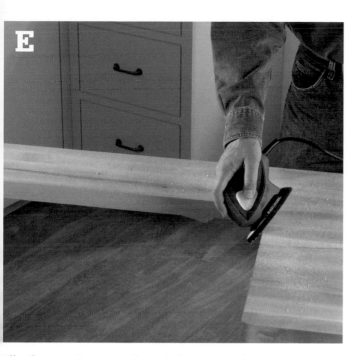

Flip the countertop and sand the cutout along the bottom edges of the opening to prevent any splintering.

Round over the top edges of the cutout with a piloted roundover bit mounted in a small router or a laminate trimmer.

Apply several coats of urethane varnish to the exposed wood around the opening. This wood will have a high level of water exposure, so take care to get a good seal. Where possible, match the finish of the countertop (if any).

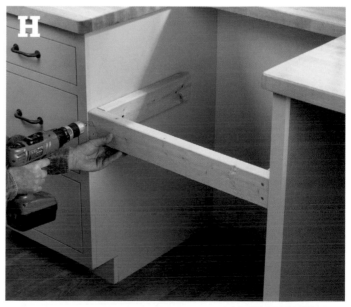

Measure and draw layout lines for a wood support frame to be attached to the adjoining cabinet walls. Attach the frame members (2 × 4) to the cabinet sides first and then face-screw through the front frame member and into the ends of side members.

(continued next page)

How to Install an Apron Sink in a Butcher Block Countertop (continued)

Cut a support platform to size from ¾" plywood or MDF then layout and cut a drain clearance hole (if your drain will include a garbage disposer, make the hole large enough to accommodate the disposer easily). Also cut holes for water supply lines if they come up through the floor and there is not enough room between the platform and the wall for the lines to fit.

Remove the countertop section containing the sink cutout, if feasible (if you can't remove the countertop, see sidebar next page). Then, screw the platform to the frame.

Set the sink on the platform and confirm that it is level with the cabinet tops by setting a straightedge so it spans the sink opening. If necessary, shim under the sink to bring it to level (if the sink is too high you'll need to reposition the frame members).

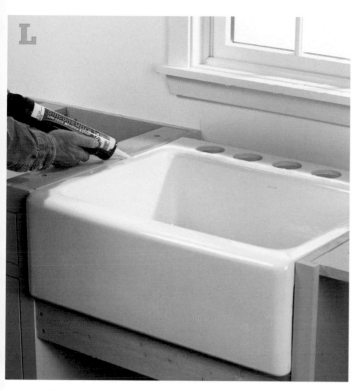

Apply silicone adhesive to the sink rim and then carefully replace the countertop section before the silicone adhesive sets up. Reattach the countertop.

Hook up drain plumbing and install the faucet. If drilling through the countertop material to install a faucet, make sure your installation hole or holes align with preformed holes in the back flange of the sink.

Option for Unremovable Countertops ▸

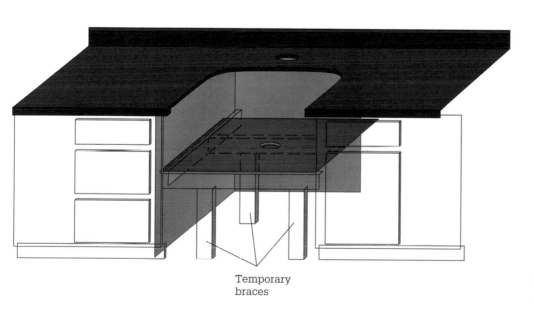

Temporary braces

If you are not able to remove the countertop, you'll need to raise the sink up against the underside of the countertop once you've caulked the rim. Create a 3-piece 2 × 4 frame and platform (as seen in Step J) but do not attach it to cabinets. Instead, support the platform with braces. With help, set the sink on the platform and raise it from below after silicone adhesive has been applied to the sink rim. When the sink rim is tight against the countertop, attach the frame members to the cabinet sides with screws.

Modern kitchen faucets tend to be single-handle models, often with useful features such as a pull-out head that functions as a sprayer. This Price Pfister model comes with an optional mounting plate that conceals sink holes when mounted on a predrilled sink flange.

Installing Faucets & Drains

Most new kitchen faucets feature single-handle control levers and washerless designs that rarely require maintenance. Additional features include brushed metallic finishes, detachable spray nozzles or even push button controls.

Connect the faucet to hot and cold water lines with easy-to-install flexible supply tubes made from vinyl or braided steel. If your faucet has a separate sprayer, install the sprayer first. Pull the sprayer hose through the sink opening and attach to the faucet body before installing the faucet.

Where local codes allow, use plastic tubes for drain hookups. A wide selection of extensions and angle fittings lets you easily plumb any sink configuration. Manufacturers offer kits that contain all the fittings needed for attaching a food disposer or dishwasher to the sink drain system.

Tools & Materials Adjustable wrench ▪ Basin wrench or channel-type pliers ▪ Hacksaw ▪ Faucet ▪ Silicone caulk ▪ Plumber's putty ▪ Flexible vinyl or braided steel supply tubes ▪ Drain components.

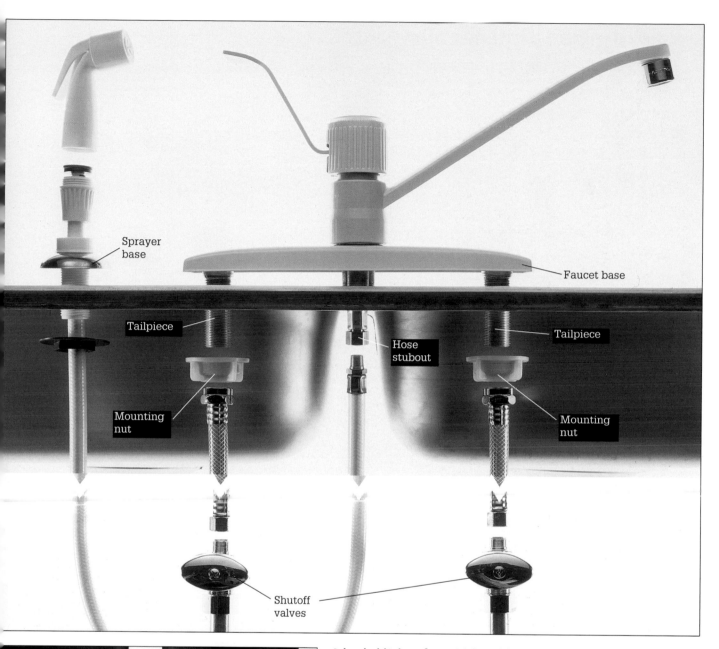

Sprayer base

Faucet base

Tailpiece

Tailpiece

Hose stubout

Mounting nut

Mounting nut

Shutoff valves

A basic kitchen faucet (above) has separate tailpieces for hot and cold water and an outlet that directs water to a separate sprayer.

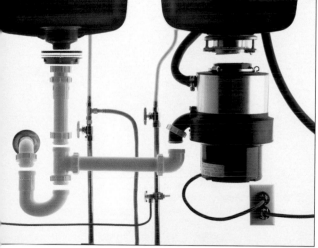

A typical drain set-up (left) for a double-bowl kitchen sink includes a garbage disposer and drain connections from a dishwasher.

How to Install a Kitchen Sink Faucet

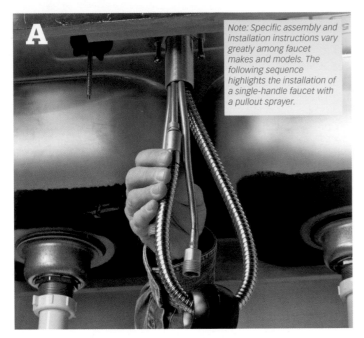

Note: Specific assembly and installation instructions vary greatly among faucet makes and models. The following sequence highlights the installation of a single-handle faucet with a pullout sprayer.

Shut off hot and cold water at the faucet stop valves. Assemble the parts of the deck plate that cover the outer mounting holes in your sink deck (unless you are installing a two-handle faucet, or mounting the faucet directly to the countertop, as in an undermount sink situation). Add a ring of plumbers' putty in the groove on the underside of the base plate.

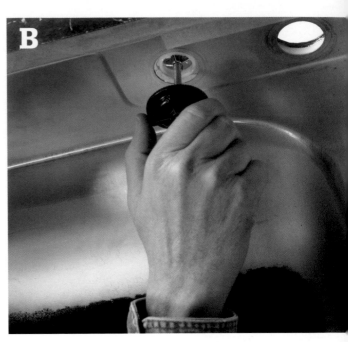

Set the base plate onto the sink flange so it is correctly aligned with the predrilled holes in the flange. From below, tighten the wing nuts that secure the deck plate to the sink deck.

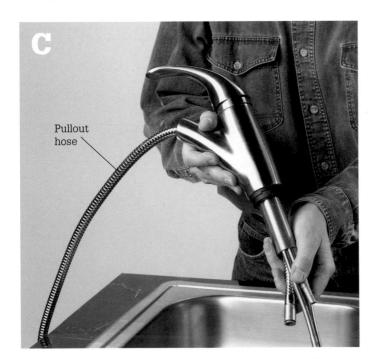

Retract the pullout hose by drawing it out through the faucet body until the fitting at the end of the hose is flush with the bottom of the threaded faucet shank. Insert the shank and the supply tubes down through the top of the deck plate.

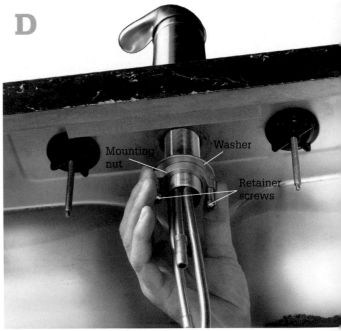

Slip the mounting nut and washer over the free ends of the supply tubes and pullout hose, then thread the nut onto the threaded faucet shank. Hand tighten. Tighten the retainer screws with a screwdriver to secure the faucet.

Slide the hose weight onto the pullout hose (the weight helps keep the hose from tangling and it makes it easier to retract the hose).

Connect the end of the pullout tube to the outlet port on the faucet body using a quick connector fitting.

Water supply tube

Hook up the water supply tubes to the faucet inlets. Make sure the lines are long enough to reach the supply risers without stretching or kinking.

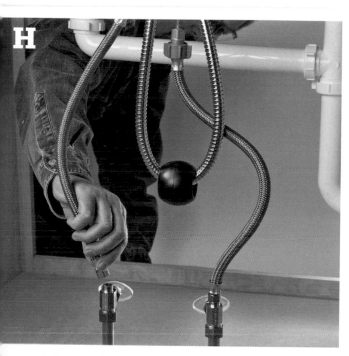

Connect the supply lines to the supply risers at the stop valves. Make sure to get the hot lines and cold lines attached correctly.

Attach the spray head to the end of the pullout hose and turn the fitting to secure the connection. Turn on water supply and test. TIP: Remove the aerator in the tip of the spray head and run hot and cold water to flush out any debris.

How to Install a Multiple Tailpiece Faucet

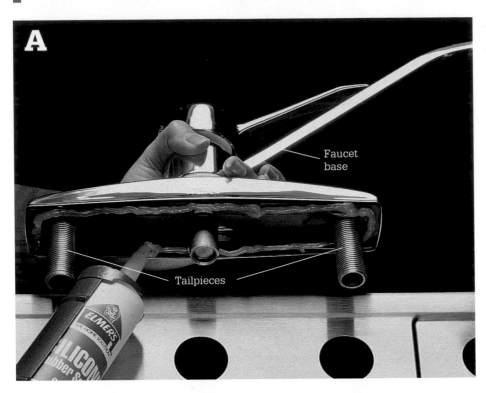

Apply a bead of silicone caulk or plumber's putty around the base of the faucet. Insert the faucet tailpieces into the sink openings. Position the faucet so the base is parallel to the back of the sink. Press the faucet down to make sure it forms a good seal with the caulk.

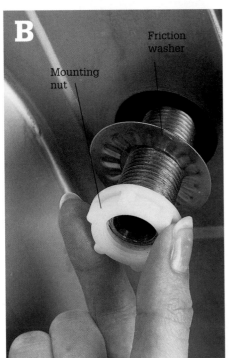

Thread the metal friction washers and the mounting nuts onto the tailpieces, then tighten with a basin wrench or channel-type pliers. Wipe away excess caulk around base of faucet.

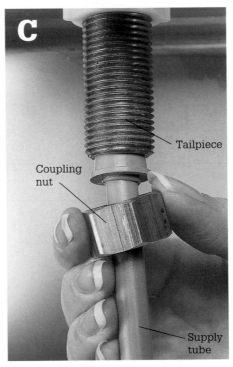

Connect flexible supply tubes to the faucet tailpieces. Tighten coupling nuts with a basin wrench or channel-type pliers.

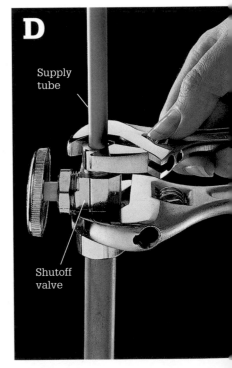

Attach the supply tubes to the shutoff valves, using compression fittings. Hand-tighten nuts, then use an adjustable wrench to tighten nuts ¼ turn. If necessary, hold valve with another wrench while tightening.

How to Attach Drain Lines

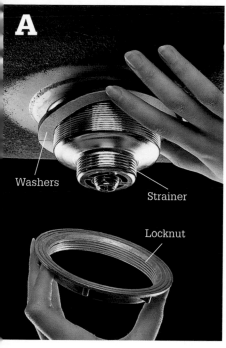

A

Washers

Strainer

Locknut

B

Insert washer

Slip nut

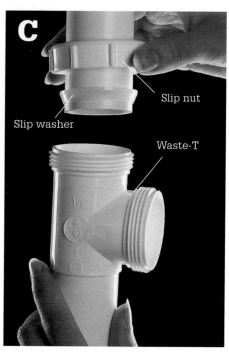

C

Slip nut

Slip washer

Waste-T

Install a sink strainer in each sink drain opening. Apply a ¼" bead of plumber's putty around bottom of the strainer flange. Insert the strainer into the drain opening. Place rubber and fiber washers over the neck of the strainer. Screw a locknut onto the neck and tighten with channel-type pliers.

Attach the tailpiece to the strainer. Place the insert washer in the flared end of the tailpiece, then attach the tailpiece by screwing a slip nut onto the sink strainer. If necessary, the tailpiece can be cut to fit with a hacksaw.

On sinks with two basins, use a continuous waste-T fitting to join the tailpieces. Attach the fitting with slip washers and nuts. The beveled ends of the washers should face the threaded portions of the pipes.

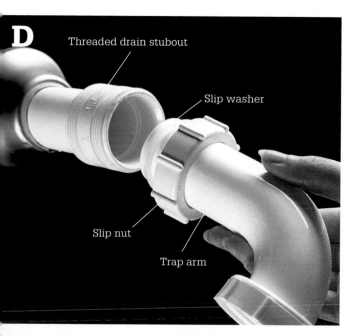

D

Threaded drain stubout

Slip washer

Slip nut

Trap arm

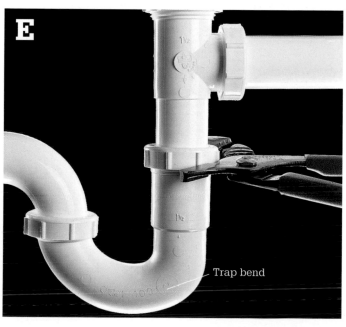

E

Trap bend

Attach the trap arm to the drain stubout, using a slip nut and washer. The beveled end of the washer should face the threaded drain stubout. If necessary, the trap arm can be cut to fit with a hacksaw.

Attach the trap bend (also called p-trap) to the trap arm, using slip nuts and washers. The beveled end of the washers should face the trap bend. Tighten all nuts with channel-type pliers.

Installing a Food Disposer

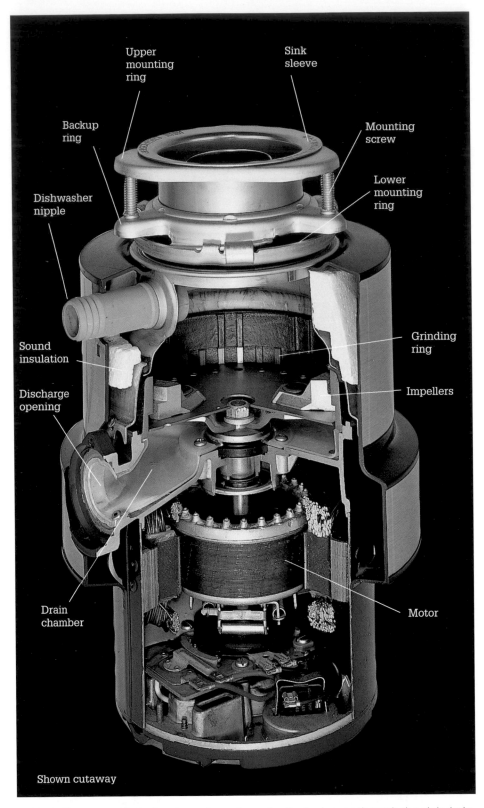

Upper mounting ring

Sink sleeve

Backup ring

Mounting screw

Dishwasher nipple

Lower mounting ring

Sound insulation

Grinding ring

Discharge opening

Impellers

Drain chamber

Motor

Shown cutaway

A food disposer grinds food waste so it can be flushed away through the sink drain system. A quality disposer has a ½-horsepower, self-reversing motor that will not jam. Other features to look for include foam sound insulation, a cast iron grinding ring, and overload protection that allows the motor to be reset if it overheats. Better food disposers have a 5-year manufacturer's warranty.

Choose a food disposer with a motor rated at ½ horsepower or more. Look for a self-reversing feature that prevents the disposer from jamming. Better models carry a manufacturer's warranty of up to five years.

Local plumbing codes may require that a disposer be plugged into a grounded outlet controlled by a switch above the sink.

Tools & Materials

Screwdriver ▪ 12-gauge appliance cord with grounded plug ▪ Wire connectors.

How to Install a Food Disposer

Remove plate on bottom of disposer. Use combination tool to strip about ½" of insulation from each wire in appliance cord. Connect white wires, using a wire connector. Connect black wires. Attach green insulated wire to green ground screw. Gently push wires into opening. Replace bottom plate.

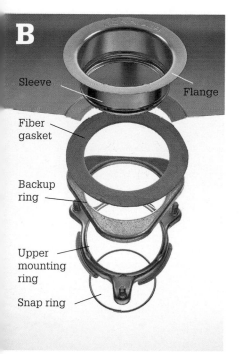

Sleeve

Flange

Fiber gasket

Backup ring

Upper mounting ring

Snap ring

Apply ¼" bead of plumber's putty under the flange of the disposer sink sleeve. Insert sleeve in drain opening, and slip the fiber gasket and the backup ring onto the sleeve. Place upper mounting ring on sleeve and slide snap ring into groove.

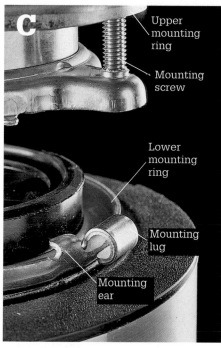

Upper mounting ring

Mounting screw

Lower mounting ring

Mounting lug

Mounting ear

Tighten the three mounting screws. Hold disposer against upper mounting ring so that the mounting lugs on the lower mounting ring are directly under the mounting screws. Turn the lower mounting ring clockwise until the disposer is supported by the mounting assembly.

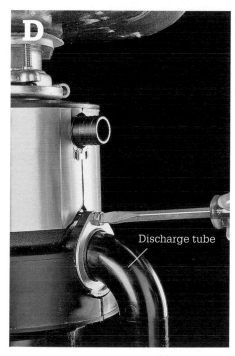

Discharge tube

Attach the discharge tube to the discharge opening on the side of the disposer, using the rubber washer and metal flange.

Dishwasher nipple

Hose clamp

If dishwasher will be attached, knock out the plug in the dishwasher nipple, using a screwdriver. Attach the dishwasher drain hose to nipple with hose clamp.

Continuous waste

Attach the discharge tube to the continuous waste pipe with slip washer and nut. If discharge tube is too long, cut it with a hacksaw or tubing cutter.

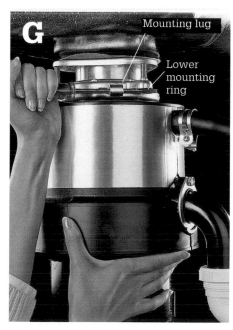

Mounting lug

Lower mounting ring

Lock disposer into place. Insert a screwdriver or disposer wrench into a mounting lug on the lower mounting ring, and turn clockwise until the mounting ears are locked. Tighten all drain slip nuts with channel-type pliers.

Installing Dishwashers

A dishwasher requires a hot water supply connection, a drain connection and an electrical hookup. These connections are easiest to make when the dishwasher is located next to the sink.

Hot water reaches the dishwasher through a supply tube. With a multiple-outlet shutoff valve or brass T-fitting on the hot water pipe, you can control water to the sink and dishwasher with the same valve.

To prevent drain water from backing up into the dishwasher, the drain hose needs to be attached to the underside of the countertop. Some local codes require the installation of an air gap.

A dishwasher requires its own 20-amp electrical circuit. For convenience, have this circuit wired into one-half of a split duplex receptacle. The other half of the receptacle powers the food disposer.

> **Tools & Materials** Screwdriver ▪ Utility knife ▪ Drill with 2" hole saw ▪ Adjustable wrench ▪ Channel-type pliers ▪ Combination tool ▪ Drain hose ▪ Waste-T tailpiece ▪ Braided steel supply tube ▪ Rubber connector for food disposer ▪ Hose clamps ▪ Brass L-fitting ▪ 12-gauge appliance power cord ▪ Wire connectors.

How to Remove a Dishwasher ▸

Remove the toe kick and access panel (if present) by unscrewing the attachment screws. Unplug the dishwasher or, if it is wired directly, turn off the power at the service panel. Remove the junction box cover and remove the wire connectors and the cable clamp. Turn off the water supply. Disconnect the water supply line from the 90° elbow. Disconnect the drain line from the waste-T or disposer. Remove the mounting screws inside the door (inset). Lower leg levelers and slide out dishwasher.

How to Install a Dishwasher

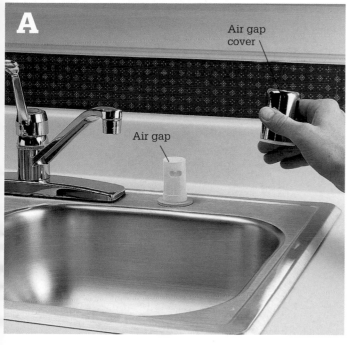

Mount air gap, using one of the predrilled sink openings. Or, bore a hole in the countertop with a drill and hole saw. Attach the air gap by tightening mounting nut over the tailpiece with channel-type pliers.

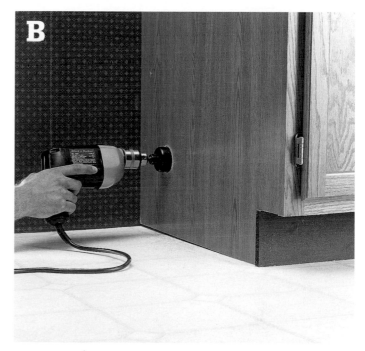

Cut openings in side of sink base cabinet for electrical and plumbing lines, using a drill and hole saw. Dishwasher instructions specify size and location of openings. Slide dishwasher into place, feeding rubber drain hose through hole in cabinet. Level the dishwasher.

Attach the dishwasher drain hose to the smaller, straight nipple on the air gap, using a hose clamp. If hose is too long, cut to correct length with a utility knife. Cut another length of rubber hose to reach from the larger, angled nipple to the food disposer. Attach hose to the air gap and to the nipple on disposer with hose clamps.

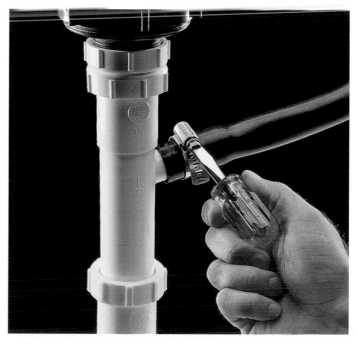

VARIATION: On sinks without food disposer, attach a special waste-T sink tailpiece to sink strainer. Attach the drain hose to the waste-T nipple with a hose clamp.

(continued next page)

How to Install a Dishwasher (continued)

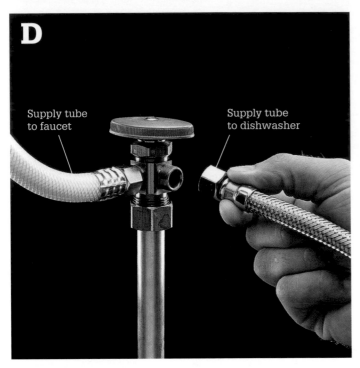

Connect dishwasher supply tube to hot water shut-off, using channel-type pliers. This connection is easiest with a multiple-outlet shutoff valve or a brass T-fitting (page 152).

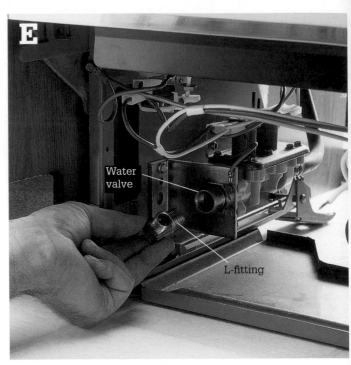

Remove access panel on front of dishwasher. Connect a brass L-fitting to the threaded opening on the dishwasher water valve, and tighten with channel-type pliers.

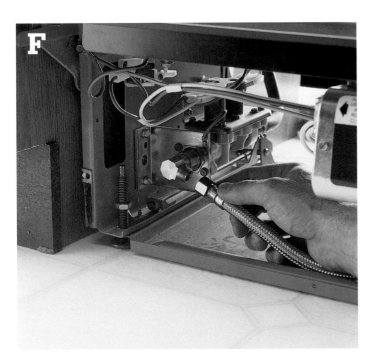

Run the dishwasher supply tube from the hot water pipe to the dishwasher water valve. Attach supply tube to L-fitting, using channel-type pliers.

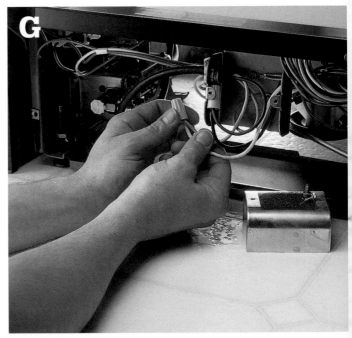

Remove cover on electrical box. Run power cord from outlet through to electrical box. Strip about ½" of insulation from each cord wire, using combination tool. Connect black wires, using a wire connector. Connect white wires. Connect green insulated wire to ground screw. Replace box cover and dishwasher access panel. Carefully slide unit into cabinet opening and level adjustable feet.

Building a short platform to raise your dishwasher makes access to the appliance easier and also lets you create a countertop area between the regular countertop height and the undersides of the cabinets.

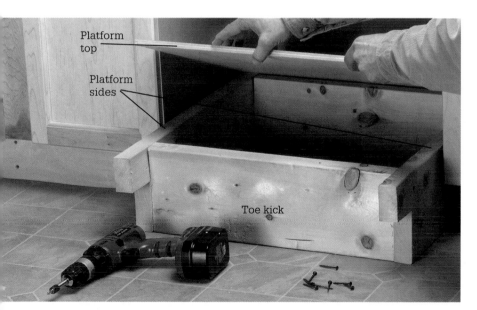

Platform top

Platform sides

Toe kick

Build a 2 × 8 platform with a plywood top to support the dishwasher. Cut a 4 × 4" notch in each platform side piece (or whichever size matches your existing toe kick space). Place the front of the platform to align with the back of the toe kick cutout. Assemble the platform with 2" screws. Cut the ½" plywood to fit the platform and attach with 1¼" screws. Cut the new countertop to size and apply edge trim to match. Attach a 1 × 3 cleat to the wall, using 2" screws. Install the countertop, using two angle irons per side and ¾" screws.

How to Install a Raised Dishwasher

Raising the dishwasher 6" to 9" makes the appliance much easier to load and unload. You'll eliminate a lot of stooping, which is especially important for those of us with touchy backs. A raised dishwasher is also much easier for wheelchair users to operate.

For an easy project, raise your existing dishwasher 8¼"—the height of a 2 × 8 and a sheet of ½" plywood. You can cover the new empty space above the toe kick with a piece of matching cabinetry. Because the platform will cover the previous access holes, you will need to cut new access holes in the side cabinets.

A raised dishwasher ideally should have at least a 12" section of countertop available on one side as a staging area for dish loading and unloading. If your dishwasher currently abuts the sink, you will need to move it, since the sink needs to have clearance of 12" on one side and 21" on the other.

You'll also need to create side panels to house the portion of the dishwasher that extends above the countertop. The easiest way to move the dishwasher into the new space is to make another, temporary box of 2 × 8 lumber and plywood the same size as the dishwasher footprint. Push this box against the dishwasher opening, pick up the dishwasher and place it on the box, then slide the dishwasher into the new opening.

Installing Refrigerators

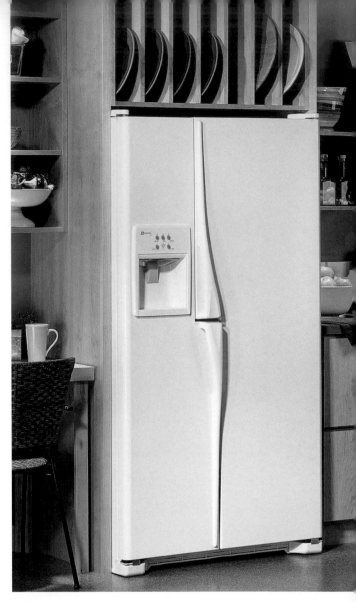

Refrigerators are heavy and bulky, and their compressors and cooling coils make them sensitive to jarring. Before moving, refer to the manufacturer's information for specific directions for your model.

If moving a refrigerator a short distance for cleaning or painting, you do not need to empty it. Otherwise, empty the refrigerator. Even if you are simply sliding the fridge out a short distance, protect the floor surface from being scratched, using heavy-duty cardboard, wood paneling or thin plywood. Tilt the refrigerator backward and slide the floor protection under the front wheels or leveling legs. Carefully continue sliding or rolling the refrigerator out. Lift the back wheels or levelers onto the floor protection. Once the refrigerator is out from the wall, unplug it. If a water supply is present, locate the shutoff valve (which may be in the basement) and turn it off. Disconnect the water supply.

Use an appliance dolly to lift the fridge from the side only—not the front or the back. If it will not fit through doorways, remove the door handles. Refer to the manufacturer's instructions before removing doors, as in-door dispensers have water lines that must be disconnected.

Protect flooring by placing heavy cardboard, wood paneling or thin plywood on the floor in front of the refrigerator location.

Refrigerators with water dispensers often have their own water filter. This filters the dispenser water and the ice-maker water, eliminating the need for an in-line water filter.

Installing a Refrigerator Ice Maker

Many refrigerators come with ice makers, which need to be attached to a water supply. The most difficult aspect is locating a water supply close to the refrigerator. Most installations involve drilling a hole through the floor and attaching the tubing to a nearby supply line in the basement.

Parts for ice-maker installation are available separately, or as kits containing saddle valve, tubing and compression fittings. Appliance stores, service centers and home centers have kits available with copper or plastic tubing. The plastic tubing can become brittle over time and possibly break, so most appliance centers recommend using copper tubing.

Tools & Materials
Adjustable wrench
- ¼" soft copper tubing • Saddle valve • Brass compression fittings.

How to Connect a Refrigerator Ice Maker

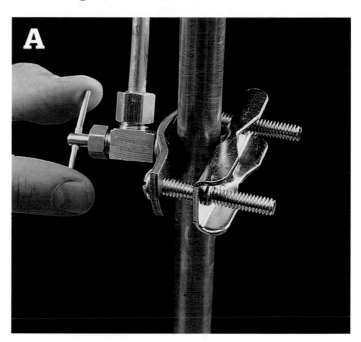

Shut off water at main shutoff valve. Attach a ¼" saddle valve to cold water pipe. Connect ¼" soft copper tubing to saddle valve with compression ring and coupling nut. Closing spigot fully causes spike inside valve to puncture water pipe. Allow 2 to 3 ft. of extra copper tubing to create a coil (see step 3).

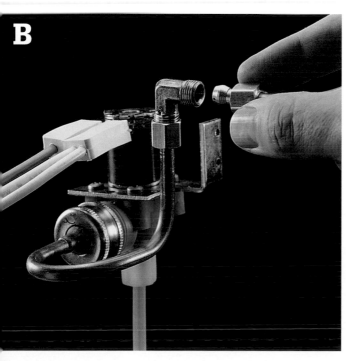

Run copper tubing to refrigerator. Connect water supply tube to the water valve tube, using a ¼" compression elbow. Slide coupling nuts and compression rings over tubes, and insert tubes into elbow. Tighten coupling nuts.

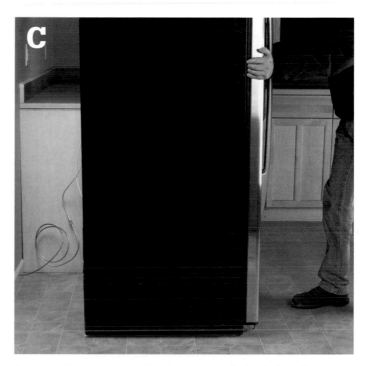

Arrange the copper coil so it won't be pinched when the refrigerator is moved back into place. Carefully roll the refrigerator into place and lock the wheels.

Installing a Hot Water Dispenser

Hot water dispensers keep small amounts of drinking water hot so you can brew tea or make instant soup right out of the tap. They're not too expensive ($100 to $300) and are relatively easy to install. Consumer models plug in to a GFCI receptacle. For water, tap into a nearby cold water supply pipe.

Hot water dispensers are also reasonably inexpensive to operate. Manufacturers suggest average use (10 cups) will cost about $.06 a day. This may actually be less than the energy cost of boiling water on a stovetop or in a microwave.

Many models also dispense cold water, and some include an inline reverse-osmosis filter.

If there is an unused fourth opening in the kitchen sink rim (after the faucet and two handles), install the hot water dispenser there. If not, drill a hole (generally 1¼") in the rim of a stainless steel sink rim. Or drill a hole into the countertop near the back rim of the sink.

The dispenser will require a 120-volt GFCI receptacle. Many sink cabinets have a receptacle that supplies a food disposer. You may be able to use the second plug for the hot water dispenser (check local code). If not, install a new circuit with a receptacle in the base cabinet.

Tools & Materials

Adjustable wrench ▪ Drill ▪ Propane torch ▪ Hot water dispenser ▪ ¼" soft copper tubing ▪ T-fitting and shutoff valve or dual-outlet shutoff valve ▪ Brass compression fittings.

Hot water dispensers keep a small amount of water piping hot and ready to use.

How to Install a Hot Water Dispenser

Slip the washers for the dispenser onto the faucet stem so the rubber washer will contact the countertop or sink rim. Insert the faucet body into the hole from above.

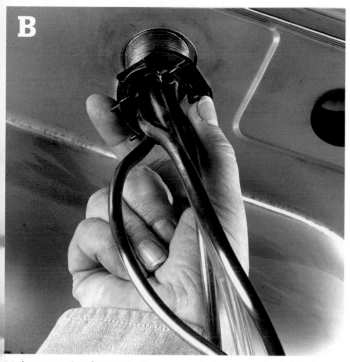

Make sure the faucet's dispenser tubes are straight. Then, with an assistant holding the dispenser head in place above the countertop, position yourself beneath the countertop. Slide the fiber washer over the dispenser tubes and onto the threaded stem. Hand-tighten the dispenser wing nut to secure the dispenser to the countertop or sink rim.

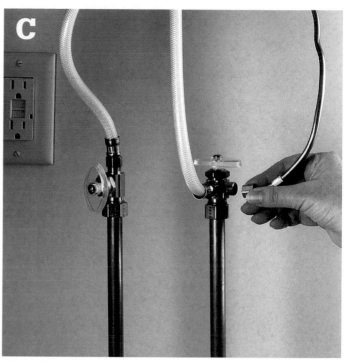

Shut off the water at the main. Attach a T-fitting and shutoff valve or a dual-outlet shutoff valve to a water supply riser. Attach the ¼" supply tube from the dispenser body to the outlet at the shutoff valve .

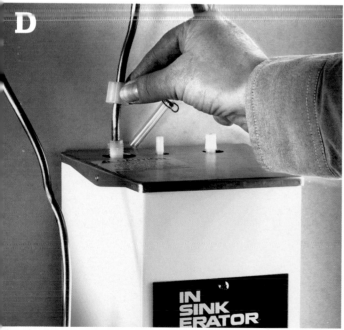

Mount the tank on the wall, locating and adjusting the mounting bracket so the tank is level and fastened securely. Do not plug in. Attach the copper supply tubing from the dispenser head to the water inlet on the dispenser tank.

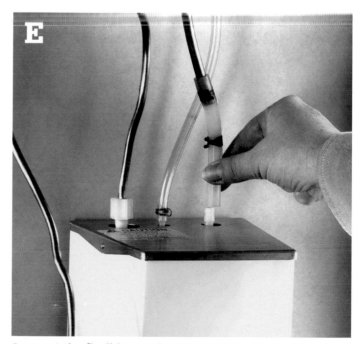

Connect the flexible supply tube from the dispenser head to the hot water outlet on the tank. If the dispenser uses a vent tube, connect it as directed by the manufacturer. Turn the water on, and depress the dispenser handle to permit water into the tank. Let the water run and watch for any leaks. Plug the heater unit into a GFCI-protected outlet. Adjust the temperature as desired.

Installing Ranges & Cooktops

When moving a range for painting or cleaning, removing it for replacement, or installing a new range, make sure you protect the flooring. Use an appliance dolly to lift the range from the side only—not the front or the back. If the range will not fit through doors, remove the oven door handle.

An electric range or cooktop must have its own dedicated 240-volt circuit. A gas range or cooktop must have the gas connections made by an authorized installer. Contact your gas provider or plumbing contractor for service in your area. Gas ranges and cooktops also need a grounded 3-hole electrical outlet to power the electronic ignition, clock and timers.

Each individual cooktop will have specific minimum clearances. Carefully read the manufacturer's instructions before beginning any cooktop installation. Installation in solid-surface material, butcher block and stone counters requires different cutout clearances (listed in the cooktop instructions) and the use of reflective aluminum tape. Check with your countertop manufacturer to make sure your cooktop installation will not damage the countertop.

Tools & Materials
Framing square ▪ Drill ▪ Jig saw ▪ Screwdriver ▪ Combination tool ▪ Cooktop with installation kit ▪ Masking tape ▪ Marker ▪ Junction box ▪ NM cable ▪ Wire connectors.

Shopping Tips ▸

- Smooth-surface cooktops require special care and cleaning supplies.
- Self-cleaning ovens (electric ranges only) are better insulated.

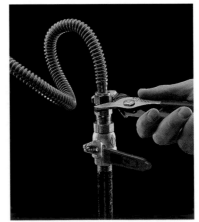

DO NOT make gas hookups yourself unless you are experienced at working with gas pipe and your local building authority allows homeowners to make connections (many municipalities prohibit unlicensed people from making gas connections).

How to Install an Electric Cooktop

Using the dimensions from the installation instructions, draw the cutting lines on masking tape on the countertop. Use a framing square to ensure all corners are square and aligned properly. Drill pilot holes, then use a jig saw to make the cuts.

Place the cooktop upside down on a protected surface and attach the foam tape as directed. Attach the mounting brackets in the specified holes.

Insert the cooktop into the countertop and attach the brackets to the cabinet sides, countertop or wood blocks, depending on stove type.

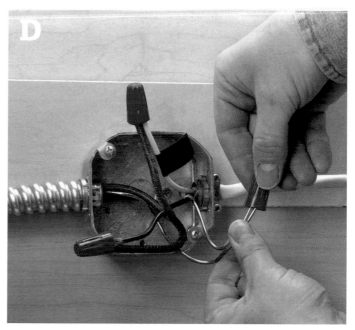

Install a junction box under the counter within the distances specified in the directions. Insert the wires from the stove conduit through a cable clamp and into the junction box. Connect the black wires; connect the red wire from the stove conduit to the white supply wire and tag the white wire with black electrical tape; connect the bare or green grounds. Close the junction box.

Installing Vent Hoods

A vent hood eliminates heat, moisture and cooking vapors from your kitchen. It has an electric fan unit with one or more filters and a system of metal ducts to vent air to the outdoors. A ducted vent hood is more efficient than a ductless model, which filters and recirculates air without removing it.

Metal ducts for a vent hood can be round or rectangular. Elbows and transition fittings are available for both types of ducts. These fittings let you vent around corners, or join duct components that differ in shape or size.

> ## Tools&Materials Tape measure ▪ Screwdrivers
> ▪ Hammer ▪ Drill ▪ Reciprocating saw ▪ Combination tool
> ▪ Metal snips ▪ Masonry drill and masonry chisel (for brick or
> stucco exterior) ▪ Duct sections ▪ Duct elbow ▪ Duct cap ▪ Vent
> hood ▪ ¾", 1½", 2½" sheetmetal screws ▪ 1¼" drywall screws
> ▪ Silicone caulk ▪ Metallic duct tape ▪ Wire connectors
> ▪ Eye protection ▪ Pencil ▪ 2" masonry nails (for brick or
> stucco exterior).

Labels on left photo: Wall cap, Elbow fitting, Vent hood, Duct, Liner, Wood panels

A wall-mounted vent hood (shown in cutaway) is installed between wall cabinets. The fan unit is fastened to a metal liner that is anchored to cabinets. Duct and elbow fitting exhaust cooking vapors to the outdoors through a wall cap. The vent fan and duct can be covered by wood or laminate panels that match the cabinet finish.

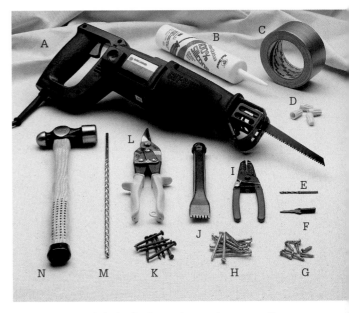

Tools & materials include: reciprocating saw with coarse wood cutting blade (A), silicone caulk (B), duct tape, (C), wire connectors (D), ⅛" twist bit (E), No. 9 counterbore drill bit (F), ¾" sheetmetal screws (G), 2½" sheetmetal screws (H), combination tool (I), masonry chisel (J), 2" masonry nails (K), metal snips (L), masonry drill bit (M), ball peen hammer (N).

How to Install a Wall-mounted Vent Hood

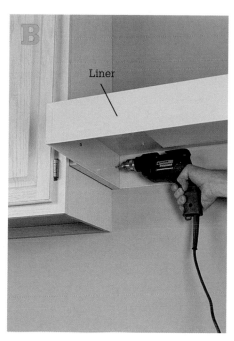

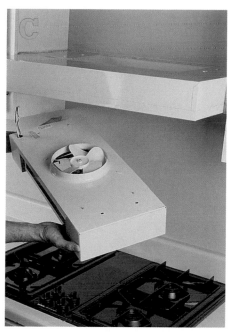

Attach ¾ × 4 × 12" wooden cleats to the sides of the cabinets with 1¼" wallboard screws. Follow the hood manufacturer's directions for setting the proper distance from the cooking surface.

Position the hood liner between the cleats and attach it with ¾" sheetmetal screws.

Remove cover panels for the light, fan and electrical compartments on the fan unit, as directed by manufacturer. Position the fan unit inside the liner and fasten it by attaching nuts to mounting bolts inside the light compartments.

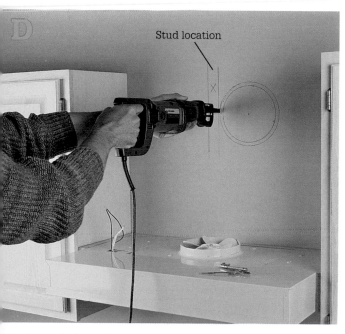

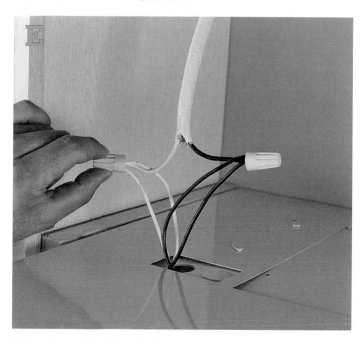

Locate studs in wall where the duct will pass, using a stud finder. Mark hole location. The hole should be ½" larger than the diameter of the duct. Complete the cutout with a reciprocating saw or jig saw. Remove any wall insulation. Drill a pilot hole through the outside wall.

Strip about ½" of insulation from each wire in the circuit cable, using a combination tool. Connect the black wires, using a wire connector. Connect the white wires. Gently push the wires into the electrical box. Replace the cover panels on the light and fan compartments.

(continued next page)

How to Install a Wall-mounted Vent Hood (continued)

F

Make duct cutout on the exterior wall. On masonry, drill a series of holes around the outline of the cutout. Remove waste with a masonry chisel and ball peen hammer. On wood siding, make the cutout with a reciprocating saw.

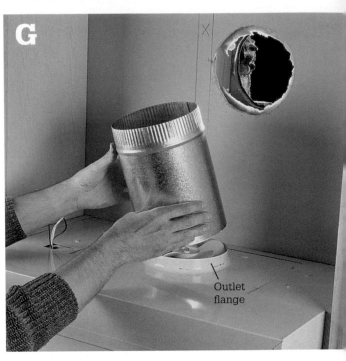

G

Outlet flange

Attach the first duct section by sliding the smooth end over the outlet flange on the vent hood. Cut duct sections to length with metal snips.

H

Drill three or four pilot holes around the joint through both layers of metal, using a ⅛" twist bit. Attach the duct with ¾" sheetmetal screws. Seal the joint with duct tape.

I

Join additional duct sections by sliding the smooth end over the corrugated end of the preceding section. Use an adjustable elbow to change directions in duct run. Secure all joints with sheetmetal screws and duct tape.

J

Install the duct cap on the exterior wall. Apply a thick bead of silicone caulk to the cap flange. Slide the cap over the end of the duct.

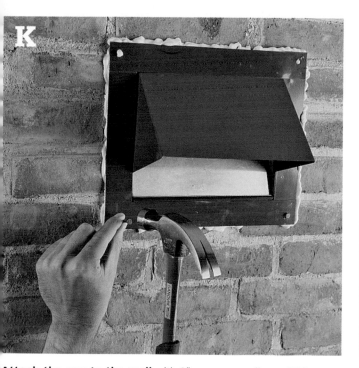

Attach the cap to the wall with 2" masonry nails, or 1½" sheetmetal screws (on wood siding). Wipe away excess caulk.

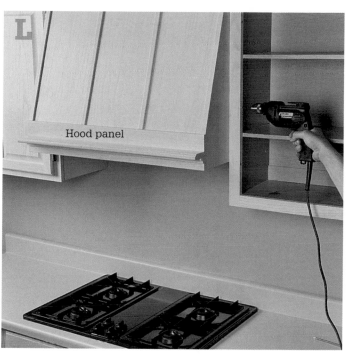

Slide the decorative hood panel into place between the wall cabinets. Drill pilot holes through the cabinet face frame with a counterbore bit. Attach the hood panel to the cabinets with 2½" screws.

Hood panel

Vent Hood Variations

Blower unit

A downdraft cooktop has a built-in blower unit that vents through the back of the bottom of a base cabinet. A downdraft cooktop is a good choice for a kitchen island or peninsula.

A cabinet-mounted vent hood is attached to the bottom of a short, 12"- to 18"-tall wall cabinet. Metal ducts run inside this wall cabinet.

Kitchen Flooring

The floor is often the largest single surface in a kitchen, and therefore has great potential for setting the kitchen's tone. Options for kitchen flooring have expanded immensely in the past few years. Many of these options are perfect for do-it-yourselfers looking to give their kitchen a stylish face-lift.

Perhaps your kitchen has a resilient sheet floor that is in good shape but is of a dated pattern. A new floating floor can be installed over existing resilient flooring in a weekend. This chapter contains information on what floating floor options are available and how to install them.

Or maybe you are more adventurous and want to install the ceramic tile floor you have always dreamed of. Information on ceramic tile options and directions on how to prepare for, cut, place and finish a ceramic tile floor are included here as well.

You'll also find information on resilient tile and sheet installation, how to remove old flooring, tips on measuring and trimming your finished floor, and many other pointers.

In This Chapter

- Project Preparation
- Measuring Your Kitchen
- Cutting Door Casing & Jambs
- Establishing Reference Lines
- Installing Laminate Flooring
- Installing Resilient Sheet Vinyl
- Installing Resilient Tile
- Installing Ceramic Tile
- Filling in Gaps

Project Preparation

Before your new floor goes in, your old flooring will probably need to be taken out and the subfloor carefully prepared for a finished surface. Project preparation is just as important as installing your floor covering and requires the same attention to detail.

If your new floor is part of a larger kitchen remodeling project, removing the existing floor is one of the first steps in the overall project, while installing the new floor is one of the last steps in the process. All other demolition and construction should be finished in the room before the floor is installed to avoid damaging the surface.

Underlayment is an important part of the preparation step. It is a layer of sheeting that's screwed or nailed to the subfloor to provide a smooth, stable surface for the floor covering. The type of underlayment you choose depends in part on the type of floor covering you plan to install.

Ceramic and natural stone tile floors usually require an underlayment that stands up to moisture, such as cementboard. Fiber/cementboard is a thin, high-density underlayment used under ceramic tile and vinyl flooring in situations where floor height is a concern. Isolation membrane is used to protect ceramic tile installations from movement that may occur on cracked concrete floors. For vinyl flooring, use a quality-grade plywood since most manufacturers' warranties are void if the flooring is installed over substandard underlayments. If you're using your old sheet vinyl flooring as underlayment, apply an embossing leveler to prepare it for the new installation (see opposite page, bottom). Most wood flooring does not require underlayment and is often placed directly on a plywood subfloor.

This section shows how to remove sheet vinyl, vinyl tile, ceramic tile, and underlayment, and how to install new plywood or cementboard underlayment. Cutting door casings, establishing reference lines and measuring for materials needed are also covered.

Plywood

Fiber/cementboard

Cementboard

Isolation membrane

Latex patching compound fills gaps, holes and low spots in underlayment. It's also used to cover screw heads, nail heads and seams in underlayment. Some compounds include dry and wet ingredients that need to be mixed, while others are premixed. The compound is applied with a trowel or wallboard knife.

Preparation Tools & Materials

Tools for flooring removal and surface preparation include: power sander (A), jamb saw (B), putty knife (C), floor roller (D), circular saw (E), hammer (F), hand maul (G), reciprocating saw (H), cordless drill (I), flat edged trowel (J), notched trowel (K), stapler (L), cat's paw (M), flat pry bar (N), heat gun (O), masonry chisel (P), crowbar (Q), nippers (R), wallboard knife (S), wood chisel (T), long-handled floor scraper (U), phillips screwdriver (V), standard screwdriver (W), utility knife (X), carpenter's level (Y).

Turn old flooring into a smooth underlayment layer for new flooring by applying an embossing leveler. Embossing leveler is a mortar-like substance that can prepare resilient flooring or ceramic tile, provided it's well adhered to the subfloor, for use as an underlayment for a new floor covering. Mix the leveler following manufacturer's directions, then spread it thinly over the floor, using a flat-edged trowel. Wipe away excess leveler with the trowel, making sure all dips and indentations are filled. Embossing leveler begins setting in 10 minutes, so work quickly. Once it dries, scrape away ridges and high spots with the trowel edge.

How to Remove Sheet Vinyl

Use a utility knife to cut the old flooring into strips about a foot wide to make removal easier.

Pull up as much flooring as possible by hand. Grip the strips close to the floor to minimize tearing.

Cut stubborn sheet vinyl into strips about 6" wide. Starting at a wall, peel up as much of the floor covering as possible. If the felt backing remains, spray a solution of water and liquid dishwashing detergent under the surface layer to help separate the backing. Use a wallboard knife to scrape up particularly stubborn patches.

Scrape up the remaining sheet vinyl and backing with a floor scraper. If necessary, spray the backing with the soap solution to loosen it. Sweep up the debris, then finish the cleanup using a wet/dry vacuum. Tip: Fill the vacuum with about an inch of water to help contain dust.

How to Remove Vinyl Tiles

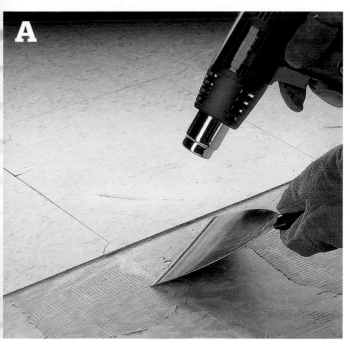

Starting at a loose seam, use a long-handled floor scraper to remove tiles. To remove stubborn tiles, soften the adhesive with a heat gun, then use a wallboard knife to pry up the tile and scrape off the underlying adhesive.

Remove stubborn adhesive or backing by wetting the floor with a mixture of water and liquid dishwashing detergent, then scrape it with a floor scraper.

How to Remove Ceramic Tile

Knock out tile using a hand maul and masonry chisel. If possible, start in a space between tiles where the grout has loosened. Be careful when working around fragile fixtures, such as drain flanges, so you don't damage them.

If you plan to reuse the underlayment, use a floor scraper to remove any remaining adhesive. You may have to use a belt sander with a coarse sanding belt to grind off stubborn adhesive.

Measuring Your Kitchen

You'll need to determine the total square footage of your kitchen before ordering your floor covering. To do this, divide the room into a series of squares and rectangles that you can easily measure. Be sure to include all areas that will be covered, such as pantries and space under your refrigerator and other movable appliances.

Measure the length and width of each area in inches, then multiply the length times the width. Divide that number by 144 to determine your square footage. Add all of the areas together to figure the square footage for the entire room, then subtract the areas that will not be covered, such as cabinets and other permanent fixtures.

When ordering your floor covering, be sure to purchase 10 to 15% extra to allow for waste and cutting. For patterned flooring, you may need as much as 20% extra.

Measure the area of the project room to calculate how much flooring you will need.

How to Measure Your Kitchen

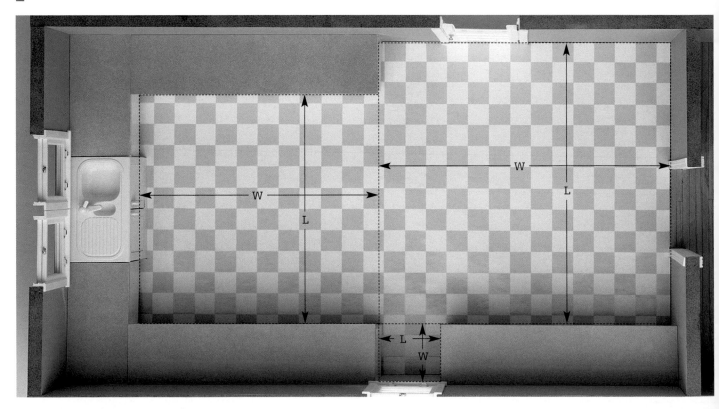

Divide the room into rectangles or squares. Include pantries and areas where movable appliances are installed. Measure the length and width of each area in inches, then multiply the length times the width. Divide that number by 144 to determine your square footage.

Cutting Door Casing & Jambs

For best results, your new flooring should fit beneath the door case molding and frame jambs, not against them. It also creates a more finished look and eliminates the intricate fitting and cutting necessary to fit flooring around molding.

It only takes a few minutes to cut the casing and jambs. If you're installing ceramic tile or parquet, keep in mind you'll be placing the flooring over adhesive, so cut about ⅛" above the top of the tile to allow for the height of the adhesive.

These directions show the casing and jambs being cut to accommodate ceramic tile. Because the tile will be placed on top of cementboard, a piece of cementboard is placed under the tile when the casing is marked.

Tools & Materials
▪ Jamb saw ▪ Floor covering.

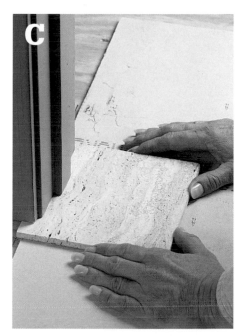

Cut the bottom of door casings and jambs the thickness of your flooring and underlayment so your floor covering will fit under it.

How to Cut Door Casing

A

Place a piece of flooring and underlayment against the door casing. Mark the casing about ⅛" above the top of the flooring.

B

Cut the casing at the mark using a jamb saw. Mark the jambs and door stops, and cut them as well.

C

Slide a piece of flooring under the door jamb to make sure it fits easily.

Establishing Reference Lines

Your first row of flooring, your first few tiles or your first piece of sheeting sets the direction for the rest of your floor. It's critical, therefore, to get off to a perfect start. You can do this by carefully planning your layout and establishing accurate reference lines.

In general, tile flooring begins at the center of the room and is installed in quadrants along layout lines, also called working lines. After establishing reference lines that mark the center of the room, lay the tile in a dry run along those lines to ensure you won't have to cut off more than half of a tile in the last row. If necessary, adjust your reference lines by half the width of the tile to form the layout lines.

For most floating floors and tongue-and-groove floors, you only need a single reference line along the starting wall. If your wall is straight, you don't even need a working line. You can place spacers along the wall and butt the first row of flooring against the spacers. However, this only works if your wall is straight. If it's bowed or out of square, it will affect the layout. The photos on the next page show options for establishing reference lines.

Tools & Materials Tape measure ∎ Chalk line ∎ Framing square ∎ Hammer ∎ 8d finish nails ∎ Spacers.

5 ft.

4 ft.

3 ft.

To check your reference lines for squareness, use the 3-4-5 triangle method. Measuring from the centerpoint, make a mark along a reference line at 3 ft. and along a perpendicular reference line at 4 ft. The distance between the two points should be exactly 5 ft. If it's not, adjust your lines accordingly.

Two Methods for Establishing Reference

Mark the centerpoint of two opposite walls, then snap a chalk line between the marks. Mark the centerpoint of the chalk line. Place a framing square at the centerpoint so one side is flush with the chalk line. Snap a perpendicular reference along the adjacent side of the framing square.

Snap chalk lines between the centerpoints of opposite walls to establish perpendicular reference lines. Check the lines for squareness using the 3-4-5 triangle method.

How to Establish Reference Lines for Wood & Floating Floors

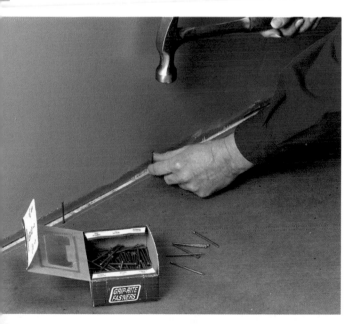

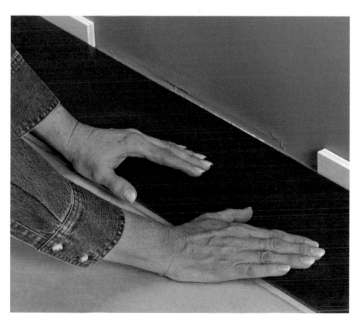

If your wall is out of square or bowed, make a mark on the floor ½" from the wall at both ends and snap a chalk line between these points. Drive 8d finish nails every 2" to 3" along the line. Use this as the reference line and butt the first row of flooring against the nails.

If your wall is straight, place ½" spacers along the wall, then butt your flooring up against the spacers.

The rich wood tones of beautiful laminate planks may cause you to imagine hours of long, hard installation work, but this is a DIY project that you can do in a single weekend. Buy the manufactured planks at a home improvement or flooring store and install laminate flooring with the step-by-step instructions offered in the following pages.

Installing Laminate Flooring

Laminate flooring comes in a floating system that is simple to install, even if you have no experience with other home improvement projects. You may install a floating laminate floor right on top of plywood, concrete slab, sheet vinyl, or hardwood flooring (follow the manufacturer's instructions). The pieces are available in planks or squares in a variety of different sizes, colors, and faux finishes—including wood and ceramic. Tongue-and-groove edges lock pieces together, and the entire floor floats on the underlayment. At the end of this project there are a few extra steps to take if your flooring manufacturer recommends using glue on the joints.

Tools & Materials Circular saw ▪ Workgloves ▪ Underlayment ▪ Kneepads ▪ Tape measure ▪ ½" spacers ▪ Scrap foam ▪ Tapping block ▪ Speed square ▪ Manufacturer glue ▪ Threshold and screws ▪ Chisel ▪ Painter's tape ▪ Rubber mallet ▪ Drawbar ▪ Finish nails ▪ Strap clamps ▪ Pencil ▪ Nail set
For shoe molding removal and replacement: Pry bar ▪ Wood shims ▪ Chisel ▪ Hammer ▪ Nail set ▪ Finish nails
For glued laminate flooring: ▪ Wood block ▪ Rubber mallet ▪ ½" spacers ▪ Strap clamps ▪ Damp cloth ▪ Plastic scraper.

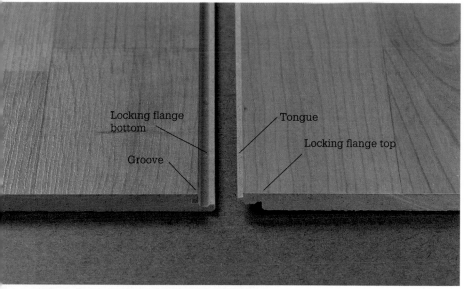

Locking flange
bottom

Groove

Tongue

Locking flange top

The joint design for laminate planks and squares is intended to make installation and replacement a breeze, while also providing a barrier from moisture and debris. Today, tongue-and-groove joints are often supplemented with positively locking flanges to provide a tight fit on both the top and bottom of the board. The tongue on one side fits into the groove of the adjacent board; then the plank is "clicked" into place by pressing down on the plank to join the flanges. Planks without the snap-together ("click") feature sometimes require glue for an extra snug fit (read the manufacturer's instructions carefully and follow all recommendations).

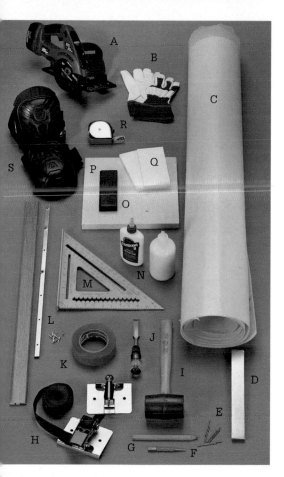

Tools and materials used to lay laminate flooring include: Circular saw (A), Work gloves (B), Underlayment (C), Drawbar (D), Finish nails (E), Nail set (F), Pencil (G), Strap clamps (H), Rubber mallet (I), Chisel (J), Painter's tape (K), Threshold and screws (L), Speed square (M), Manufacturer glue (N), Tapping block (O), Scrap foam (P), 1/2" Spacers (Q), Tape measure (R), Kneepads (S).

▌Terms You Need to Know

Subfloor—The base layer of wood or plywood that supports the underlayment and surface flooring.

Underlayment—The intermediate layer between the surface floor and the subfloor.

Floating floors—Floors that are not fastened to the subfloor or underlayment, but rather "float" on top. The flooring is held together with a snap-together, interlocking system.

Glueless laminate flooring (also called "click-floors")—Laminate flooring that does not require glue for installation, but instead relies upon tight tongue-and-groove joints. No-glue flooring is far easier to install and repair than glued laminate flooring, but it may not be as resistant to moisture—so avoid installing it in bathrooms or basements.

Glued laminate flooring—Laminate flooring that requires glue at each plank joint in order to effectively seal together the tongue-and-groove planks.

Drawbar—A metal bar used to pull together the final two planks in a row. There are two hooks—one to attach to the end of a plank close to the wall (where a rubber mallet would not fit to tap the final plank into the adjacent plank), and one on the other end to pull the plank in tight with the adjacent board.

Strap clamps—A device used to hold several planks together tightly while adhesive in between joints dries.

How to Install Laminate Flooring

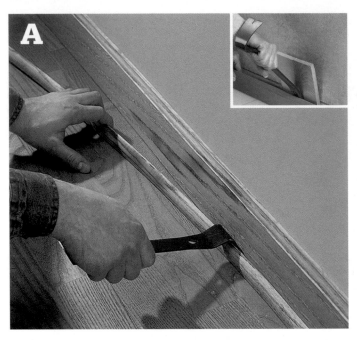

Remove the shoe molding by wedging a pry bar between the shoe molding and baseboards and pry outward. Continue along the wall until the entire shoe is removed. Next, place a scrap board against the wall and use a pry bar to pull the baseboard away from the wall (inset). Maintain the gap with wood shims. Number the sections for easy replacement. Drive protruding nails in floor ⅛" below the surface with a nail set.

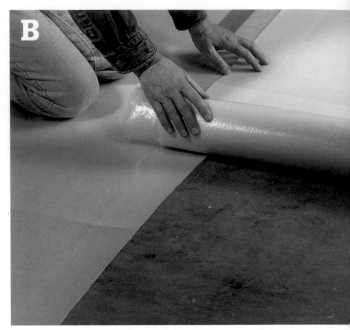

To install the underlayment, start in one corner and unroll the underlayment to the opposite wall. Cut the underlayment to fit, using a utility knife or scissors. Overlap the second underlayment sheet according to the manufacturer's recommendations, and secure the pieces in place with adhesive tape.

Tip ▸

- **Laminate flooring, like hardwood,** can shrink or expand when the temperature or humidity in a room changes. This movement can cause planks to buckle, so be sure to allow your new laminate flooring stock to acclimate to the conditions in your house. Simply keep the planks in the room where they will be used for a few days prior to installation.

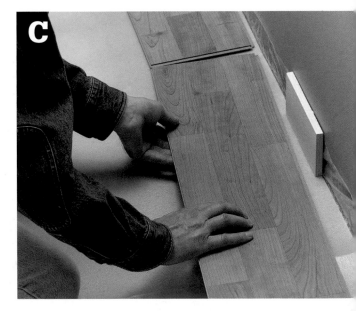

Working from the left corner of the room to right, set wall spacers and dry lay planks (tongue side facing the wall) against th wall. The spacers allow for expansion. If you are flooring a room more than 26 ft. long or wide, you need to buy appropriate-sized expansion joints. Note: Some manufacturers suggest facing the groove side to the wall.

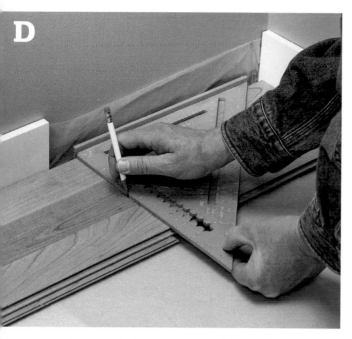

Set a new plank right side up, on top of the previously laid plank, flush with the spacer against the wall at the end run. Line up a speed square with the bottom plank edge and trace a line. That's the cutline for the final plank in the row.

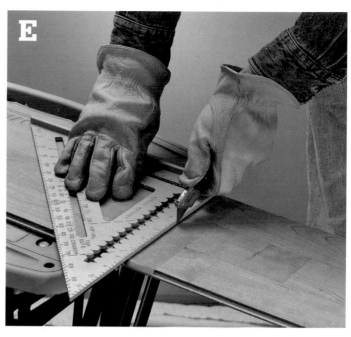

Press painter's tape along the cutline on the top of the plank to prevent chips when cutting. Score the line drawn in Step D with a utility knife. Turn the plank over and extend the pencil line to the backside.

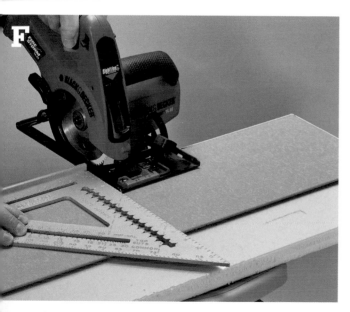

Clamp the board (face down) and rigid foam insulation or plywood to a work table. The foam discourages chipping. Clamp a speed square on top of the plank, as though you are going to draw another line parallel to the cutline—use this to eye your straight cut. Place the circular saw's blade in front (waste side) of the actual cutline.

To create a tight fit for the last plank in the first row, place a spacer against the wall and wedge one end of a drawbar between it and the last plank. Tap the other end of the drawbar with a rubber mallet or hammer. Protect the laminate surface with a thin cloth.

(continued next page)

How to Install Laminate Flooring (continued)

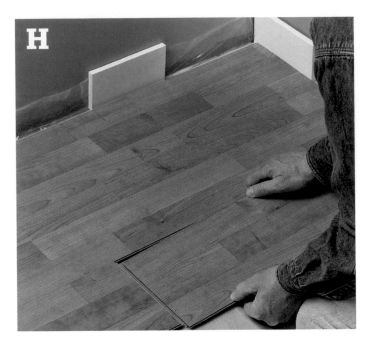

Continue to lay rows of flooring, making sure the joints are staggered. Staggering joints prevents the entire floor from relying on just a few joints, thus preventing the planks from lifting. Staggering also stengthens the floor, because the joints are shorter and evenly distributed.

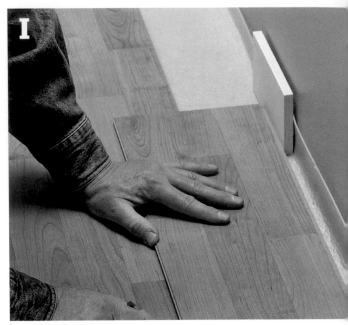

To fit the final row, place two planks on top of the last course; slide the top plank up against the wall spacer. Use the top plank to draw a cutline lengthwise on the middle plank. Cut the middle plank to size using the same method as in Step D (only now you are "ripcutting" a lengthwise cut). The very last board must be cut lengthwise and widthwise to fit.

Tip ▸

- **To stagger joints,** first check the manufacturer's instructions to determine what the minimum distance should be between the staggered joints. The range is usually between 8" and 18" (minimum). The first plank in the second row can sometimes be the waste piece from the cut you made at the end of the last run. But if you don't have a long enough scrap, the first plank in each row should alternate between being ⅓ and ⅔ the length of a full plank. This creates a pattern that is not only pleasing to the eye, but it ensures a solid installation.

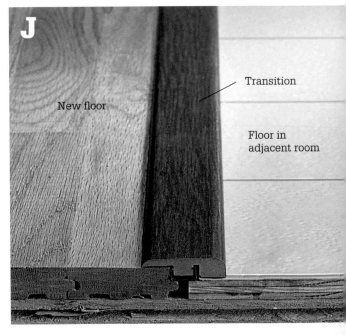

New floor

Transition

Floor in adjacent room

Install transition thresholds at room borders where the new floor joins another floor covering. These thresholds are used to tie together dissimilar floor coverings, such as laminate flooring and wood or carpet. They may also be necessary to span a distance in height between flooring in one room and the next.

How to Work Around Obstacles

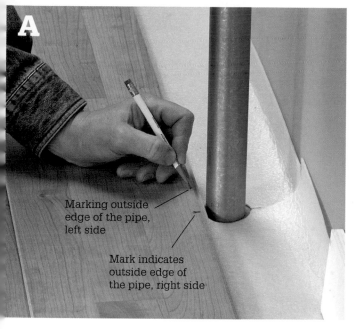

Marking outside edge of the pipe, left side

Mark indicates outside edge of the pipe, right side

Position a plank end against the spacers on the wall next to the obstacle. Use a pencil to make two marks along the length of the plank, indicating the points where the obstacle begins and ends.

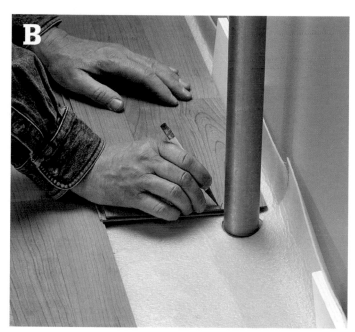

Once the plank is snapped into the previous row, position the plank end against the obstacle. Make two marks with a pencil, this time on the end of the plank to indicate where the obstacle falls along the width of the board.

Use a speed square to extend the four lines. The space at which they all intersect is the part of the plank that needs to be removed to make room for the obstacle to go through it. Use a drill with a Forstner bit, or a hole saw the same diameter as the space within the intersecting lines, and drill through the plank at the X. You'll be left with a hole; extend the cut to the edges with a jigsaw.

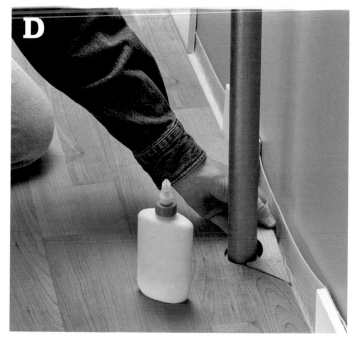

Install the plank by locking the tongue-and-groove joints with the preceding board. Fit the end piece in behind the pipe or obstacle. Apply manufacturer-recommended glue to the cut edges, and press the end piece tightly against the adjacent plank. Wipe away excess glue with a damp cloth.

Most resilient flooring is made from vinyl. The higher the percentage of vinyl in the product, the higher the quality of the floor. In solid vinyl flooring (left), the design pattern is built up from solid layers of vinyl. Vinyl composition flooring (center) combines vinyl with filler materials. Printed vinyl flooring (right) relies on a screen print for its color and pattern. The print is protected by a vinyl-and-urethane wear layer.

Installing Resilient Sheet Vinyl

Preparing a perfect underlayment is the most important phase of resilient sheet vinyl installation. Cutting the material to fit the contours of the room is a close second. The best way to ensure accurate cuts is to make a cutting template. Some manufacturers offer template kits, or you can make one by following the instructions on the opposite page. Be sure to use the recommended adhesive for the sheet vinyl you are installing. Many manufacturers require that you use their glue for installation. Use extreme care when handling the sheet vinyl, especially felt-backed products, to avoid creasing and tearing.

Tools & Materials Linoleum knife ▪ Framing square ▪ Compass ▪ Scissors ▪ Non-permanent felt-tipped pen ▪ Utility knife ▪ Straightedge ▪ ¼" V-notched trowel ▪ J-roller ▪ Stapler ▪ Flooring roller ▪ Chalk line ▪ Heat gun ▪ ¹⁄₁₆" V-notched trowel ▪ Vinyl flooring ▪ Masking tape ▪ Heavy butcher or kraft paper ▪ Duct tape ▪ Flooring adhesive ▪ ⅜" staples ▪ Metal threshold bars ▪ Nails.

How to Cut Vinyl

Use a linoleum knife or utility knife and a straightedge to cut resilient flooring. Make sure to use a sharp knife blade, and change blades often. Always make cuts on a smooth surface, such as a scrap of hardboard placed under the flooring.

How to Make a Cutting Template

Place sheets of heavy butcher paper or brown wrapping paper along the walls, leaving a ⅛" gap. Cut triangular holes in the paper with a utility knife. Fasten the template to the floor by placing masking tape over the holes.

Follow the outline of the room, working with one sheet of paper at a time. Overlap the edges of adjoining sheets by about 2" and tape the sheets together.

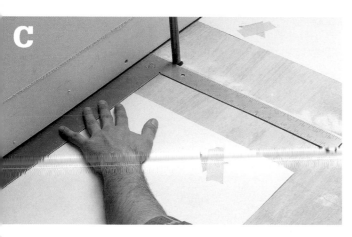

To fit the template around pipes, tape sheets of paper on either side. Measure the distance from the wall to the center of the pipe, then subtract ⅛".

Transfer the measurement to a separate piece of paper. Use a compass to draw the pipe diameter on the paper, then cut out the hole with scissors or a utility knife. Cut a slit from the edge of the paper to the hole.

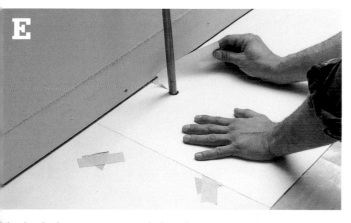

Fit the hole cutout around the pipe. Tape the hole template to the adjoining sheets.

When completed, roll or loosely fold the paper template for carrying.

How to Install Perimeter-bond Sheet Vinyl

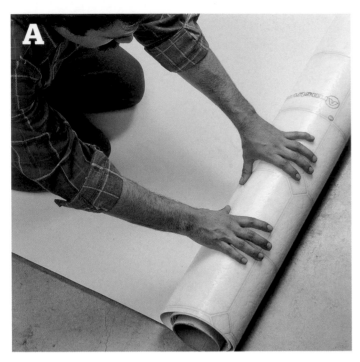

Unroll the flooring on any large, flat, clean surface. To prevent wrinkles, sheet vinyl comes from the manufacturer rolled with the pattern side out. Unroll the sheet and turn it pattern-side up for marking.

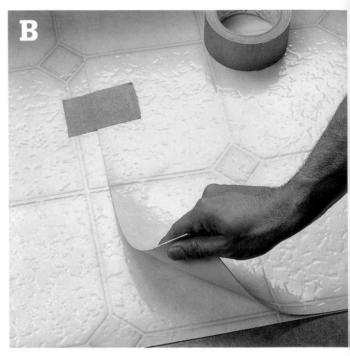

For two-piece installations, overlap the edges of the sheets by at least 2". Plan to have the seams fall along the pattern lines or simulated grout joints. Align the sheets so the pattern matches, then tape the sheets together with duct tape.

Position the paper template over the sheet vinyl and tape it in place. Trace the outline of the template onto the flooring using a non-permanent felt-tipped pen.

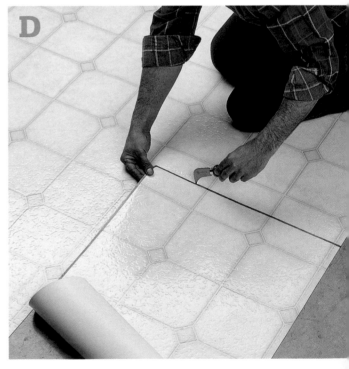

Remove the template. Cut the sheet vinyl with a sharp linoleum knife or a utility knife with a new blade. Use a straightedge as a guide for making longer cuts.

Cut holes for pipes and other permanent obstructions. Cut a slit from each hole to the nearest edge of the flooring. Whenever possible, make slits along pattern lines.

Roll up the flooring loosely and transfer it to the installation area. Do not fold the flooring. Unroll and position the sheet vinyl carefully. Slide the edges beneath undercut door casings.

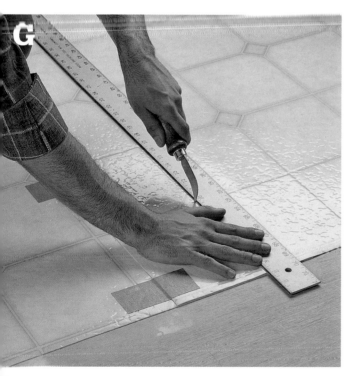

Cut the seams for two-piece installations using a straightedge as a guide. Hold the straightedge tightly against the flooring, and cut along the pattern lines through both pieces of vinyl flooring.

Remove both pieces of scrap flooring. The pattern should now run continuously across the adjoining sheets of flooring.

(continued next page)

How to Install Perimeter-bond Sheet Vinyl (continued)

Fold back the edges of both sheets. Apply a 3" band of multipurpose flooring adhesive to the underlayment or old flooring, using a ¼" V-notched trowel or wallboard knife.

Lay the seam edges one at a time onto the adhesive. Make sure the seam is tight, pressing the gaps together with your fingers, if needed. Roll the seam edges with a J-roller or wallpaper seam roller.

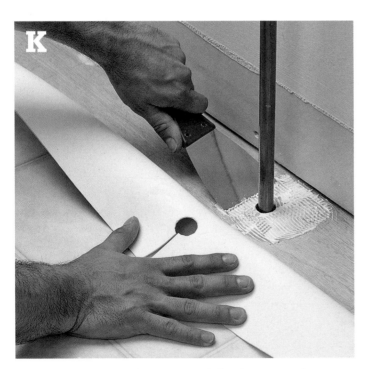

Apply flooring adhesive underneath flooring cuts at pipes or posts and around the entire perimeter of the room. Roll the flooring with the roller to ensure good contact with the adhesive.

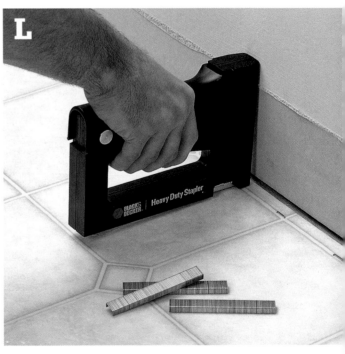

If you're applying flooring over a wood underlayment, fasten the outer edges of the sheet with ⅜" staples driven every 3". Make sure the staples will be covered by the base molding.

How to Install Full-spread Sheet Vinyl

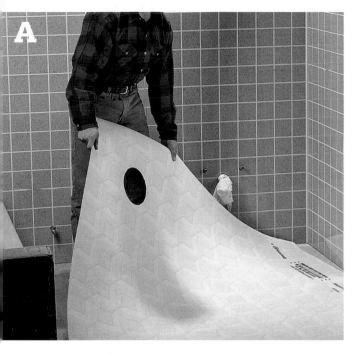

Cut the sheet vinyl using the techniques described on pages 246 and 247 (steps A to H).

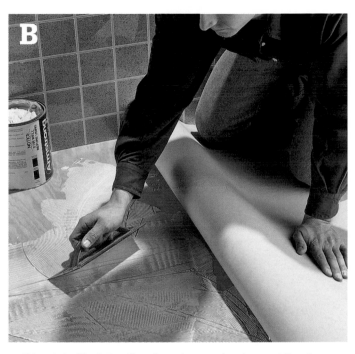

Pull back half of the flooring, then apply a layer of flooring adhesive over the underlayment or old flooring using a ¼" V-notched trowel. Lay the flooring back onto the adhesive.

Roll the floor with a heavy flooring roller, moving toward the edges of the sheet. The roller creates a stronger bond and eliminates air bubbles. Fold over the unbonded section of flooring, apply adhesive, then lay the flooring down and roll it. Wipe up any adhesive that oozes up around the edges of the vinyl, using a damp rag.

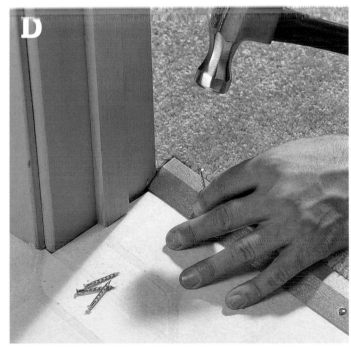

Measure and cut metal threshold bars to fit across doorways. Position each bar over the edge of the vinyl flooring and nail it in place.

Installing Resilient Tile

As with any tile installation, resilient tile requires carefully positioned layout lines. Before committing to any layout and applying tile, conduct a dry run to identify potential problems.

Keep in mind there's a difference between reference lines (see page 237) and layout lines (see below). Reference lines mark the center of the room and divide it into quadrants. If the tiles don't lay out symmetrically along these lines, you'll need to adjust them slightly, creating layout lines.

Once layout lines are established, installing the tile goes fairly quickly, especially if you're using self-adhesive tile. Be sure to keep joints between the tiles tight and lay the tiles square.

Tiles with an obvious grain pattern can be laid so the grain of each tile is oriented identically throughout the installation. You can also use the quarter-turn method, in which each tile has its pattern grain running perpendicular to that of adjacent tiles. Whichever method you choose, be sure to be consistent throughout the project.

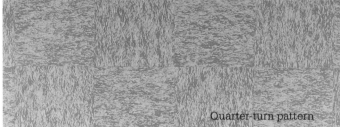

Check for noticeable directional features, like the grain of the vinyl particles. You can set the tiles in a running pattern so the directional feature runs in the same direction (top), or in a checkerboard pattern using the quarter-turn method (bottom).

Tools&Materials   Tape measure ▪ Chalk line ▪ Framing square ▪ Utility knife ▪ 1/16" notched trowel (for dry-back tile) ▪ Resilient tile ▪ Flooring adhesive (for dry-back tile).

How to Establish Tile Layout Lines

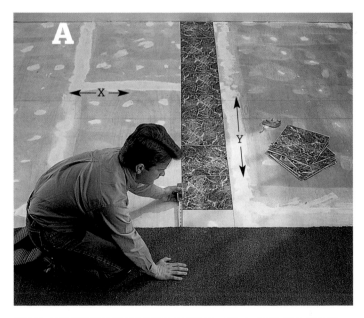

Snap perpendicular reference lines with a chalk line. Dry-fit tiles along layout line Y so a joint falls along reference line X. If necessary, shift the layout to make the layout symmetrical or to reduce the number of tiles that need to be cut.

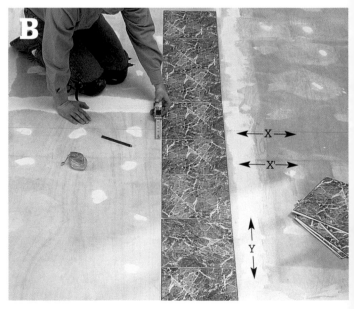

If you shift the tile layout, create a new line that's parallel to reference line X and runs through a tile joint near line X. The new line, X', is the line you'll use when installing the tile. To avoid confusion, use a different colored chalk to distinguish between lines.

Dry-fit tiles along the new line, X'. If necessary, adjust the layout line as in steps A and B.

If you adjusted the layout along X', measure and make a new layout line, Y', that's parallel to reference line Y and runs through a tile joint. Y' will form the second layout line you'll use during installation.

How to Install Self-adhesive Resilient Tiles

Once your reference lines are established, peel off the paper backing and install the first tile in one of the corners formed by the intersecting layout lines. Lay three or more tiles along each layout line in the quadrant. Rub the entire surface of each tile to bond the adhesive to the floor underlayment.

Begin installing tiles in the interior area of the quadrant, keeping the joints tight between tiles.

(continued next page)

Note: Tile to be cut shown inverted for clarity; tiles should be faceup for marking.

Finish setting full tiles in the first quadrant, then set the full tiles in an adjacent quadrant. Set the tiles along the layout lines first, then fill in the interior tiles.

To cut tiles to fit along the walls, place the tile to be cut (A) faceup on top of the last full tile you installed. Position a ⅛"-thick spacer against the wall, then set a marker tile (B) on top of the tile to be cut. Trace along the edge of the marker tile to draw a cutting line.

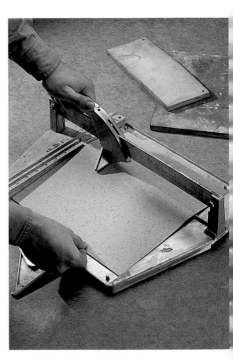

TIP: To mark tiles for cutting around outside corners, make a cardboard template to match the space, keeping a ⅛" gap along the walls. After cutting the template, check to make sure it fits. Place the template on a tile and trace its outline.

Cut tile to fit using a utility knife and straightedge. Hold the straightedge securely against the cutting line to ensure a straight cut.

OPTION: You can use a ceramic-tile cutter to make straight cuts in thick vinyl tiles.

Install cut tiles next to the walls. If you're pre-cutting all tiles before installing them, measure the distance between the wall and installed tiles at various points in case the distance changes.

Continue installing tile in the remaining quadrants until the room is completely covered. Check the entire floor. If you find loose areas, press down on the tiles to bond them to the underlayment. Install metal threshold bars at room borders where the new floor joins another floor covering.

How to Install Dry-back Tile

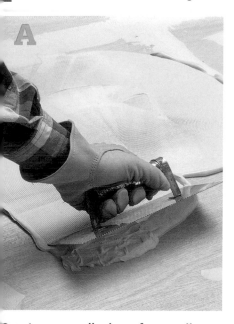

Create perpendicular reference lines and dry-fit tiles to establish the final layout. Apply adhesive around the intersection of the layout lines using a trowel with 1/16" V-shaped notches. Hold the trowel at a 45° angle and spread adhesive evenly over the surface.

Spread adhesive over most of the installation area, covering three quadrants. Allow the adhesive to set according to the manufacturer's instructions, then begin to install the tile at the intersection of the layout lines. You can kneel on installed tiles to lay additional tiles. When the first three quadrants are completely tiled, spread adhesive over the remaining quadrant, then finish setting the tile.

Installing Ceramic Tile

Ceramic tile installation starts with the same steps as installing resilient tile. You snap perpendicular reference lines and dry-fit tiles to ensure the best placement.

Work in small sections so the mortar doesn't dry before the tiles are set. Use spacers between tiles to ensure consistent spacing. Plan an installation sequence to avoid kneeling on set tiles. Be careful not to kneel or walk on tiles until the designated drying period is over.

Tools&Materials

¼" square-notched trowel ▪ Rubber mallet ▪ Tile cutter ▪ Tile nippers ▪ Hand-held tile cutter ▪ Needle-nose pliers ▪ Grout float ▪ Grout sponge ▪ Soft cloth ▪ Small paintbrush ▪ Thin-set mortar ▪ Tile ▪ Tile spacers ▪ Grout ▪ Latex grout additive ▪ Wall adhesive ▪ 2 × 4 lumber ▪ Grout sealer ▪ Tile caulk.

How to Install Ceramic Floor Tile

A

Make sure the subfloor is smooth, level and stable. Spread thin-set mortar on the subfloor for one sheet of cementboard. Place the cementboard on the mortar, keeping a ¼" gap along the walls. Fasten it in place with 1¼" cementboard screws. Place fiberglass-mesh wallboard tape over the seams. Cover the remainder of the floor.

B

Draw reference lines and establish the tile layout (see pages 236 to 237). Mix a batch of thin-set mortar, then spread the mortar evenly against both reference lines of one quadrant, using a ¼" square-notched trowel. Use the notched edge of the trowel to create furrows in the mortar bed.

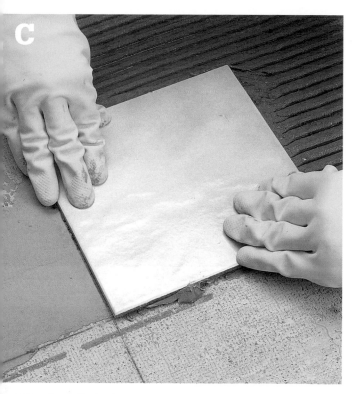

Set the first tile in the corner of the quadrant where the reference lines intersect. When setting tiles that are 8" square or larger, twist each tile slightly as you set it into position.

Using a soft rubber mallet, gently tap the central area of each tile a few times to set it evenly into the mortar.

Variation: For large tiles or uneven stone, use a larger trowel with notches that are at least ½" deep.

Variation: For mosaic sheets, use a ³⁄₁₆" V-notched trowel to spread the mortar and a grout float to press the sheets into the mortar. Apply pressure gently to avoid creating an uneven surface.

(continued next page)

How to Install Ceramic Floor Tile (continued)

To ensure consistent spacing between tiles, place plastic tile spacers at the corners of the set tile. With mosaic sheets, use spacers equal to the gaps between tiles.

Position and set adjacent tiles into the mortar along the reference lines. Make sure the tiles fit neatly against the spacers.

To make sure the tiles are level with one another, place a straight piece of 2 × 4 across several tiles, then tap the board with a mallet.

Lay tile in the remaining area covered with mortar. Repeat steps B to G, continuing to work in small sections, until you reach walls or fixtures.

Measure and mark tiles to fit against walls and into corners (see page 252). Cut the tiles to fit. Apply thin-set mortar directly to the back of the cut tiles, instead of the floor, using the notched edge of the trowel to furrow the mortar.

Set the cut pieces of tile into position. Press down on the tile until each piece is level with adjacent tiles.

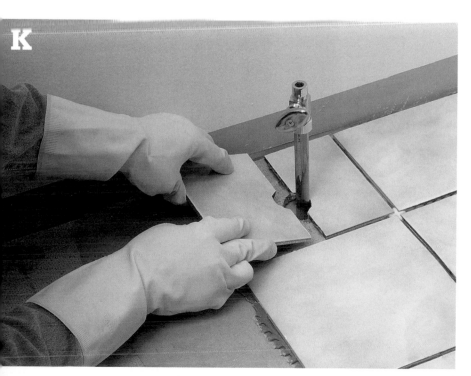

Measure, cut and install tiles that require notches or curves to fit around obstacles, such as exposed pipes or toilet drains.

Carefully remove the spacers with needlenose pliers before the mortar hardens.

(continued next page)

How to Install Ceramic Floor Tile (continued)

Apply mortar and set tiles in the remaining quadrants, completing one quadrant before starting the next. Inspect all of the tile joints and use a utility knife or grout knife to remove any high spots of mortar that could show through the grout.

Install threshold material in doorways. If the threshold is too long for the doorway, cut it to fit with a jig saw or circular saw and a tungsten-carbide blade. Set the threshold in thin-set mortar so the top is even with the tile. Keep the same space between the threshold as between tiles. Let the mortar set for at least 24 hours.

Prepare a small batch of floor grout to fill the tile joints. When mixing grout for porous tile, such as quarry or natural stone, use an additive with a release agent to prevent grout from bonding to the tile surfaces.

Starting in a corner, pour the grout over the tile. Use a rubber grout float to spread the grout outward from the corner, pressing firmly on the float to completely fill the joints. For best results, tilt the float at a 60° angle to the floor and use a figure-eight motion.

Use the grout float to remove excess grout from the surface of the tile. Wipe diagonally across the joints, holding the float in a near-vertical position. Continue applying grout and wiping off excess until about 25 square feet of the floor has been grouted.

Wipe a damp grout sponge diagonally over about 2 square feet of the floor at a time. Rinse the sponge in cool water between wipes. Wipe each area only once since repeated wiping can pull grout back out of joints. Repeat steps O to R to apply grout to the rest of the floor.

Allow the grout to dry for about 4 hours, then use a soft cloth to buff the tile surface and remove any remaining grout film.

Apply grout sealer to the grout lines, using a small sponge brush or sash brush. Avoid brushing sealer on to the tile surfaces. Wipe up any excess sealer immediately.

Filling in the Gaps

With most flooring projects you will have gaps between walls and floor that need to be covered, as well as at thresholds, between rooms and around small obstacles, such as pipes. For every situation, there is a molding to fit your needs.

A floor isn't truly finished until all of the pieces are in place. These moldings help give your floors a professional look. The names for moldings may differ slightly between manufacturers. Marble thresholds and vinyl cove molding (not pictured) are available for tile and resilient flooring applications.

Wood molding is used for a smooth transition between the hardwood in the dining area and the tile in the adjoining room.

T-moldings span transitions between hardwood floors and other floors of equal height. These products are usually glued in place.

Reducer strips provide a transition between a wood floor and an adjacent floor of a lower height. One edge is grooved to fit the tongue in the hardwood.

Carpet reducers (A) are used to finish off and create a smooth transition between flooring and carpeting.

Stair nosing (B) is used to cover the exposed edges of stairs where the risers meet the steps. It is also used between step-downs and landings.

Baby threshold (C) is used in place of baseboards and quarter round in front of sliding glass doors or door thresholds, to fill the gap between the floor and door.

Reducer strips (D), also called transition strips, are used between rooms when the floors are at different heights and composed of different materials.

Overlap reducers (E) are also used between rooms when one floor is at a different height than an adjoining room.

T-moldings (F) are used to connect two floors of equal height. They are also used in doorways and thresholds to provide a smooth transition. T-moldings do not butt up against the flooring, allowing the wood to expand and contract under it.

Baseboards (G) are used for almost all types of floors and are available in a wide variety of designs and thicknesses. They are applied at the bottom of walls to cover the gap between the floor and walls.

Quarter round (H), similar to shoemolding, is installed along the bottom edge of baseboard and sits on top of the floor. It covers any remaining gaps between the floor and walls.

Kitchen Lighting

Lighting does many jobs in the kitchen. It can set the mood, illuminate the task at hand, highlight a detail, or simply be beautiful to look at. Important as lighting is, a great many kitchens are poorly lit.

One common kitchen lighting problem is the centrally placed ceiling fixture with no other lighting sources. Unfortunately, this central fixture creates strong shadows at every workstation because the cook's body is always between the light source and the work area. Fortunately, this can be remedied in a number of creative and beautiful ways highlighted in this chapter.

Another kitchen lighting scheme, considered a step up from the single fixture, was the suspended ceiling with banks of fluorescent lights. The problem with fluorescent lighting is that it can make everything look green. In this chapter you will learn that light sources have different effects on color.

We'll cover lighting for tasks, accent and ambient lighting, and decorative lighting, using photo examples of each. Also included are how-to directions for installing track and cable lighting, under-, in-, and above-cabinet lighting, recessed lights and a ceiling fan with light fixture.

In This Chapter

- Removing Electrical Fixtures
- Installing Track Lighting
- Installing Low-voltage Cable Lighting
- Under-cabinet Lighting
- Installing In-cabinet & Above-cabinet Lighting
- Replacing a Ceiling-mounted Fixture
- Replacing a Hanging Light Fixture

Removing Electrical Fixtures

Many of the following lighting projects begin with removing an electrical fixture—either a receptacle or a lighting fixture. Whenever you remove an electrical fixture, carefully follow the instructions on this page. The neon circuit tester is an inexpensive yet vital tool for preventing potentially fatal electrical shocks. Remember that simply turning a wall switch off does not guarantee that all wires in a fixture will be without power.

Tools & Materials — Circuit tester
- Screwdriver.

How to Remove Electrical Fixtures

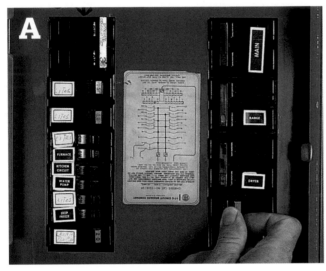

Shut off the electrical power to the kitchen circuits at the main service panel.

Remove the bases and coverplates from lights and other electrical fixtures. Be careful not to touch the wires until they have been tested for power.

Test the circuit wires for power, using a neon circuit tester. Touch one probe to a grounding screw, and the other to each circuit wire connection. If the circuit tester light glows, turn off the main circuit breaker, and retest.

When you are sure the power is off, disconnect the fixture or receptacle from the circuit wires.

Installing Track Lighting

Track lights give you the ability to precisely aim light fixtures. They are ideal for illuminating work areas and dining spaces.

It's easy to replace your central ceiling fixture with a surface-mounted lighting track. Additional tracks can be added, using L- or T-connectors.

Tools & Materials

Circuit tester ■ Screwdriver ■ Track lighting kit.

Track lighting makes it easy to create custom lighting effects. The individual fixtures can be arranged to provide focused task lighting or supply indirect lighting to brighten a dark corner.

How to Install Track Lighting

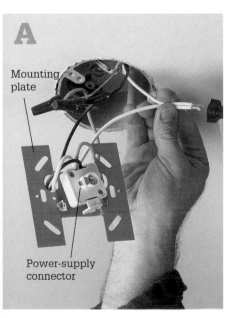

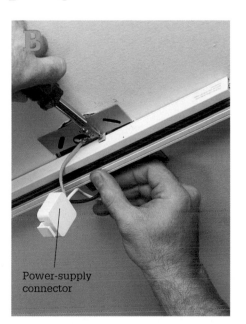

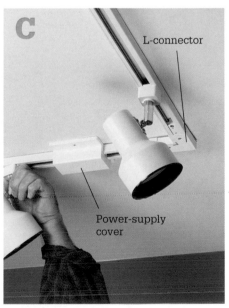

Connect the power-supply connector to the circuit wires, using wire connectors. Then, attach the mounting plate to the electrical box.

Mount the first track to the ceiling, screwing it into framing members or using toggle bolts. Secure the track to the mounting plate with screws. Snap the power-supply connector into the track.

Install additional tracks, connecting them to the first track with L- or T-connectors. Install the power-supply cover. Cap bare track ends with dead-end pieces. Position the light fixtures as desired.

Installing Low-voltage Cable Lighting

This unique fixture system is a mainstay of retail and commercial lighting and is now becoming common in homes. Low-voltage cable systems consist of a transformer and two parallel, current-carrying cables to suspend and provide electricity to fixtures mounted anywhere on the cables. The system's ease of installation, flexibility and the wide variety of whimsical and striking individual lights available make it perfect for all kinds of spaces. Low-voltage cable light systems are ideal for situations where surface-mounted track is undesirable or impossible to install. Most fixtures use the MR16 halogen bulb, which provides very white, focused light—excellent for accent lighting.

How to Install Low-voltage Cable Lighting

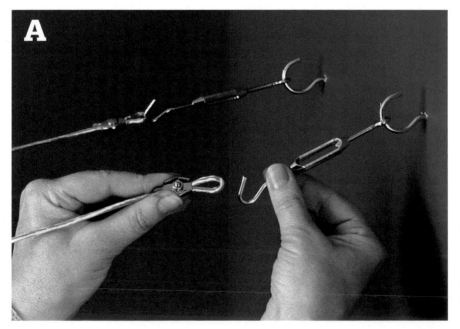

A

Tools & Materials
Neon circuit tester
■ Screwdriver ■ Low-voltage cable lighting system ■ Wire connectors.

Screw the cable hooks into the walls, 6 to 10" apart. (Make sure the hooks hit wall framing, or use wall anchors.) Cut the cable to the length of the span plus 6" extra for loops. Make loops with the provided fasteners, and attach the cables. Adjust the turnbuckles until cables are taut. Turn off the power at the service panel, and test the circuit with a neon tester. Remove the old fixture if you are replacing an existing fixture.

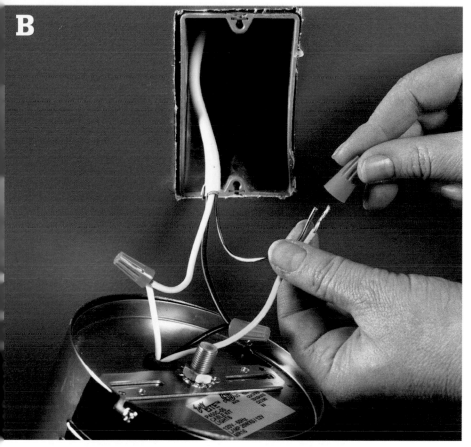

B

If you are not replacing an old fixture, install a new electrical box for the power supply and route cable to it from nearby receptacle (see pages 268 to 269). Leave 11" of extra cable for making connections, and secure it in the box with a cable clamp. Remove 10½" of sheathing from the end, and strip ¾" of insulation from the ends of the wires. Install the mounting strap for the transformer onto the fixture box with the provided screws. Remove the cover from the transformer, and connect the black transformer wire to the black circuit wire. Connect the white transformer wire to the white circuit wire, and connect the ground transformer wire to the grounding wire. Attach the transformer to the wall, and replace the cover.

C

Connect the two low-voltage leads from the transformer to the parallel cables. The low-voltage leads can be connected at any point on the cable and can be cut to any length. Connect the leads to the cables using the screw-down connectors provided. (It doesn't matter which lead is connected to which cable.) Make sure the screw is tight enough to pierce the insulation. Once the leads are attached, it's safe to restore the power. The 12-volt current is safe, and it's easier to adjust the lights when they're on.

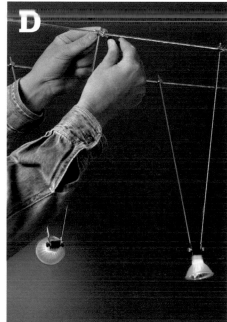

D

Attach the fixtures with the connectors supplied by the manufacturers (fixtures connect in a variety of ways), and adjust the beams as necessary. Make sure you don't add more fixtures than the transformer can support.

Under-cabinet Lighting

Under-cabinet lights come in numerous styles, including mini-track lights, strip lights, halogen puck lights, flexible rope lights and fluorescent task lights (covered here).

This installation shows hard-wiring a series of fluorescent under-cabinet lights and installing a new wall switch control.

Consult your electrical inspector about code requirements regarding the type of cable required (some may require armored cable) and the power source from which you draw. Some codes may not allow you to draw power for light fixtures from small appliance circuits. Also make sure the wattage of the new lights does not exceed the safe capacity of the circuit.

Tools & Materials
Neon circuit tester ▪ Utility knife ▪ Wallboard saw ▪ Hammer ▪ Screwdriver ▪ Drill and hole saw ▪ Jig saw ▪ Wire stripper ▪ Under-cabinet lighting kit ▪ 12-2 NM cable ▪ Pigtail wiring ▪ Twist-on wire connectors ▪ Plastic switch box ▪ Switch.

How to Install Hard-wired Under-cabinet Lighting

Shut off the power to the receptacle you plan to draw power from, then use a neon circuit tester to confirm the power is off. Disconnect the receptacle from its wiring. Locate and mark the studs in the installation area. Mark and cut a channel to route the cable, using a utility knife. In order to ease repair of the wallboard when finished, we cut a 6"-wide channel in the center of the installation area.

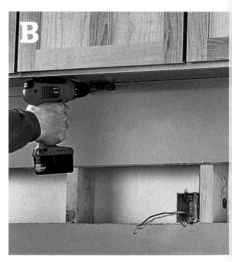

Drill holes through the cabinet edging and/or wall surface directly beneath the cabinets where the cable will enter each light fixture. Drill 5⁄8" holes through the studs to run the cable.

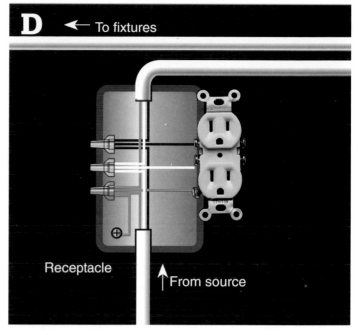

Install a plastic switch box by nailing it to the stud. Route a piece of 12-2 cable from the switch location to the power source. Route another cable from the switch to the first fixture hole. If you are installing more than one set of lights, route cables from the first fixture location to the second, and so on.

Strip 8" of sheathing from the ends of the switch-to-power cable. Clamp the cable into the receptacle box. Using plastic wire connectors, pigtail the white wires to the silver terminal on the receptacle and the black wires to the brass terminal. Pigtail the grounding wires to the grounding screw in the electrical box. Tuck wiring into the electrical box and reattach the receptacle.

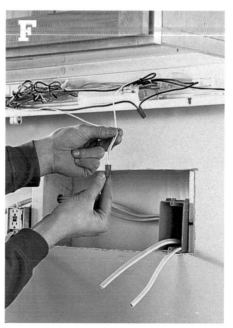

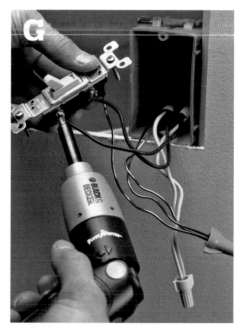

Remove the access cover, lens and bulb from the light fixture. Open the knockouts for running cables into the fixture. Insert the cables into the knockouts and secure the clamps. Strip 8" of sheathing from the cables. Attach the light fixture to the bottom of the cabinet with screws.

Use wire connectors to join the black, white and ground leads from the light fixture to each of the corresponding cable wires from the wall, including any cable leading to additional fixtures. Re-attach the bulb, lens and access cover to the fixture. Repeat this process for any additional fixtures.

Strip 8" of sheathing from each cable at the switch and clamp the cables into the switch box. Join the white wires together with wire connectors. Connect each black wire to a screw terminal on the switch. Pigtail the ground wires to the grounding screw on the switch. Install the switch and coverplate; restore power. Patch removed wallboard.

Installing In-cabinet & Above-cabinet Lighting

Cabinets are great places for a variety of lighting. While under-cabinet lights make great task and accent lighting, cabinet tops and insides are great for concealing ambient sources.

Tools & Materials

Neon circuit tester ▪ Drill ▪ Hole saw ▪ Fish tape ▪ Cable stripper ▪ Combination tool ▪ Mini low-voltage recessed light ▪ 120 volt-12 volt transformer ▪ Fluorescent light fixture ▪ Wire connectors ▪ Nonmetallic cable.

How to Install In-cabinet Lights

A

Use a hole saw to make a hole in the top of the cabinet or in a shelf. Depress the spring clips on the side of the light and fit it into the hole. The two wires should be on top.

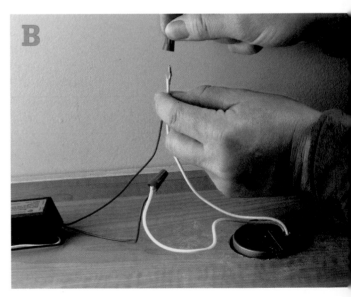

B

Connect the light to transformer wires or to the next light in the series with wire connectors. The simplest way to install a transformer for these lights is to use a plug-in transformer. You can install a switch for the receptacle or you can use a plug-in transformer with a built-in switch. For larger, built-in cabinets, hardwire the transformer and use a standard or dimmer switch as with under- or above-cabinet lights.

How to Install Above-cabinet Lights

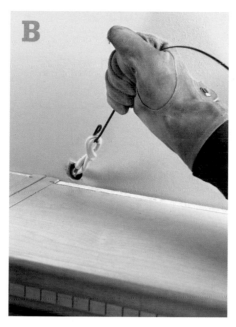

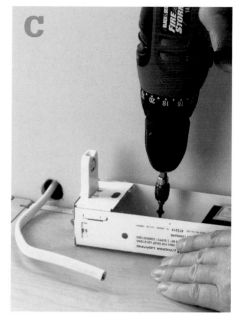

Turn off power to the circuit and confirm that the power is off, using a neon circuit tester. Drill a ⅝" hole through the wall surface directly above the cabinets where the cable will enter each light fixture.

Route an NM cable from a nearby receptacle to a switch, as you would for under-cabinet lighting (see pages 268 to 269). Route cable from the switch to the hole above the cabinet. Use a fish tape to pull the cable up through the wall behind the cabinet. Pull about 16" of cable through the hole.

Use a fluorescent fixture that will be entirely concealed by the trim on the front edge of the cabinet top. (Lighting stores sell low-profile fluorescent fixtures.) Remove the lens and the cover from the fluorescent fixture. Attach the light fixture to the back of the cabinet top with screws.

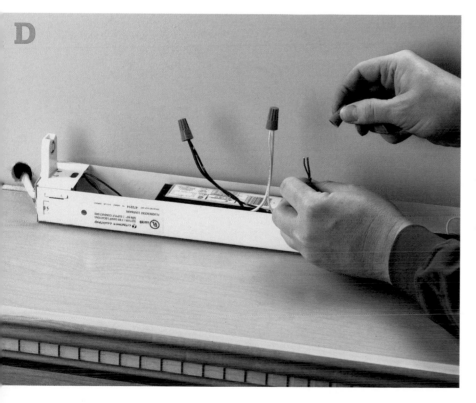

Remove a knockout from the fixture, and route the cable into the fixture, leaving 11" extra for making connections. Secure it with a cable clamp. Remove 10½" of sheathing from the cable and strip ¾" of insulation from each of the wires. Using wire connectors, connect the black circuit wire to the black fixture wire, the white circuit wire to the white fixture wire, and the grounding circuit wire to the fixture grounding wire. Tuck the wires into the fixture, replace the cover and lens, and install a bulb. Install the switch, and restore the power.

Installing a new ceiling fixture can provide more light, along with an aesthetic lift.

Replacing a Ceiling-mounted Fixture

Ceiling fixtures don't have any moving parts and their wiring is very simple, so, other than changing bulbs, you're likely to get decades of trouble-free service from a fixture. This sounds like a good thing, but it also means that the fixture probably won't fail and give you an excuse to update a room's look with a new one. Fortunately, you can don't need an excuse. Upgrading a fixture is easy and can make a dramatic impact on a room. You can substantially increase the light in a room by replacing a globe-style fixture by one with separate spot lights, or you can simply install a new fixture that matches the room's décor.

Tools & Materials   Light fixtures
▪ Voltage sensor ▪ Screwdrivers ▪ Wire stripper.

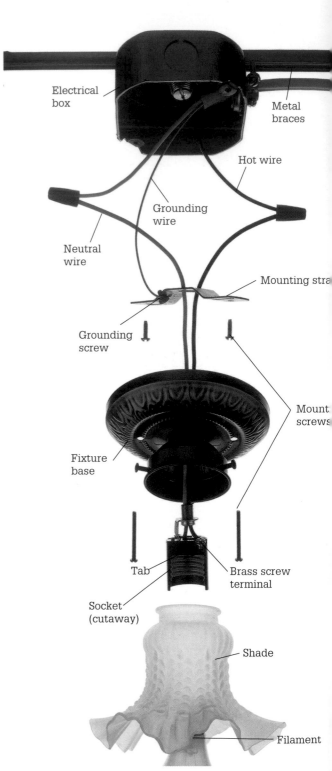

Electrical box
Metal braces
Hot wire
Grounding wire
Neutral wire
Mounting strap
Grounding screw
Mount screws
Fixture base
Tab
Brass screw terminal
Socket (cutaway)
Shade
Filament

No matter what a ceiling light fixture looks like on the outside, they all attach in basically the same way. An electrical box in the ceiling is fitted with a mounting strap, which holds the fixture in place. The bare wire from the ceiling typically connects to the mounting strap. The two wires coming from the fixture connect to the black and white wires from the ceiling.

How to Replace a Ceiling-mounted Light Fixture

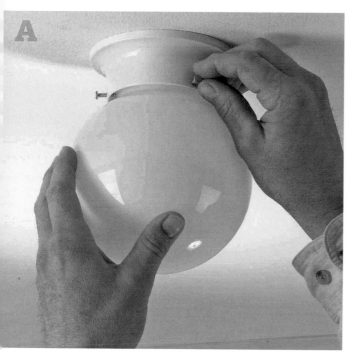

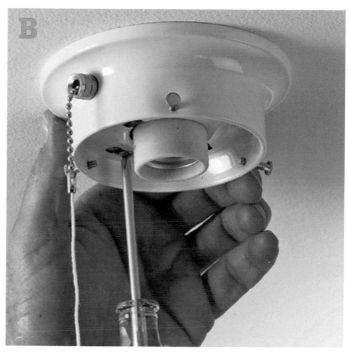

Begin by turning off the power to the fixture. Remove the globe by unthreading the globe (turning it counterclockwise) or by loosening the three screws that pinch the globe in place (the screws usually go through a collar around the base of the globe). Next, remove the lightbulbs from the fixture.

Detach the old light from the ceiling electrical box. Most traditional fixtures use two long screws to secure the fixture base to the metal electrical box in the ceiling. Have a helper hold the fixture with one hand so it doesn't fall, while you use a screwdriver to remove the two screws. Gently pull the light straight down, exposing the wiring that powers the fixture.

Before you touch the wires that feed the existing light, use a voltage sensor to verify that the circuit is now dead. With the fixture's switch in the on position, insert the sensor's probe into the electrical box and hold the probe within ½" of the black wires inside. If the sensor beeps or lights up, then the circuit is still live, and you'll need to trip the correct breaker to disconnect power to the fixture. If the sensor does not beep or light up, the circuit is dead and you can proceed safely.

(continued next page)

D

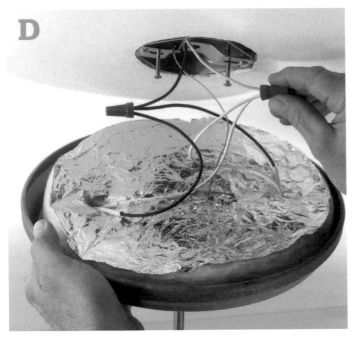

Once you have verified that the power to the light is off at the main panel, remove the fixture by disconnecting the wires. After removing the wire connectors, pull the fixture completely away from the box.

E

Before you install the new fixture, check the ends of the wires coming from the ceiling electrical box. They should be clean and free of nicks or scorch marks. If they're dirty or worn, clip off the stripped portion with your combination tool. Then, strip away about ¾" of insulation from the end of each wire.

F

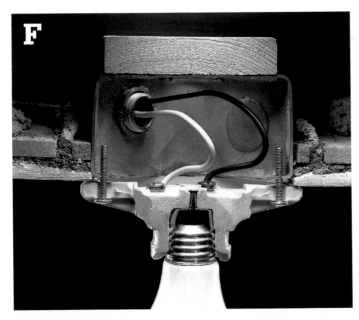

Now, take a look at the electrical box. Most fixtures installed in the last few decades are attached to a mounting strap, a strip of metal reaching from one side of the electrical box to another and attached with two screws. Older light fixtures were often mounted directly to the holes in the box, a less safe installation that doesn't meet current electrical codes.

G

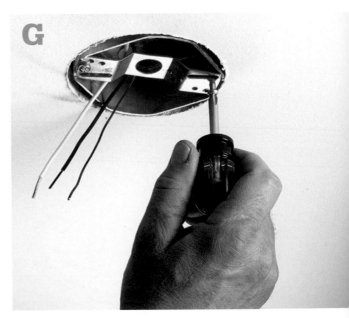

If the box doesn't have a mounting strap, attach one. One might be included with your new fixture; otherwise, you can buy one at any hardware store or home center.

H

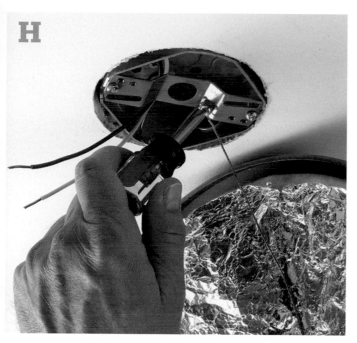

You will probably find a bare copper wire in the box. Connect this wire to the screw near the center of the mounting strap. Wrap the wire clockwise around the screw and turn the screw until it is snug.

I

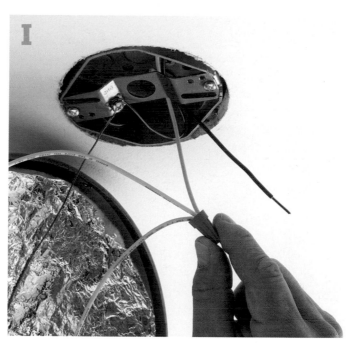

Set the new fixture on top of a ladder or have a helper support it. You'll find two short wires—called leads—coming from the fixture, one white and one black. If the ends of the leads are not already stripped, remove about ¾" of insulation from each wire end. Hold the white lead from the fixture next to the white wire from the ceiling. Push the ends into a wire connector, and twist the connector clockwise until it is snug.

J

Now connect the black wire to the black lead with a wire connector in the same way. Give both connections a gentle tug to make sure the connectors are tight.

K

Tuck the wire connections into the ceiling box on either side of the mounting strap. Secure the light to the ceiling box by driving the fixture's mounting screws through the holes in the fixture base and into the strap.

L

With the fixture secured to the box, you can install the lightbulbs and shades. Each fixture is a little different; follow the manufacturer's instructions. Once the bulbs are in, restore power to the fixture and test it.

Replace a Hanging Light Fixture

Chandeliers and other hanging fixtures exist in a huge variety of styles, so chances are good that you might acquire a house with a chandelier you find less than attractive. Of course, you might also have a chandelier stop working for some reason. Either way, they're easy enough to replace.

A properly installed chandelier has more bracing behind it than a standard ceiling fixture, so don't try to replace a simple ceiling globe with a 50-pound chandelier. You'll likely find a broken chandelier on your dining room table if you do.

Replacing an old chandelier is a quick and easy way to make a big change to a room's character, not to mention the quality of its light.

Tips for Hanging Heavy Fixtures ▶

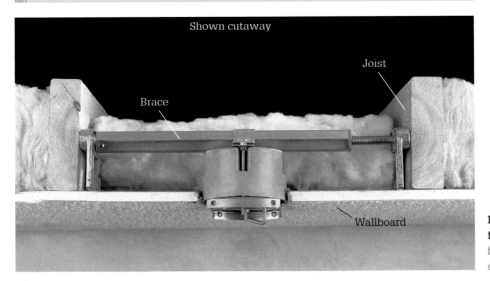

Shown cutaway

Joist

Brace

Wallboard

Heavy chandeliers and ceiling fans are suspended from electrical boxes that are secured between ceiling joists with heavy-duty braces.

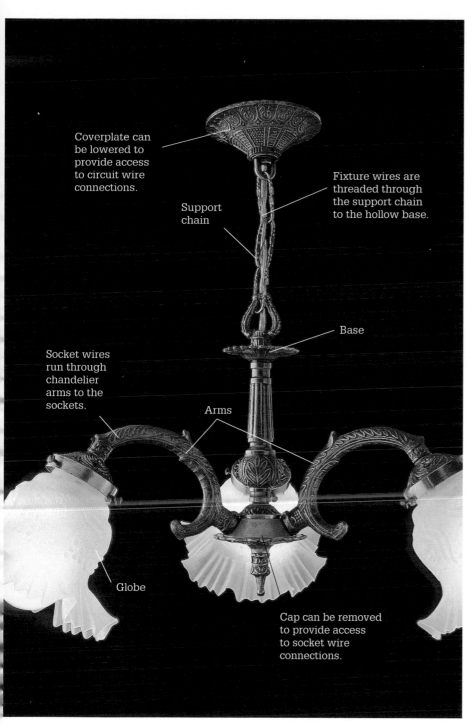

Coverplate can be lowered to provide access to circuit wire connections.

Support chain

Fixture wires are threaded through the support chain to the hollow base.

Base

Socket wires run through chandelier arms to the sockets.

Arms

Globe

Cap can be removed to provide access to socket wire connections.

Combination tool

Screwdriver

Voltage sensor

Replacement chandelier

Tools and materials for replacing a hanging light fixture include the new fixture, a voltage sensor or multimeter, a wire stripper or combination tool, a screwdriver and mounting hardware.

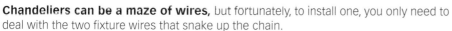

Chandeliers can be a maze of wires, but fortunately, to install one, you only need to deal with the two fixture wires that snake up the chain.

How to Install a New Chandelier

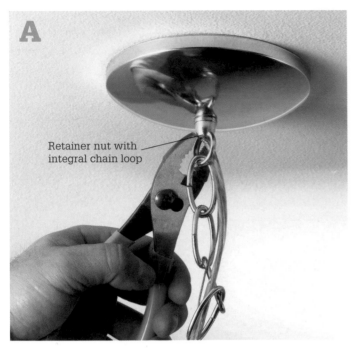

A

Retainer nut with integral chain loop

Remove the old light fixture. To gain access to the wiring connections, unfasten the retainer nut that secures the coverplate for the electrical box. On some chandeliers (such as the one above), the ring that holds the support chain for the chandelier is integral to the retainer nut, so unfastening it will mean the fixture is being supported only by the electrical wires.

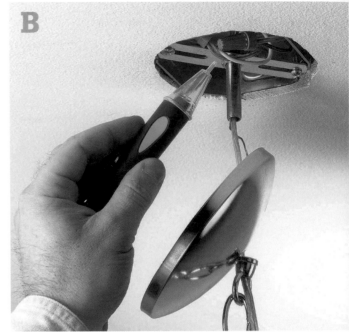

B

Turn off the power to the old fixture at the main service panel. Use a voltage sensor to verify that the circuit is dead. With the light switch turned on, insert the sensor's probe into the electrical box within ½" of the wires inside. If the sensor beeps or lights up, then the circuit is live and you've shut off the wrong circuit. Shut off additional circuits until the probe confirms that you've shut off the correct one.

Safety Tip ▶

Chandeliers are heavy, as you will learn very quickly when you're removing or installing one. It's better to rig up some means of temporary support for the fixture than to rely on a helper to hold it or—worse still—try to hold it yourself (you will need both hands to make the connections). One solution is to position a tall stepladder directly below the work area so you can rest the fixture on the top platform. And just in case the fixture falls, remove all the bulbs and globes before you do any of the work.

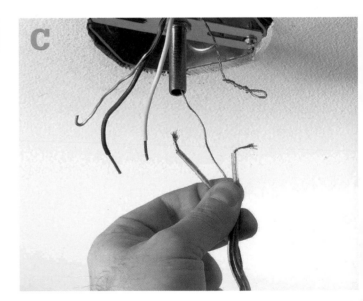

C

Remove the wire connectors from all the wires in the box and separate the wires. If the support chain is still attached, unscrew the mounting nut from the end of the threaded nipple inside the box. Disconnect the bare copper wire from the screw near the center of the mounting strap. Pull the old wires down through the threaded nipple.

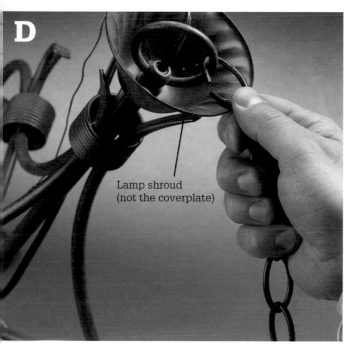

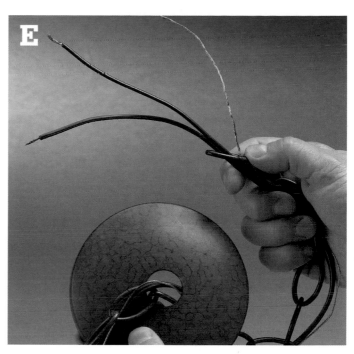

Adjust the length of the support chain on the new chandelier (if necessary) so it will hang at the desired height when mounted. This is normally done by disconnecting the chain from the support ring on the fixture, removing the required number of links and then reattaching the chain.

There will be two insulated wires and a bare copper ground wire woven in with the chain on your new fixture. There should be 6" to 12" of extra wire at the top of the chain. If the ends of these wires aren't stripped, use your combination tool to strip away ¾" of insulation.

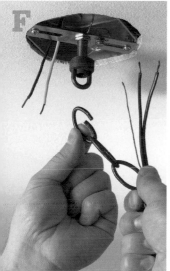

Hang the new fixture from the threaded nipple (unless the chain support nut is integral to the coverplate retainer, as in step A). You may need to screw the threaded nipple farther into the mounting plate so it does not extend past the coverplate. Or, you may need to replace the mounting strap and nipple with correctly sized hardware (usually provided with the new fixture). Make the wire connections, including attaching the bare copper wire to the grounding screw on the mounting strap.

Carefully tuck the wires into the electrical box and then tighten the retainer for the coverplate so it is snug against the ceiling. Restore power and test the fixture.

Photo Contributors

Abruzzo Kitchens
Jim Dase Kitchens Designer
www.abruzzokitchens.com
p. 92 (both)

Armstrong Floors
www.armstrong.com
pp. 70, 72, 74, 75 (bottom)

Asko
www.asko.com
p. 217

Buddy Rhodes Concrete
www.buddyrhodes.com
p. 52 (bottom)

Cambria
www.cambria.com
p. 55

Daltile
www.daltile.com
p. 185

Dewitt Designer Kitchens
www.dewittdesignerkitchens.com
p. 158

DuPont Corian
www.corian.com
p. 54 (top)

Eco Floors
www.ecofloors.com
p. 228

Elkay
www.elkay.com
p. 36, 65 (bottom)

Expanko, Inc.
Cork and rubber flooring
www.expanko.com
p. 7

GE Appliances
www.geappliances.com
p. 29 (bottom), 69, 111

Green Mountain Soapstone Company
www.greenmountainsoapstone.com
p. 57

IKEA
www.ikea.com
pp. 76, 80, 81 (bottom)

Kitchenaid
www.kitchenaid.com
pp. 61, 188

Kitchoo
www.kitchoo.com
© 2006 Kitchoo: p. 63

Kraftmaid
www.kraftmaid.com
pp. 15 (bottom), 23 (bottom), 41, 89, 132, 238

Maytag
www.maytag.com
p. 218

Mill's Pride
www.millspride.com
p. 78-79, 265

National Kitchen and Bath Association
www.nkba.org
p. 19 (top): NKBA/ Jan Regis
p. 28: NKBA/ Marcy Wells
p. 29: NKBA/ Huber
p. 33: (top): NKBA/ Lori Carrol
p. 35: NKBA/ Gilmer
p. 262: NKBA/ Judy Hunt

Pergo
www.pergo.com
p. 52 (top)

Plato Woodworking
www.platowoodwork.com
p. 13 (bottom)

Price Phister
www.pricephister.com
p. 206

SieMatic Corporation
www.siematic.com
pp. 4, 21, 39-40, 43 (bottom), 45 (bottom), 120-121

Sinkerator
www.sinkerator.com
p. 220

Snaidero
www.snaidero.com
pp. 8-9, 17 (top)

Teragren
Fine bamboo flooring, panels and veneer
www.teragren.com
pp. 25, 27

Urban Homes, N.Y.:
www.uhny.com
pp. 31 (top), 90-91 (all)

Wilsonart
www.wilsonart.com
pp. 51, 82

Wolf Appliance Company, LLC.
www.wolfappliances.com pp. 62, 222

Photo Credits

Alamy
www.alamy.com
© Elizabeth Whiting & Associates/ Alamy: pp. 6-7, 18 (bottom), p. 34
© VIEW Pictures Ltd/ Alamy: p. 19 (bottom)

Todd Caverly
©Todd Caverly: p. 71 and for the following:
    G.M. Wild Construction, Inc.: pp. 13, 22, 23 (top), 56 (top), 68, 110
    Lorraine Construction: pp. 30, 71

Collinstock, LLC
www.collinstock.com
© Collinstock/ Greg Premru: p. 11 (bottom)
© Collinstock/ Andrea Rugg: p. 81 (top)

Corbis
www.corbis.com
© Corbis/ Royalty Free: p. 130

Tony Giammarino
Giammarino & Dworkin
© Tony Giammarino: pp. 11 (top),
    20 (both), 50, 60, 66, 67, 73 (bottom), 150
and for the following:
    www.homemasons.com: pp. 14, 26 (both), 43 (top), 45 (top), 48
    Lobkovich Kitchen Designs, www.lobkovich.com: p. 32
    K. Kowach, designer: p. 44
    Kitchen Designworks, 804.262.0006: p. 58 (top)

Susan Gilmore
www.susangilmorephoto.com
© Susan Gilmore
for Laural Ulland Architecture, www.laurelulland.com: p. 59 (bottom)

Karen Melvin
Minneapolis, MN
© Karen Melvin for the following designers:
    David Samcla, Samela Architect. p. 10
    Vujovich Design build: p. 12
    Rebekah Fellers Interiors, Cincinnati, Ohio: p. 16
    Sala Architects: p. 17 (bottom)
    Knapp Cabinetry: p. 24
    Cornelius Interior Design, Minneapolis: p. 54 (bottom)
    Pappas Design: p. 75 (top)
    Senn and Youngdahl Fine Builders: p. 83 (top)
    Jenn-Air Appliances: p. 85
    Jon Monson — The Landschute Group, Inc.: p. 86-87

Northlight Photography/ Roger Turk
www.nlpinc.com
© Northlight Photography/ Roger Turk
    p. 56 (bottom), 83 (top)

Eric Roth Photography
www.ericrothphoto.com
© Eric Roth: p. 46; for Tom Catalano p. 15;
    for Thomas Buckborough p. 53

Jessie Walker
www.jessiewalker.com
pp. 31 (bottom), 33 (bottom)

Resources

Air-Conditioning and Refrigeration Institute
703-524-8800
www.ari.org

American Institute of Architects
800-242-3837
www.aia.org

American Lighting Association
800-274-4484
www.americanlightingassoc.com

American Society of Interior
Designers
202-546-3480
www.asid.org

Association of Home Appliance Manufacturers
202-872-5955
www.aham.org

Center for Inclusive Design & Environmental Access
School of Architecture and
Planning University of Buffalo
716-829-3485
www.ap.buffalo.edu

Center for Universal Design
NC State University
919-515-3082
www.design.ncsu.edu

Construction Materials Recycling Association
630-548-4510
www.cdrecycling.org

Energy & Environmental Building
Association
952-881-1098
www.eeba.com

Energy Star
888-762-7937
www.energystar.gov

International Association of
Lighting Designers
312-527-3677
www.iald.org

International Residential Code Book International Conference
of Building Officials
800-284-4406
www.icbo.com

Kitchen Cabinet Manufacturers
Association
703-264-1690
www.kcma.org

Lighting Design Lab
877-604-6592
www.lightingdesignlab.com

National Association of Home Builders (NAHB) Research Center
800-638-8556
www.nahbrc.com

National Association of the
Remodeling Industry (NARI)
847-298-9200
www.nari.org

National Kitchen & Bath Association (NKBA)
800-843-6522
www.nkba.org

National Wood Flooring Association
800-422-4556
www.woodfloors.org

Resilient Floor Covering Institute
301-340-8580
www.rfci.com

The Tile Council of America
864-646-8453
www.tileusa.com

U.S. Environmental Protection Agency-Indoor Air Quality
www.epa.gov

Reference Charts

Converting Measurements

To Convert:	To:	Multiply by:
Inches	Millimeters	25.4
Inches	Centimeters	2.54
Feet	Meters	0.305
Yards	Meters	0.914
Square inches	Square centimeters	6.45
Square feet	Square meters	0.093
Square yards	Square meters	0.836
Cubic inches	Cubic centimeters	16.4
Cubic feet	Cubic meters	0.0283
Cubic yards	Cubic meters	0.765
Ounces	Milliliters	30.0
Pints (U.S.)	Liters	0.473 (Imp. 0.568)
Quarts (U.S.)	Liters	0.946 (Imp. 1.136)
Gallons (U.S.)	Liters	3.785 (Imp. 4.546)
Ounces	Grams	28.4
Pounds	Kilograms	0.454

To Convert:	To:	Multiply by:
Millimeters	Inches	0.039
Centimeters	Inches	0.394
Meters	Feet	3.28
Meters	Yards	1.09
Square centimeters	Square inches	0.155
Square meters	Square feet	10.8
Square meters	Square yards	1.2
Cubic centimeters	Cubic inches	0.061
Cubic meters	Cubic feet	35.3
Cubic meters	Cubic yards	1.31
Milliliters	Ounces	.033
Liters	Pints (U.S.)	2.114 (Imp. 1.76)
Liters	Quarts (U.S.)	1.057 (Imp. 0.88)
Liters	Gallons (U.S.)	0.264 (Imp. 0.22)
Grams	Ounces	0.035
Kilograms	Pounds	2.2

Lumber Dimensions

Nominal - U.S.	Actual - U.S.	METRIC
1 × 2	¾ × 1½"	19 × 38 mm
1 × 3	¾ × 2½"	19 × 64 mm
1 × 4	¾ × 3½"	19 × 89 mm
1 × 5	¾ × 4½"	19 × 114 mm
1 × 6	¾ × 5½"	19 × 140 mm
1 × 7	¾ × 6¼"	19 × 159 mm
1 × 8	¾ × 7¼"	19 × 184 mm
1 × 10	¾ × 9¼"	19 × 235 mm
1 × 12	¾ × 11¼"	19 × 286 mm
1¼ × 4	1 × 3½"	25 × 89 mm
1¼ × 6	1 × 5½"	25 × 140 mm
1¼ × 8	1 × 7¼"	25 × 184 mm
1¼ × 10	1 × 9¼"	25 × 235 mm
1¼ × 12	1 × 11¼"	25 × 286 mm
1½ × 4	1¼ × 3½"	32 × 89 mm
1½ × 6	1¼ × 5½"	32 × 140 mm
1½ × 8	1¼ × 7¼"	32 × 184 mm
1½ × 10	1¼ × 9¼"	32 × 235 mm
1½ × 12	1¼ × 11¼"	32 × 286 mm
2 × 4	1½ × 3½"	38 × 89 mm
2 × 6	1½ × 5½"	38 × 140 mm
2 × 8	1½ × 7¼"	38 × 184 mm
2 × 10	1½ × 9¼"	38 × 235 mm
2 × 12	1½ × 11¼"	38 × 286 mm
3 × 6	2½ × 5½"	64 × 140 mm
4 × 4	3½ × 3½"	89 × 89 mm
4 × 6	3½ × 5½"	89 × 140 mm

Liquid Measurement Equivalents

1 Pint	= 16 Fluid Ounces	= 2 Cups
1 Quart	= 32 Fluid Ounces	= 2 Pints
1 Gallon	= 128 Fluid Ounces	= 4 Quarts

Converting Temperatures

Convert degrees Fahrenheit (F) to degrees Celsius (C) by following this simple formula: Subtract 32 from the Fahrenheit temperature reading. Then, multiply that number by 5/9. For example, 77°F - 32 = 45. 45 × 5/9 = 25°C.

To convert degrees Celsius to degrees Fahrenheit, multiply the Celsius temperature reading by 9/5. Then, add 32. For example, 25°C × 9/5 = 45. 45 + 32 = 77°F.

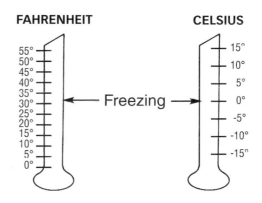

Index

Index (continued)

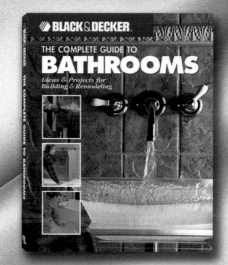

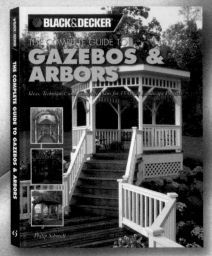
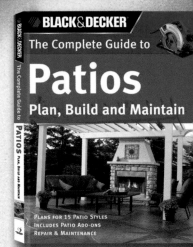